SACRAMENTAL POETICS
AT THE DAWN OF SECULARISM

*Cultural Memory*
*in*
*the*
*Present*

*Mieke Bal and Hent de Vries, Editors*

# SACRAMENTAL POETICS
# AT THE DAWN OF SECULARISM

*When God Left the World*

*Regina Mara Schwartz*

STANFORD UNIVERSITY PRESS

STANFORD, CALIFORNIA

Stanford University Press
Stanford, California

Printed in the United States of America on acid-free, archival-quality paper

Library of Congress Cataloging-in-Publication Data

Schwartz, Regina M.
  Sacramental poetics at the dawn of secularism : when God left the world /
Regina Mara Schwartz.
     p. cm. — (Cultural memory in the present)
  Includes bibliographical references and index.
  ISBN 978-0-8047-5667-9 (cloth: alk. paper)—ISBN 978-0-8047-5833-8 (pbk. :
alk. paper) 1. English poetry—Early modern, 1500–1700—History and criticism.
2. Christian poetry, English—Early modern, 1500–1700—History and criticism.
3. Christianity and literature—England—History—17th century.  4. Rites and
ceremonies in literature.  5. Aesthetics, Modern—17th century.  6. God in
literature.  7. Ritual in literature.  I. Title.

PR545.R4.S39  2008
820.9'3823                                    2007037710

Typeset by Westchester Book Group in 11/13.5 Adobe Garamond

This book was published with the assistance of Northwestern University.

*In the Christian tradition, an initial privation of body goes on producing institutions and discourses that are the effects of and substitutes for that absence: multiple ecclesiastical bodies, doctrinal bodies, and so on. How can a body be made from the word? This question raises the other haunting question of an impossible mourning: "Where art thou?" These questions stir the mystics.*

—MICHEL DE CERTEAU, *THE MYSTIC FABLE*

# Contents

*Preface*

The Eucharist has always been mysterious to me. As a Jewish child, nothing in my tradition could prepare me for such a ritual. The *separation* between the Creator and his Creation is the fundamental tenet of Judaism.[1] God may have spoken, but in disembodied words. God may have molded man, but man could not mold God. The divine was utterly unimaginable and to create any image was the ultimate idolatry. Maimonides, among others, inveighed against naïve readings of the Bible that took anthropomorphism literally. As for God, "He gives orders without appearing" as a contemporary philosopher wryly observed.[2] Certainly God does not manifest himself in bread, does not give himself to man to be materially ingested.

And yet, I also knew that the Eucharist was the heart of Christianity: it was taking communion that made my Christian friends Christian, and taking communion that even created the Church itself. How did that happen? I wanted to understand how a wafer could become God. Passover offered little help, for the matzoh we ate to commemorate the Exodus was neither God, nor Moses or Elijah—it was only bread that was flat because the ancient Israelites had to flee before it had time to rise. Flat bread becoming God, and for that matter, God becoming man—this was completely different.

My fascination prompted me to attend Mass now and then, but when it came to communion, I would leave church inconspicuously (or so I imagined). And then one wet Sunday in London, alone and free of obligations, I seized the opportunity to attend services at St Giles at Cripplegate, the church John Milton attended (when he attended) and his burial place. Doubtless, I thought I would be communing with the soul of the poet who has engaged so much of my imaginative life. I encountered, however, another communion. Singing hymns his father had composed, and wondering how Milton, that iconoclastic "sect of one," felt about joining in any communal ritual he did not invent himself, I heard my own voice blending with the other voices in the congregation, and I distinctly felt the comforts of community.

Until communion. When the priest invited everyone to forge the mystical body of God by partaking of the body and blood of Christ together, to accept the invitation Christ himself offered at the last supper to "take, eat, and do this in remembrance of me," my fellow feelings dissipated with the awareness that I could not join. But why not, I asked myself? No one here will prevent me, no one knows me, knows that I am Jewish, and as far as my faith is concerned, I need not bother myself too much, for I could take communion as a scholar of ritual, adopting an anthropological pose. And so, instead of electing to stay behind in my pew while everyone filed past me toward the altar, I resolved to join the movement forward. But while I gave my limbs the command to stand and walk, they did not move. Frozen and embarrassed, I began to reassure myself that I was neither sinner nor convert, but someone who simply wanted to join. I tried again, loath to interrupt my spiritual communion by failing to complete that last ritual gesture, but again I was unable to move.

What had happened? Did my terror that Yahweh would strike me down for committing idolatry overcome me? Oh yes. Did I fear that my anthropological experiment was disrespectful of others' meaningful experience? Indeed. Was I afraid that if I ate Christ's body, I would turn into a Christian? That too. But clarification of my inability to take communion only emerged during the years I worked on this study. Then, on a pilgrimage to Santiago de Compostela, it came. There, I had another opportunity to take communion among dear friends in the small chapel at Ignatius Loyola's house that we visited during our journey. A private Mass had been arranged for our group. This time, I did not fear the wrath of an ancient Israelite deity nor did I have any reason to question my respect for communion or the gravity of my intentions. Indeed, they were so serious that the priest and I had discussed the question of my taking communion at considerable length. But that day began with my visit to Guernica where harrowing visions of human violence cry out from museums and memorials; so, when the priest spoke movingly of Christ's sacrifice, I was haunted by the specter of war victims, including my own ancestors.

On that day I knew that I could not take communion because the world was not yet redeemed. When I explained to the priest that if ever justice reigns, then I will surely be able to take in the body of the Lord, he nodded sadly, so sadly. It is, therefore, with genuine sympathy for those who felt real hunger for the real presence, the sacramental presence of the Lord, that I try to heed the responses of Reformation poets. Rather than import an Enlightenment arch-secularism back to a time when the sacramental world view was challenged, that is, rather than offer another reading of the cultural productions of the Reformation through post-Reformation secular lenses (that celebrate reason as liberation from the bondage of human superstition), I try to listen to the many people who believed that human pain was the legacy of Adam's sin, that human nature was first made in the image of God and subsequently tarnished, and that only the sacrifice of God could restore it. I want to be attentive to how deeply felt the loss of God was in a world once believed to be filled with "the glory of the Lord."[3]

EVANSTON

PASSOVER 2007

# Acknowledgments

This study is conceived as a sequel to *The Curse of Cain: The Violent Legacy of Monotheism*. That book, Part 1 of a project to explore the social and cultural legacies of ancient religion in modern life, focused on the ways that ancient Near Eastern conceptions haunt modern Western understandings of collective identity—a legacy that includes not only a vision of universal love but also identity defenses too often invoked to justify violence. Here, I return to the question of ancient religion in modernity to uncover another cultural legacy toward the sacred, not violent, but creative.

As I was writing, I presented pilot versions of chapters at the International Milton Symposium in Bangor, Wales, the annual conference on theology and philosophy at Villanova University, on mysticism at the University of Chicago, the Sixteenth-Century Studies Annual Conference in Toronto, the South Central Modern Language Association Convention in San Antonio, and at a conference on Religion and Culture at Oxford University. Everywhere, I profited from the helpful advice of audience members. An earlier version of the chapter on Milton appeared in *Religion and Literature* and on Herbert in *Questioning God in the Millennium*, ed. Jack Caputo. I was helped, in the final stages, by Deborah Masi, Virgil Brower, and Brian Maxson.

This work is dedicated to Rosanne, my mother, who so incarnated goodness that I have far more experiential understanding of the doctrine of the incarnation than a Jewish person should! And as the Passion did not mean the end of divine goodness, so her recent departure does not signal the loss of her infinite goodness.

SACRAMENTAL POETICS
AT THE DAWN OF SECULARISM

## PART I

POESIA MYSTICA

# 1

## Sacramental Poetics

The Oracles are dumb,
No voice or hideous hum
   Runs through the arched roof in words deceiving.
*Apollo* from his shrine
Can no more divine,
   With hollow shriek the steep of *Delphos* leaving.
No nightly trance, or breathed spell,
Inspires the pale-ey'd Priest from the prophetic cell.

The lonely mountains o're,
And the resounding shore,
   A voice of weeping heard, and loud lament;
From haunted spring and dale
Edg'd with poplar pale,
   The parting Genius is with sighing sent,
With flow'r-inwov'n tresses torn
The Nymphs in twilight shade of tangled thickets mourn.
—John Milton, "On the Morning of Christ's Nativity," 173–88[1]

"Man is unavoidably a sacramentalist and his works are sacramental in character," writes the poet David Jones.[2] My effort to draw attention to a sacramental poetics is heir to a long discourse that links *Ars to Sacre*, both before and after the Christian Church Fathers explored the connection of art and the sacred. The explicit debts of literature to religion are immense: from medieval Corpus Christi plays to Victorian devotional poetry, from Renaissance cantos to Romantic symbolism, from Donne's sonnets to Eliot's quartets. The relation is multifaceted: the poet as inspired prophet, the poet as a creator in the image of the Creator, words as grounded in the Word, inspiration as divine prompting, language as liturgical, drama as ritual, poetry as hymn. And despite recent trends in more scientifically oriented criticism—involving questions of textual production and dissemination—a theological and philosophical study of literature continues unabated.[3]

Nonetheless, we should still heed Jones's warning: "The terms 'sacrament' and 'sacramental' are apt to give off overtones and undertones that for a number of disparate reasons have a kind of narrowing effect. Thus, for Christians and especially for the Catholic Christian, those terms carry a specialized meaning and a special aura surrounds them. On the other hand, for secularized man in general, and especially for post-Christians or anti-Christians such terms are suspect or uncongenial. So that in various opposing ways the wide significance and primary meaning is obscured."[4] This "primary meaning," Jones suggests simply, is sign-making. Mankind has, "for about fifty millenn[ia] . . . made works, handled material, in a fashion that can only be described as having the nature of a sign. We have ample archeological evidence to show us that paleolithic man was a sacramental animal, . . . this creature juxtaposed marks on surfaces [that] had not merely utile, but significant, intent; that is to say a 're-presenting,' a 'showing again under other forms,' an 'effective recalling' of something [that] was intended."[5]

The human urge to make signs is not at all restricted to the rituals of the Church, of any church. Not only are the arts characterized by the activity of sign-making; "ultimately, the very work of the sign implies the sacred." Somehow, a sign seems to inevitably evoke the sacred. But how? First, because it works by evoking something beyond itself, something that transcends the sign. Insofar as it evokes something beyond, the sign participates in transcendence, and transcendence—whether vertical or horizontal, above or beyond our comprehension, control, and use—is the realm of mystery. We can point to it, sign it, and by doing so evoke it, and sometimes even more, manifest it. As Jacques Maritain summarized, for the scholastic philosophers, "sign is that which renders present to knowledge something other than itself." *Signum est id quod repræsentant aliud a se potentiæ cognoscenti.* A *sign manifests.*[6] And as Augustine says simply, "Signs, when they pertain to divine things, are called sacraments."[7] Even for Aristotle, a metaphor is not simply ornate language; it bears truth, like riddles that communicate a truth almost incommunicable to human minds.

Like signification, the riddle of transubstantiation, for Leibniz, resists solution, on the one hand, and complete obscurity, on the other. "*By virtue of being a metaphor* it testifies to something other than the rational order of things" but in a manner that appears intelligible.[8] Riddles, like that of transubstantiation, issue from the "voice of prophets, monsters, messengers and the gods at the pivotal moments of destiny for many reasons, but chief among these is the vast discontinuity between human and divine experience. Charged on several occasions with speaking the 'unspeakable,' is it any wonder Tiresias sometimes resorts to what sound like riddles? The wonder is that he can speak at all."[9] Mystery is not hopelessly lost to us; it is manifest by virtue of an utterance that says more than it can say.

When Samuel Johnson draws a distinction between didactic poetry and devotional poetry, he affirms the didactic, for it concerns the works of God rather than God Himself. Devotional poetry, on the other hand, faces two difficulties: the first is that while religion is truth, art is necessarily fictional; the second is that when devotion is honest, the poetry that results is poor: "poetical devotion cannot often please. . . . Contemplative piety, or the intercourse between God and the human soul, cannot be poetical" for "to ask for mercy from the Creator is a higher state than poetry can confer." But both his conception of what religious devotion is and his understanding of what counts as excellent poetry, indeed, as poetry itself, inform this judgment.

Poetry pleases by exhibiting an idea more grateful to the mind than things themselves afford. This effect proceeds from the display of those parts of nature which attract, and the concealment of those which repel the imagination: but religion must be shewn as it is; suppression and addition equally corrupt it; and such as it is, it is known already. From poetry the reader justly expects, and from good poetry always obtains, the enlargement of his comprehension and elevation of his fancy; but . . . Omnipotence cannot be exalted; Infinity cannot be amplified; Perfection cannot be improved.[10]

As if he were addressing Johnson before his time, Herbert takes up the very problem that preoccupies him here: the incommensurability of verse to its sacred subject. Herbert, the poet who wrote in "Jordan (I)," "Who sayes that fictions only and false hair / Become a verse? Is there in truth no beautie?" would surely agree with Johnson that theology is "too sacred for fiction, and too majestick for ornament." And yet Herbert finds a way—a compelling way—to write indisputably devotional verse. In his lyric, "A True Hymn," he concludes that "although the verse be somewhat scant, / God doth supplie the want." And then, in its final lines, the speaker expresses his lack: "*O, could I love!* and stops: *God writeth, Loved.*"[11] Herbert never makes the claim that his verse is adequate to his subject, that he can describe God; to the contrary, he writes verse about that inadequation. The true poem is only manifest in the last word, one written by God, if in the poet's hand: "*Loved.*" Herbert's poetry does not try to offer a mental or sensory picture of the miracle of divine love; it does not try to contain its subject. Rather it somehow depicts a miracle that language can only point toward.

The art of language is to point beyond itself, swelling toward significance beyond what is strictly signified. Maritain noted the important distinction between the *making* of art and the *contemplation* of metaphysics: "the more-real-than-reality," which both seek, "metaphysics must attain in the nature of things, while it suffices to poetry to touch it in any sign whatsoever."[12] With its evocation of images and sounds, indeed, an entire sensory reservoir, poetry is especially suited to the surplus of meaning. And because drama, opera, and ritual call upon multiple senses, they have a similar evocative power. Sometimes this surplus is so great that a kind of sensory exhilaration or confusion sets in: we seem to taste what we feel, to hear what we see. At the Eucharist, does the believer see God in the wine, taste him in the wafer, smell him in the incense, hear him in the hymns, or is God made present by means of all of these and more than all of these? Unsurprisingly, the blurring of sensory distinctions, synaesthesia, marks the "spiritual senses" for apprehending God in the mystical tradition.

Mining a sensory reservoir is also a hallmark of sacramental poetry—a poetry that is sacramental, not because it is an object of worship (an idol, an artifact), not because it is believed to be a sacred leftover of a divine presence (a relic), but sacramental in that it does not contain what it expresses; rather, it expresses far more than it contains. Sacramental poetry points to a meaning greater than and beyond itself. Valéry has written about poetry in ways that sound remarkably like a description of liturgy: "All at once this text is no longer one of those intended to teach us something and to vanish as soon as that something is understood; its effect is to make us live a different life, breathe according to this second life; and it implies a state or a world in which the objects and beings found there, or rather their images, have other freedoms and other ties than those in the practical world. . . . all this gives us the idea of an enchanted nature, subjected as by a spell to the whims, the magic, and the powers of language."[13] A sacramental poetry is a poetry that signifies more than it says, that creates more than its signs, yet does so, like liturgy, through image, sound, and time, in language that takes the hearer *beyond* each of those elements.[14]

Beyond sign-making, there is another component of sacramentality: efficacy. The catechism of the Council of Trent addresses this aspect clearly: "A sacrament is a thing subjected to the senses, which has the power not only of signifying but also of effecting grace."[15] Rites make something *happen*. While many arguments took place about what made sacraments effective—the agency of Christ, the faith of the believer, the signs themselves, signs empowered by Christ[16]—the question of the efficacy of the sacraments and was never in doubt. They confer grace and create a world. And although philosophers and poets have debated the nature of the efficacy of art—its source located in inspiration, in the artist, or adhering in the work itself—they also agree on the fundamental efficacy of art: *to manifest a world*. This is the basis of the otherwise audacious comparison of the artist to the Creator as well as the metaphor of the Creator as supreme Artist. In the Augustinian tradition as it is elaborated by Eriugena and Bonaventure, the human artist imitates the supreme Artist, God. Here, art is not in the thing or in the work of making it; it "dwells beyond the life and presence of the artist himself," in divine art.[17] A sacramental poetics is not any sign-making, then, for it entails a radical understanding of signifying, one that points beyond the life and presence of the artist, to manifest a new world; in Valéry's phrase, "a second life." A sacramental poetics, hence, is not afflicted by embarrassment at the poverty of signs, at the inept ways in which language falls short of conveying the sacred. In it, signs are empowered to be effective—if not to confer grace, then to change their hearer; if not to grant him eternity, then to manifest a world.

To further illuminate this sacramental poetics, it is helpful to turn to the quintessential sacrament in Christianity, the Eucharist, and to chart its movement from ritual to poetry. Obviously, by "movement," we do not mean that the Eucharist has *left* the Church; it certainly has not. But a striking and in many ways counter-intuitive phenomenon took place during the Reformation when the doctrine of transubstantiation was rejected by many Reformers. Aspects of the Eucharist began showing up in the poetry of the Reformation, albeit in completely unorthodox ways. The world manifest by the ritual was now manifest in poetry: a universe infused with divinity, a dialogue between God and man, physical union, a realm of justice. Sacramental poetics does not begin with these early modern poets, and while they were often preoccupied with the Eucharist, this is not what makes their poetry sacramental, for this is not a poetics of theme. Rather, the Eucharist is a limited case that we can pursue here, to interrogate why and how the impulse that informs the ritual could govern the poetry, how the spiritual cravings for communion with divinity addressed so fully by the Eucharist could also be addressed in poetry. As sign-making characterizes the sacrament of the Eucharist, it also does poetry, which is similarly engaged in making present what is absent—not just in select figures of speech, like prosopopoeia, but in the very poetic enterprise. In this case, sign-making assumes a special form: in the Incarnation, the sign is identical to its referent. "The union of God and man in a single person is the union of divine art and one of its works in a single being. . . . God can make a masterpiece by uniting himself to his work."[18] In Christ the work of art is also the Artist. And this identity can enable us to venture further in our understanding of a sacramental poetics—as one in which the artist becomes indistinguishable from his art. The expression and the subject that produce it are joined inseparably: in a deep sense, we see the artist in his work. Conversely, a sacramental understanding of participation enfolds the reader or viewer into this process. Entering the world of the poem, he participates in its discoveries, seeing what it sees, hearing what it says, feeling what it feels. No mere spectator of the work, the viewer is changed during his encounter with it, rendering a sacramental poetics effective.

## The Eucharist

As the central religious controversy of the Reformation, the Eucharist was a lightning rod, a focus where tremendous energy gathered, or better, a lightning bolt—for it jolted sensibilities into a new world order. Over the question of the Mass, heads rolled and ink spilled; religious institutions convulsed at the birth of new theologies and rituals and the defamation and reformation of old ones. Debates about the Eucharist became the occasion for the worldview we regard as "modern" to begin to be articulated. When the dust settled after the Reformers had redefined the Eucharist, understandings of the material and immaterial, the visible and invisible, immanence and transcendence were revised. Theology, metaphysics, aesthetics, and politics were re-imagined. This fledgling modernism swept into its purview a vast array of concerns and disciplines—from the linguistic to the political, from the anthropological to the cosmological, from the private sanctuary of belief to the public forum of state ceremony. In the course of questioning the Eucharist, justice and sacrifice, cosmos and creation, community and love, language and image were all implicated. These in no way exhaust the enormous theological implications of the Eucharist, but they do allow us to witness how questions so urgent for theology become the domain of secular thought as the ethical, the ontological, the erotic and the symbolic.[19] That is why the Eucharist is a rich site for investigation about the infusion of sacramentality into the secular world.

Until the Reformation, the Eucharist was largely understood as the offering of the sacramental body of Christ. While that sacrifice was made historically on the cross, with his gift of the Eucharist, Christ enabled the rest of humanity to share in his sacrifice—in the *sacramental* offering of his body and blood. The Eucharist offered the communicant participation in the sacrifice of Christ, with all its benefits, as surely as God entered history and became man in the Incarnation. The organic image of the body was especially suited to accommodating both social differentiation (the parts of the body) and social cohesion (the one body).[20] The image of the body also suggested an intimacy lost in later Newtonian mechanistic metaphors: not only the social body but also each believer was changed decisively by partaking of the host.

His sinful body formerly devoted to death was now cleansed for eternal life. He was no longer an exile from God, for he could enjoy a share of his divinity. He was no longer in exile from the created world, for he was now materially joined to it through the body of God. His fallen language did not inevitably fail, dooming him to misunderstanding and missed communication, for now, the words of institution—*hoc est enim corpus meum*—broke through the tragedy of fallen signification. With justice restored, our social bond embodied, our dead flesh made to live, and our participation in divine love assured, the Eucharist brought salvation into a fallen world, restoring paradisal harmony.

In the Mass the redemption of the world, wrought on Good Friday for once and for all, was renewed and made fruitful for all who believed. Christ himself, immolated on the altar of the cross, became present on the altar of the parish church, body, soul, and divinity, and his blood flowed once again, to nourish and renew Church and world. As kneeling congregations raised their eyes to see the Host held high above the priest's head at the sacring, they were transported to Calvary itself, and gathered not only into the passion and resurrection of Christ, but into the full sweep of salvation history as a whole. . . . The sacrifice of the Mass was the act by which the world was renewed and the Church was constituted, the Body on the corporas the emblem and the instrument of all truly human embodiment, whether it was understood as individual wholeness or as rightly ordered human community.[21]

In the Roman world, "sacrament" meant "taking an oath" and there the most extreme sacrament was the oath of the gladiator who was even willing to give his body and blood. By sharing the sacramental body of Christ, the communicant made such an oath but also entered a new body, the body of the Church, which was created through participation in the sacrament.

None of this was the achievement of modernist symbolic thinking. In none of this did the logic of a sign standing for something else, an "absent signified," prevail. In the sacramental Eucharist, the body of God was materially and spiritually present in the host and the fact that the wafer bled now and then offered ample miraculous testimony. As John Keble explained in his introduction to *The Works of Richard Hooker*, "The primitive apostolical men, being daily and hourly accustomed to sacrifice and to dedicate to God even ordinary things . . . God omnipresent was so much in their thoughts, that what to others would have been mere symbols, were to them designed expressions of his Truth, providential intimations of his Will. In this sense, the whole world, to them, was full of sacraments."[22]

When the priest invoked Christ's words—"This is my body"—the meaning of those words was not ever-eluding. The intimate relation between the event, the words, and their meaning was not arbitrary, for the interpretation as well as the historical and linguistic event were divinely given. Together, event and its interpretation constituted "revelation."[23]

Since Saint Augustine, ancient tradition distinguished between two classes of symbols. Some were *signa propria*, that is, things we use to designate something else, things that are therefore "instituted" to signify. Thus, they were called *instituta* or "intentional," or *voluntaria* (Bonaventure). . . . The other category consisted of things (*res*) that, in addition to their proper meanings, received from God the function of designating other things. These were realities of nature (things, persons, numbers, places, times, gestures, etc.) but transposed (*translata*) into signs by the divine will. These *signa naturalia* escaped the human codifications of meaning. . . . They were the province of a "spiritual" or divine hermeneutics.[24]

This "divine hermeneutics" did not deny the distance between beings and divinity; but it did claim that they could be bridged by the will and design of God.

It should come as little surprise that during the Reformation, this premodern understanding of sacramentality was relentlessly assaulted. Because sacramental thinking is completely alien to the way modern secularism has conceived matter, space, time, and language, in a sense it had to be almost dismantled for modernism to be born. "God's body cannot be here and at the right hand of the Father," said a logic of physical space that trumped the sacred space of sacramentality. "Man cannot eat God" said a logic of human physiology that, turning a deaf ear to the liturgy of sacramentality, went so far as to equate the claim of participation in the divine with cannibalism. "A priest cannot sacrifice God" claimed a logic of authority that denied the mystery of sacramental agency and accused man of trying to exercise power over the divine. "A sign can only stand for, that is, stand in for what it signifies, which is necessarily absent" said a logic of representation that defied the participation of the sign in its referent.[25] Not only rituals, but also altars, priestly vestments, church music, paintings, and sculptures were stripped down in a surge of iconoclasm that took these "signs and wonders" of God for idols. In this way, Reformers chipped away at sacramentality until the body of sacramental experience was reduced beyond recognition, and, for some, this meant that God might be leaving the world—yet once more.[26]

God or the gods have left the world repeatedly. In ancient Greece, with the rise of democracy, Plato dismissed tradition to insist that the new order had to be justified in Reason. The gods left again with the decline of the ancient "pagan" world and the rise of the Judeo-Christian civilization. The standard reading of this shift is that the organic totality of the ancient universe, in which religion was an immediate element in people's lives, was lost, and religion came to refer to a transcendent power—no longer the pre-Christian gods, but the One transcendent God, the supreme Being. Again, the gods departed with the rise of modernity: here, a medieval universe full of sacramental meanings gave way to the notion of the infinite mechanistic universe. They left again with the rise of modern industrial civilization and the secular political order: at the end of the nineteenth century, in the epoch of nihilism signaled by Nietzsche's "God is dead." And again, when postmodernity claimed the end of big narratives. It seems that God is abandoning the world, or dying, all the time.

To those who feel some longing for a mythical past, for a time when a transcendent presence would have governed their creation, the dying of the gods is mournful. To those who feel constrained by the notion of transcendence, the departing gods are a sign of hope. For the first temperament, culture seems to be on a downward spiral away from the essence of the religious toward an empty logic; for the second, secularization is an upward spiral away from superstition toward the light of reason. Of course, neither is a complete picture and neither is free of distortions. Undoubtedly, the departure of the gods brings both gains and losses.

Quoting Hölderlin, Heidegger describes modernity as the age of the "flight of the gods" (especially the Greek gods), a departure that has left an era of spiritual vacuity. "No god any longer gathers men and things unto himself, visibly and unequivocally, and by such gathering disposes the world's history and man's sojourn in it."[27] Only when men lived "in the sight of the gods" (*Angesicht der Götter*) were they able to compose themselves as a people.[28] Authentic poets, however (like Hölderlin), are attuned to the desolation of the present, giving their poetry a sense of deep loss. Hölderlin's mature poetry, for Heidegger, is marked by its "holy mourning (*heilige trauernden*)," a mourning of the departure of the gods.[29] Heidegger understands great art as establishing a community by means of a collective vision of art, but for him, since the late Middle Ages, society has produced no great art in this sense.[30] Nonetheless, while he finds modernity so spiritually impoverished that it cannot even name the gods, I see the poets of early modernity as actively engaged in retrieving the holy when its cultural presence seemed most threatened. Far from being the disclosure of emptiness, their work is an expression of the sacred.

When Reformers gave up the doctrine of transubstantiation (even as they held on to revised forms of the Eucharist), they lost a doctrine that infuses all materiality, spirituality, and signification with the presence of God. Their world was shaken by reformers' challenges to the medieval system of sacramentality, challenges to the sacred order as they had known it, an order that regulated both their actions and beliefs. Reformation poets had two responses to this loss. One was to mourn: they mourned the passing of a world alive and redolent with meaning.

> And new Philosophy calls all in doubt,
> The Element of fire is quite put out;
> The Sun is lost, and th'earth, and no mans wit
> Can well direct him where to looke for it.
> And freely men confesse that this world's spent,
>
> . . . . . . . . . . . . . . .
>
> 'Tis all in peeces, all coherence gone;
> All just supply, and all Relation:
>
> . . . . . . . . . . .
>
> This is the worlds condition now . . .
> (John Donne, "The First Anniversary: The Anatomy of the World")

Another response was to displace their longing for that sacred world onto other cultural forms, to accommodate sacramentalism to modernity. The movement from the sacrament to the sacramental was not, however, an explicit recovery of previous figures of transcendence, nor a deliberate effort to deliver a wholesale transfer from one cultural formation, the institutional church, to another, *ars poetica*. Nonetheless, many of the values embraced and encoded in ritual life found their way into broader cultural expressions, including the domains of the state and the arts. In their impulse to hold fast to the sacred even while the modern sciences challenged its presuppositions, early moderns forged innovative responses to the looming threats of a godless world. The premise of this study is that we still have much to learn from the sixteenth and seventeenth-century thinkers and writers who lived at the dawn of modernity and at the end of the long era when a religious worldview was dominant.

When the body of God left the altar, where it had redeemed human sin, the hope for justice did not disappear—it became the province of tragedy. The commemoration of sacrifice became both urgent and challenging in Shakespearean tragedy, raising the pressing question, how do murders differ from sacrifice? How is divine justice fulfilled rather than violated? Furthermore, if God left the world materially, he did not leave a realm of dead matter behind. Matter participated in a vitalist cosmic body. And so, in the poetry of John Milton, who inveighed vociferously against the doctrine of transubstantiation, we are offered a vision of the unfallen cosmos as always materially transubstantiating—naturally, without ritual or priest. Then too, the eucharistic longing for divine love did not simply give way to an empty carnality or a severe asceticism. Instead, the early modernists culled an erotic spiritual tradition from their mystical resources. In the poetry of John Donne, the union and communion achieved by the material combining with the body of God is manifest most fully in erotic love and its sexual consummation. Another concern proved groundless: that with the meaning of *hoc est enim corpus meum* altered, along with its system of signification, language would degenerate into a babel of sounds. Instead, it issued in the mystery of communication, of conversation. George Herbert writes of the communion as an exalted conversation with God, and his speaker engages in that conversation in his lyrics. Not only in poetry, but also in portraits and processions, the early modern period was marked by extraordinary creativity, a time when new cultural expressions of the sacred were woven from the strands of older ones.

In one sense, then, this book asks what happened when God seemed to leave the world yet once more, at the very dawn of secularism, when the host no longer became the mystical body of God through a miracle, but became a symbol, when divine cosmology no longer revealed divine providence, but offered a universe of dead matter, when language no longer effected miraculous transformations—like turning a wafer into God's body—but only conventionally signified some thing, when bodies joined in physical love became not a glimpse of transcendence but mere sex, when tragedy became not a challenge to divine justice but mere crime, and the visible referred, not beyond itself to an invisible mystery, but to raw power and possession. In another sense, the book questions the tidiness of these assumptions, critiquing the dominant myth of secularization that has marked the modern period.[31] My contention is that instead of God leaving the world without a trace, the very sacramental character of religion lent itself copiously to developing the so-called secular forms of culture and that these are often thinly disguised sacramental cultural expressions.

Sometimes this process was not so easy, for when these "secular" cultural expressions tried to fall back on a sacred metaphysics, it was not always there. And without it, they were more difficult to sustain. For instance, if the Church were no longer the mystical body of Christ, it would not be surprising for it to become a legalistic institution. If matter cannot turn into the body of Christ, it would not be surprising for it to become pure extension. Without the Eucharist and the sacramental system it was a part of, it would not be surprising if the sociality forged by ritual gave way, initially, to commemoration of a one-time miracle, and eventually, to mere spectacle. In the protracted process of "secularization," the understanding of community has evolved from the domain of theology to statecraft, transforming (reducing or elevating?) covenant into contract. But where has the understanding of sacramentality, of the material manifestation of God, gone? When we drink wine we can toast *"salute," "la chaim," "cin cin,"* in a foreign tongue—but we are only engaging in a debased allusion to the Latin words that effect a miracle: we are not changed thereby and we do not hope thereby to change the world. In contrast, the believer *is* changed decisively by partaking of the host. What do we now have that could possibly even begin to satisfy the needs met by the Eucharist—for cleansing human fault and overcoming death, for achieving communal justice and peace?

And yet we know that cultural forms persist stubbornly, especially religious ones, and the persistence of the mystery of the Eucharist in early modernity was no exception. Poetry grasped for it through language; the nation grasped for it through symbolizing community; love longed for it through mutual devotion; materialism clung to it through vitalism. We are still haunted by the Eucharist, haunted not only by its promise of divinity but also by its promise of justice. Nonetheless, is something not lost in these translations into modernist echoes? Surely a feeling of profound loss reverberates through the work of the early modern writers, a keen sense that something is missing, a real hunger for the real presence of God.

Of course no one claimed at the time to be bent on destroying sacramentality. They only applied an early modern logic to phenomena that were heretofore governed by premodern sacramental assumptions. Furthermore, it is tempting, but dangerously misleading, to assume that the modern worldview took hold in one cataclysmic upheaval during the Reformation, when that was clearly not the case. Debates over the Eucharist were not coherently impelled by modernism alone and certainly those debates did not *cause* the new thinking but only reflected it. Instead, secular philosophy, the sciences, political and legal theory, and the arts moved in fits and starts, more and less indebted to their sacramental forebears. Certainly no overt secularism was being deliberately proposed: no one denied that Christ died to save mankind. But when the sacramental worldview was losing hold, the cracks in its foundation began to show in its pivotal ritual.

The first changes were tentative and, with hindsight, seem contradictory. For example, Luther vowed to tear down the Mass, asserting that if he could tear down the Mass, he could tear down the Church. To him, the doctrine of transubstantiation implicitly granted the priesthood the power to deliver miracles, to change bread into the body of Christ with their words, and so he inveighed against the presumption of the priesthood to "offer" Christ as a sacrifice. Having vigorously asserted that priests claimed for themselves such miraculous agency, Luther just as energetically denied that they could have it. The mystery of *hoc est enim corpus meum* was simply hocus-pocus.

Nonetheless, Luther still insisted that Christ was really present in the Eucharist, "in, with, and under" the bread and the wine, and for his recourse to this rather awkward "consubstantiation" that seemed to endorse just about everything about the old sacrament except the priest's agency and a miraculous transformation of substance, more radical Reformers dubbed him "Dr. Pussyfoot." But they were hardly more consistent. Zwingli, for instance, did not embrace the doctrine of Real Presence: for him, the bread only *represented* Christ who was not sacrificed again in the Mass. But for all of his embrace of symbolic signification, Zwingli still maintained that a community was mysteriously constituted through the ritual of the Eucharist; indeed, for him, the real body of Christ was the collective community of believers who shared the ritual. When early modernists reframed the Eucharist, their intention was not to destroy it, but only to reform it. And so, bringing their fledgling modern sensibility to a medieval sacramental vision, they only nipped and tucked—transubstantiation became consubstantiation and then a doctrine of Real Presence—but in the end, with an adjustment here about space, there about time, here about agency, there about symbols, they tried to accommodate a sacred worldview to one of burgeoning modernism. The fit was uncomfortable at best.

Most of the Reformation poets who lived on the brink of this new world embraced, predictably, a spiritual—not material—presence of

Christ in the Eucharist. "Thy teeth shall not do him violence, neither thy stomach contain his glorious body. By faith he is seen, by faith he is touched, by faith, he is digested."[32] But this left them with a persistent nostalgia for that physical presence, a nostalgia that could reach just shy of heresy. Despite Reformers' consensus that the Mass does not re-enact the sacrifice of Christ, that it only commemorates it. Shakespeare is clearly preoccupied with representing the *sacrifice* of the Eucharist. When he offers the murderous *Othello* posing as a priest sacrificing at the altar, his tragedy draws a troubling relation between murder and sacrifice. Milton imagined both a paradisal Eucharist and a transubstantiating universe. For John Donne, the miracle of the Eucharist is the miracle, so rarely achieved, of combining with the other: mind, soul, *and* body. Herbert begins his monumental anthology of lyrics, *The Temple*, with "The Altar" (not a communion table that suggests a symbolic meal), and at the end, in his final lyric, "Love (III)," the guest eats the meat offered by the host. Perhaps these poets feared losing communion with God altogether, feared that divinity and humanity were locked in a tragic separation that left man wallowing in his sin, like the Catholics who responded to the spiritual understanding of divine presence: "in believing in Christ by faith—which is but an apprehension of the understanding—we do no more really eate the body of Christ than doth the hungrye man his dinner when he apprehendeth and desireth it but cannot have it."[33] In any event, their preoccupation with the substance of the Eucharist does suggest that many Reformed poets hungered, even, as their Catholic detractors would have it, were condemned "to apprehend and desire" a dinner that they could only imagine—however compelling their imaginings.

# 2

## Mystical and Political Bodies

> It is, it seems to me, in the sixteenth century that we detect the first signs of a modern reflection upon politics and religion; it is then that a new sensitivity to the question of the foundations of the civil order is born as a result of the combined effects of the collapse of the authority of the Church and of the struggles that accompanied the Reformation, as a result both of the assertion of the absolute right of the Prince and of the challenges to that right.
> —Claude Lefort, *Democracy and Political Theory*

The disenchantment of the world does not occur once, for all time; rather, it occurs gradually and repeatedly, to a greater or lesser degree, with each major revision in a world order believed to be governed by divine laws with divinely appointed leaders to interpret those laws. Eventually, even that premise is challenged: a world ordered by men who use reason to pursue a common good and experimentation to explain what had been mysterious is on the horizon. In this transition toward secularization, "divine otherness, whatever its shape, [is] transported into the social space and the nonhuman [is] incorporated into the structure of human ties. The main thing is that from now on the instituting force is made visible and accessible, whether in the guise of a place, an institution or an individual nature."[1]

The fate of sacramentality during the Reformation is part of this longer narrative of gradual secularization. For the contemporary philosopher Marcel Gauchet, the movement from the religious (wherein the invisible Other was regarded as the foundation of the world) to the beginnings of secularization (wherein that invisible transcendent power is appropriated by the immanent social sphere) occurred with the birth of each of the "axial religions," Judaism, Christianity, and Buddhism. Such codification of the "religious" was, ironically, the beginning of its own demise.

> The power of a few individuals to act in the name of the gods is the barely perceptible, yet irreversible step toward everyone having an influence on the god's decrees—the imperceptible yet definite beginning of a collective grasp on the previously sacrosanct order. . . . Political domination, which decisively entangles the gods in history, will prove to be the invisible hoist lifting us out of the religious.[2]

This compelling description of the appropriation of the gods and the manipulation of their power—the invisible becoming visible—is an especially apt account of the genealogy of the "mystical body" of the Eucharist. In its early uses, *corpus mysticum*, the mystical body, referred to the consecrated host in the liturgy, not to the body of the Church members. The community of Christians was called the *corpus Christi*, not the *corpus mysticum*. In the middle of the twelfth century, these meanings were reversed. The church, eager to assert the real presence of the human and the divine Christ against spiritualizing challenges, began to refer to the host as the *corpus Christi*, the body of Christ. That is, the term that originally signified the Christian Church then began to designate the consecrated host, and vice versa: the term used for the host, *corpus mysticum*, was gradually transferred to the Church. This process was codified when Boniface VIII in 1303 issued the bull *Unam sanctam* to remind political entities that they functioned not independently but within the body of the Church: "Urged by faith we are bound to believe in one holy Church, Catholic and also Apostolic . . . without which there is neither salvation nor remission of sins . . . which represents *one mystical body*, the head of which is Christ, and the head of Christ is God."[3] Thereafter, "mystical body" which originally had a sacramental, liturgical meaning, came to refer more and more to a social and political entity. To more fully grasp the course of sacramentality, then, we must descend from the heights of mystical poetry to the depths of practical politics.

According to Henri de Lubac and Michel de Certeau, two changes had a profound impact on the way religious life was instituted in the medieval period: the specialization of the elite classes, including the priest-hood, and the organization of the Church into a more centralized body whose theology was more technical, doctrinal, and professionalized.[4] The Fourth Lateran Council (1215) made sacramental practice "the instrument of a campaign to free Christians from the grip of the first large popular here-sies, autonomous communal movements, and growing secular powers. . . . In order to be convincing, they mobilized the rhetorical devices of images and exempla, thereby using, already at this early date, the technique of 'showing in order to inspire belief.' "[5] So concerted was this effort to bring the visible under institutional aegis that the period witnessed a surge of in-terest in theories of perspective, optics, and "pictorial composition" that had no small stake in making visible the invisible.[6]

In this climate, the Eucharist was given a strategic function: to consolidate the Church, by positing not just the equivalence but the identity between mystical reality and the visible and by making that de-pend upon hierarchical authority. Hence, the Eucharist became a miracle made possible through the power of the Church—a power seemingly prior to the miracle. In this way, the Eucharist became a locus where the Church could exercise its control over the sacred. "This Eucharistic 'body' was the 'sacrament' of the *institution,* the visible instituting of what the institution was meant to become, its theoretical authorization and its pastoral tool."[7] This co-optation of the Eucharist also vastly accentuated the institution's hierarchy, formalism, and legalism. The distinction be-tween this later understanding of the sacrament and its origins is not trivial. It is the profound difference between a hierarchical institution appropriating the right to dispense the medicine of the Eucharist versus the belief that the Eucharist itself has the sacramental power to create a healthy social body. Mystery is the domain beyond human control, but here *sacramentality* (the Latin translation of the Greek *musterion*) is no longer contrasted to *instrumentality* for the mystery itself has been instrumentalized.

This kind of interchange of the sacramental with the institutional, the mystery with the social order, was thorough enough that by the Eliza-bethan period jurists could create a doctrine of the king's two bodies, drawing upon both the tradition of the *corpus mysticum* and classical impe-rial claims, to imagine a natural and an eternal body for the king.[8] Again and again, their rhetoric stresses the invisibility of the immortal body politic: "the Body politic is a Body that cannot be seen or handled;[9] . . . for the politic capacity is invisible and immortal."[10] Ernst Kantorowicz himself refers to the doctrine of the two bodies as *mystical.* "Mysticism" is in fact the first word in his introduction to his lengthy tome,[11] the term he uses to sum up what he will discuss, the term he invokes at the beginning of his first chapter—"that mystical talk with which the English crown jurists enveloped and trimmed their definitions of kingship and royal capacities"—and as he continues, this allusion to mysticism becomes more explicit: the doctrine of the two bodies includes a mystical union of them, one that mimics the logic of the hypostatic union of the two natures of Christ.[12] The mystical becomes the political.

His thesis is that a fundamentally incarnational understanding of transcendence is ultimately co-opted by the state to suggest that, as Christ had both human and divine persons, so the King has a mortal and immortal body. And while the "transference of definitions from one sphere to another, from theology to law" may not be so remarkable because the "*quid pro quo* method—the taking over of theological notions for defining the state—had been going on for many centuries,"[13] energies were concentrated on that task by Tudor English jurists. Theirs was not the effort of a few idiosyncratic jurists, but a widespread cultural vocabulary that spread by means of royal iconography.[14] This included a process wherein "under the *pontificalis maiestas* of the pope, who was styled also as 'Prince' and 'true emperor', the hierarchical apparatus of the Roman Church tended to become the perfect prototype of an absolute and rational monarchy on a mystical basis, while at the same time the state showed increasingly a tendency to become a quasi-Church or mystical corporation."[15] In one of the more influential co-optations of its sacramental meaning, then, the mystical body came to refer more and more to the absolute monarch and to the body of the monarchy, the nation.[16]

On the scaffold, Charles I claimed, "I go from a corruptible crown to an incorruptible one."[17] When his head was displayed, people ran to soak handkerchiefs in his blood: "The blood of that sacred body."[18] An instant demand arose for relics when miracles "wrought by his blood" were reported. The account of his martyrology was published as *Eikon Basilike: The Portraiture of his sacred Maiestie in his solitude and suffering,* with a frontispiece depicting Charles holding a crown of thorns, his earthly crown at his feet, which rested on the globe. In Claude Saumaise's *Defensio regio pro Carolo I*, he blames the separation of the political from the natural body of the king for laying the groundwork that could lead to regicide:

At the time of Edward II two Despensers, to maintain their own power, wanted to distinguish between the political and the natural body of the monarchy. This did great harm to both kings and kingdoms because, when the subjection due to the king was directed more to his political body than to his physical body, it became permissible for subjects to remove the sovereign, if he was weak or unjust or if he violated the law; and this could be done just as well through force. This was the worst possible conclusion and one deduced from a false proposition thought up and invented with specious pretexts, since now, at the subjects' will, the king could put down his scepter along with his life. So long as royal power was inseparable from the person of the monarch, the sovereign, even if he committed a crime, could not be punished like a private person, because his majesty and person were inseparable.[19]

The consequences of the many entanglements of the sacrament with politics are extensive: here, the sacrament is corralled into serving a doctrine of absolute political rule. Such use suggests the reduction of the divine to an idol, one imagined as the most powerful individual imaginable rather than as an unknowable deity. In this way, a doctrine that had originally militated against any form of human domination by reserving the "head" of the body for God alone was used, ironically enough, to legitimate precisely the opposite—human, instead of divine rule—with all of the trappings of divinity now showered upon all-too-human leaders, whether emperor, pope, or prince. And the more divine absolutism was elaborated, the more it could be used to justify earthly absolutism. Paradoxically, when the theological doctrine of the Eucharist was most spiritualized, it was most politically manifest in the state. *With the real material body of Christ denied, it is "substantialized" in the body of the nation.* This eucharistic political theology has moved far from its origins as a theological concept: then, the body of God did not allude to the joining of the emperor and the state. Instead, it alluded to the mystery of God becoming man and of man participating in divinity.

When the icons of the suffering naked body of Christ are replaced by images of the monarch—clothed in velvets, silks, and pearls—and when images of suffering give way to displays of authority, then the mystery of the sacrifice of Christ conferring redemption becomes an echo of a lost order in what has become an ideological and theological nexus of wealth and power. We need only compare the language of the host to the language of the crown. The bread and wine "not only represent this exceeding love of our Saviour in giving His Body to be broken, and His Blood to be shed for us, but it likewise seals to us all those blessings and benefits which are procured for us by His death and passion, the pardon of sins, and power against sin."[20] Even when Anglicans did not want to focus on the sacrifice for doctrinal reasons, they still alluded to the broken body. But in contrast to divine love conferring "blessings and benefits against sin and mortality," the monarchy offers *rule*: "In the figure of the Crown, the government and polity of the realm are presented; for in the gold, the government of the Community is known, and in the flowers of the Crown, raised and adorned with jewels, the Honor and Office of the King or Prince is designated."[21]

In Shakespeare's play, when Richard II divests himself of the immortal office, the rhetoric of divine kingship dissolves, and tellingly, Richard contrasts the king with very different figures of the religious:

> I'll give my jewels for a set of beads,
> My gorgeous palace for a hermitage,
> My gay apparel for an almsman's gown,
> My figured goblets for a dish of wood,
> My scepter for a palmer's walking staff,
> My subjects for a pair of carved saints
> And my large kingdom for a little grave,
> A little little grave, an obscure grave; . . .
> (*Richard II*, III.iii.147–54)

He may be histrionic, but Richard's metaphors are carefully chosen: jewels, gorgeous palace, gay apparel, figured goblets, subjects, and a kingdom are contrasted to rosary beads, a hermitage, an almsman's gown, a dish of wood, the palmer's staff, carved saints, and a little grave. Apparently, old metaphors of poor piety had not altogether departed from Tudor England; instead, they lingered to rebuke the claims of divinity made by the powerful wealth of the state. Because kingship has been defined as property and possession, when Richard loses his wealth and his subjects, he loses the kingdom. In contrast, when divinity is understood as mystery, Christ divests all possession, including his life, and only thereby achieves the kingdom. Hence, it is only when Richard finally gives up his crown that his metaphors become most Christlike: "yet you Pilates / Have here delivered me to my sour cross, / And water cannot wash away your sin" (IV.i.240–43). The gap between kingship and divinity opens widest here; the irony even depends upon that gap. Despite the rhetorical labors of propagandists and lawyers to borrow legitimacy from the sphere of the sacred, a mortal ruler could not plausibly claim the mystery of God, the Incarnation, or the Eucharist. Those efforts were all part of the political drive to harness the ineffable for control—not to embrace the mystery.

For many theologians, the corporate body created through communion with the body of Christ was neither monarchial nor republican, but, at its heart, mystical—not subject to institutions. The tradition offered not only *corpus* understood as polity, but also *mysticum*, the mystery of the sacrament. Because no comprehension, no manipulation, and hence, no control over this mystery could occur, the process of translation into the state—even trying to undergird monarchy with mystical understanding—was inevitably doomed. Despite the anxious rhetorical claims that the body politic was *immortal, ineffable,* and *invisible,* it was continually made visible in state portraits and processionals, rendered manipulable through the machinations of court politics, and it was liable to lose its immortality, as it did when Charles I lost his "Body natural" and "the Body politic"—the entire institution of monarchy—went with him. The process of making visible and immanent what had been invisible and transcendent results in an extremely precarious organic theory of the state. Without transcendence to anchor it, any mortal authority claimed on that ground is vulnerable.[22] In this sense, surely the dissolution of monarchy was *already* inherent in the adoption of this religious, fundamentally incarnational understanding of monarchy.

Nonetheless, throughout appropriations of the Eucharist, the hunger for mystery surfaced again and again, even as the "mystical body" was borne through an often instrumental history. For even as the concept of *corpus mysticum* ebbed and flowed through political uses, it always harbored its early potential—its reference to the consecrated host by which Christ was made present once again through the mystery, by which the faithful participated in the project of sanctifying the community. Just as, initially, the Church was constituted by the Eucharist, by the very reception of the body and blood of Christ, and not the other way around, so the earlier Eucharist implied a consensus model of community in which

members of the mystical body collectively give birth to a community in
which sacramentality is "dispensed" evenly.

The model of sociality in the early doctrine of the sacrament is both
proto-egalitarian and participatory. No one has more or less of that body.
All participate in divinity. All are qualified—not by abstractions like republican "virtue," not by a liberal theory of rights—but by materially partaking of Christ. "If you are the body and members of Christ, your
mystery is laid on the Table of the Lord, your mystery you receive. To that
which you are you answer Amen, and in answering you assent. For you
hear the words, The body of Christ, and you answer Amen."[23] Not an elite
priesthood, but all "that eatest My flesh and drinketh My blood abideth in
Me, and I in Him" (John 26:18): "This then," Augustine comments on
John, "is to eat that food and to drink that drink, to abide in Christ and to
have Him abiding in oneself."

While the later Middle Ages came to arrogate this sacramental power
to an elite class who controlled the dispensing of sacramentality, many Reformation theologians were moved to ask, how do we return to this earlier
understanding of a communion and community without hegemony? In
Justin Martyr's depiction, the eucharistic community in its entirety constitutes the only possible kingdom of priests: "God receives not sacrifices
from any except through His priests. God therefore testifies beforehand
that *all* who . . . offer the sacrifices which Jesus the Christ commanded,
that is, at the Eucharist of the bread and the cup, which are offered in
every part of the world by Christians, are acceptable to Him."[24] In his
utopian vision, the revolutionary Abiezer Coppe (1619–72) reframed the
Eucharist as radically communist: "The true Communion amongst men,
is to have all things common, and to call nothing one hath, ones own."[25]
In this way, a mysterious common participation in divinity was invoked in
the rhetoric of the most radical of English revolutionaries.[26]

The hunger for mystery reached a crisis during the period that denied
the mystery of transubstantiation, the Reformation. In a popular devotional
book of the seventeenth century, Christopher Sutton's *Godly Meditations
upon the Most Holy Sacrament of the Lord's Supper* (1630), the bread and
wine do not change at their consecration; nonetheless, "We acknowledge
that the dignity of this Sacrament is greater than words can express, yea,
than the mind of man is able to conceive. If any will exact the efficacy of those
five words, 'for this is My body,' we answer, 'It is a great mystery.' "[27] Hooker

denied transubstantiation on the one hand, rejected the understanding of the host as symbolic commemoration, on the other, and argued eloquently for understanding of the sacraments as participation, "Namely the reall participation of Christe and of life in his bodie and bloode by meanes of this sacrament."[28] For him, "grace, element and word" all comprise the sacrament: it cannot be defined as such with the exclusion of grace, and hence cannot be reduced to symbols.[29] "All things are therefore partakers of God, they are his ofspringe, his influence is in them, and the personall wisdom of God is for that verie cause said to excel in nimbleness or agilities, to pearce into all . . . to goe through all, and to reach unto everie thinge which is."[30] Hooker can ground his doctrine of real presence in "participation" and still reject transubstantiation. Indeed, and interestingly, it was often the Reformers who were most eager to condemn the doctrine of transubstantiation, including John Milton, who clung to the mystery most fervently. What was at stake with the loss of the mystery of the host? Not so much: just a vision of a redeemed world, eternal life, justice, participation in a community constituted by consent rather than by rule, and by even more—love.

## Idolatry: Images and Imagination

"And truly, he that in heart and by argument maintaineth the sacrifice of the Mass to be propitiatory for the quick and the dead is an idolator; as also he that alloweth and commendeth creeping to the cross, and such like idolatrous actions . . .
—Reginald Scot, *Discoverie of Witchcraft* (1584)

The commandment against idol worship encompassed two sins: "outward idolatry of the hand, which is when men make an image or similitude, and erect and set it up for religious use" and "inward idolatry of the heart, which is when men misconceiving God, do worship him according to their misconceit."[31] Henry Wilkinson warned the House of Commons in 1643, "Let it not be said of any of you that you carry any idols in your hearts which are the greatest stumbling blocks."[32] Idols include the "invisible conceits and imaginations of our mind."[33] A strain of contemporary philosophy shares Elton's suspicion of the idol of the brain, also referred to as the idols of the mind, the eye, and the heart. These have their contemporary analogue in the "idol of the concept" and are the more or less explicit heirs of mystical theology.

Like the political legacy, the philosophical afterlife of the eucharistic debates endures. For the twentieth-century philosopher and theologian Jean-Luc Marion, the image itself is not an idol—only the apprehension of the viewer can determine if that image is an idol or an icon. "The idol makes the divine available, secures it, and in the end distorts it. . . . As idol, the concept itself arranges a presence of the divine in our image, a god who reflects back to us our experience or thought."[34] The idol is a god we have fashioned for ourselves. It projects our wants, our violence, our fears, and reflects back to us only ourselves. "Hence its prodigious political effectiveness: it renders close, protective, and faithfully sworn the god who identifying himself with the city [the nation, the people], maintains an identity for it."[35] In the end, Marion claims that the idol "is characterized solely by the subjection of the divine to the human conditions for experience of the divine." For the idol, the divine is "prey to be captured (Paul, Philippians 2:6)," whereas the authentic divine "does not *belong to* us but befalls us."[36]

For another contemporary philosopher, Emmanuel Levinas, only when we have abandoned our idols can justice prevail. The ethical demand of the Other must be invisible and prior to any question of being. One can only affirm one's Being before another's right to be: "My being-in-the-world or my 'place in the sun,' my being at home, have these not also been the usurpation of spaces belonging to the other man whom I have already oppressed or starved, or driven out into a third world; are they not acts of repulsing, excluding, exiling, stripping, killing? . . . [A kind of fear must precede being:] A fear for all the violence and murder my existing might generate, in spite of its conscious and intentional innocence."[37] And he concludes his courageous *Ethics as First Philosophy*: "To be or not to be—is that the question? Is it the first and final question? The question par excellence or the question of philosophy [is] *not* 'why being rather than nothing' but how being *justifies* itself." This leads to his wholesale revision of the entire project of Western metaphysics, with his objection to all forms of thought that submit the Other to the overview of an objectifying reason, that is, in his terms, to idolatry. "Just as a theoretical analysis of God borders on blasphemy to him, so an ontological thematization of the Other distorts the Other's very epiphany."[38] For Levinas, the irruption of the mystery of another person bears the overwhelming ethical responsibility that the irruption of the divine does; indeed, this—the face of the Other—is his understanding of divinity.

Before being, Levinas stresses the priority of the ethical. And like Levinas, Marion stresses, before being, the priority of the given, more accurately, of given-ness or donation; he objects that God cannot be made subject to the "concept of being." Why are these thinkers and others with them so intent to move beyond the concept of Being? Both fear the scandal of God being contaminated by the finiteness of Being. I would add my own suspicion: that the concept of Being has been contaminated by *possession.* After all, one of the meanings of Being that Aristotle offers is "property." The contemporary philosophical version of idolatry includes *possessing* the concept—idolatrous, in the sense of delimiting, describing, and manipulating the concept. To own the concept, to possess Being, is to turn a world that is independent and animate into one that is subject to the process of my thought; it is to turn the Other into an object, but not just any object, *my* object. What, then, is the objection to idolatry if not ultimately an objection to the violence of possession?

All of these idolatries of possession reduce the Other to use, whether economic, material, or even spiritual use. Idolatry, then, is not only about the worship of images, or about mistaking an *image* of god for the true god, or about mistaking a vehicle for the referent. Nor is it only about the worship of false gods. It encompasses wider meanings than the idolatry of "replacement" wherein worship of the wrong object is substituted for worship of the right one. It also includes the radical understanding voiced succinctly by Wittgenstein: "All that philosophy can do is to destroy idols. And that means not making any new ones—say out of the 'absence of idols.'"[39] Marion joins Wittgenstein in the radical implications of idolatry: "Visible idolatry is no more refuted by substituting one image for another, than conceptual idolatry collapses before another 'concept of God.' Idolatry is finally effaced only before the *absence* of a concept, an absence that is definitive and that initiates another approach to God—as the 'unknown God' (Acts 17:23–24)." Here, he joins company with the tradition of mystical theology articulated by Pseudo-Dionysius as the negative way to the divine and Nicholas of Cusa's "learned ignorance."

The Hebrew term for idolatry, *avodah zarah,* literally means "strange worship" and that strangeness registers in two senses: as the worship of a strange thing, but also as a strange way of worshipping. It is especially those who are sensitive to the limits of language and thought, whether ancient, like Pseudo-Dionysius, medieval, like Nicholas of Cusa, or modern,

like Emmanuel Levinas and Jean-Luc Marion, who have also been sensitive to the dangers of erecting new idols. Fixing an image of God (hence,
possessing it) is a denial of divine freedom, and for many thinkers, this is
the essence of idolatry.[40] They too have distinguished between the object
of worship—if it is false or misleading, leading to a false life, one devoted
to the wrong pursuit, an unworthy cause—and the manner of worship,
one that approaches the object in a troubling way. And like them, the
many Reformers preoccupied with idolatry sought not only to prevent
worship of a false god, but also to preserve the true One from "use." They
feared an instrumentality that sought to control the domain of mystery.
What they helped to enable, however, was arguably a new instrumentality—
not of the Eucharist by the Church, but of the sacred by the state.

How did this fear of the loss of mystery, this suspicion of idolatry,
play out at the beginnings of modernism? Throughout their rhetoric, Reformers ranging from high Anglicans to radical Puritans accused the Roman church of idolatry and the Roman Mass of being an exercise in idol
worship. While complaints varied from doctrine to hermeneutics, from
ritual acts to ritual setting, the fear of idolatry was common ground. The
two central theological controversies of the Reformation, over the Eucharist and iconoclasm, were not so distinct, then, informed as they both
were by the impulse to destroy the idol. John Knox compares the idolatry
of the Mass to ancient pagan idolatry of wood and stone, adding the qual-
ification that "the poor God of bread is the most miserable of all other
idols."[41] Cranmer did not mince words: "the people being superstitiously
enamored and doted upon the Mass . . . [this] Idolatry were taken for god-
liness and religion."[42] And the very worst of all idolatries was the worship
of the host: the "cake idol," "the god of bread," the "idol of the altar."[43]

The history of iconoclasm in the early modern period has been carefully recovered by historians, and while it is needless for me to rehearse
their accounts, I do want to highlight their conclusion: for two centuries
the systematic destruction of religious art—exquisite works of painting,
sculpture, and relief—was mandated by the state; it was believed that this
destruction of images would help to alter the beliefs of the people.[44] Much
of England's Reformation was battled over the "scenes and the ceremoni-
als," that is, the performance of rites and the apprehension of ornament in
parish churches. "The fabric of worship, its setting, circumstance, and
manner—the 'scenico apparatu' or scenic apparatus, as John Jewel called

it—was more striking, more unavoidably perceptible to most worshippers than specific or subtle alterations in the content of belief."[45] In the end, belief and the scene of belief were inseparable; iconoclasts destroyed images in order to change doctrine: "the fate of imagery was intimately associated with changes in the doctrine of the Eucharist, and iconoclasm time and again played an important part in determining the course of reforming events."[46] Zwingli's charge that the scholastics brought "the veneration of images . . . into the world along with their doctrine of transubstantiation" was not isolated.[47] Often, the abolition of imagery was a step that preceded, and to some degree made inevitable, the abolition of the Mass. In fact, the abolition of the Mass in Wittenberg, Strasbourg, and Zurich immediately followed the desecration of images in each place.

While the campaign against images began earlier,[48] during Edward VI's reign England engaged in astonishing acts of destruction of the legacy of medieval art—stone sculpture, painting, metallurgy, wood carving, stained glass. By 1960, even tombs were being smashed, prompting Elizabeth to intervene with an injunction forbidding the defacement of tombs and the smashing of glass windows. Interestingly, her proclamation forbids not only "the breaking or defacing of any parcel of any Monument, or tomb, or grave" but also makes it prohibited "to breake any image of kings, princes, or nobles, estates of this realm, or any other." While Jewel inveighed against religious images in his *Apology*, a Catholic polemicist, Nicholas Sanders, could mock Jewel for the obvious contradiction: "Breake if you dare the Image of the Queenes Majestie, or Arms of the Realme."[49] His target was well aimed, for when crosses were torn down, coats of arms were erected in their place—even on rood screens.

The age of Elizabeth confronts us with a startling fact: sixteenth-century England saw more destruction of images than any culture in the history of iconoclasm, including the ravages of the Byzantine movement eight centuries earlier.[50] And yet, in a seeming contradiction, Elizabeth's reign is marked by the elaboration of the most extensive iconography of any monarch in English history. Christ could not be made visible nor could the mother of God be represented, but the visage of the Queen was everywhere to be seen, embodying the nation in virginal purity, prosperity, and nobility. Bible frontispieces depicting Elizabeth supported by the virtues would have been seen by nearly all Englishmen; official documents included illuminations of the Queen as an "icon" of royal power; engravings and woodcuts of her image were circulated; seals and coins, like Hilliard's remarkable Second Great Seal, sought to depict the divinity of the Queen's rule.[51] Between the medallions crafted out of base metal and the cameos and miniatures worn as talismans by the upper classes, Elizabethan England was arguably engaged in a ubiquitous cult of the royal image.[52]

Representations of the monarch proliferated at the same time as the systematic destruction of statues in churches, the tearing down of crosses, smashing of funerary monuments, melting down of silver plates, burning of exquisite tapestry and carving, and the obliteration of fine art. While Church iconography was destroyed and Church ceremonies were strongly curtailed, the state was simultaneously embracing images and processionals full of pomp and ceremony. Could the era really have been oblivious to the contradiction? Or was it cynically and deliberately arrogating authority from the Church to itself?[53] There can be little doubt that the iconoclastic impulse was sincere: everywhere reformers' rhetoric expresses the impulse to bring the Church back to its founding purity. But precisely because they understood the power of the image, they could not have been unaware of the power of its use for galvanizing nationalism. Even as it attenuated the substantial character of the Church, the state constructed itself as a substantial entity. If the once-material body of Christ was now a metaphor, conversely, the metaphor of "the state" was now materialized, in spades.

The state sought to arrogate to itself the power of the sacred, seeing it as strengthening arguments for succession, consolidation, and legitimacy of power. At first, the state tried to hold mystery in tension with its substantial identity: "it pleaseth almightie God to communicate by sensible meanes those blessings which are incomprehensible."[54] It could do so by echoing former rituals, with their allusion to a transcendent power beyond human manipulation. The triumphal entry of the Queen replaced processing with the host, the Saints' Holy Days were radically reduced but the Queen's Holy Day was introduced; the images of the miracle working Christ and his mother were replaced with "portraits," better understood as "icons" of Elizabeth.[55] Doubtless, some of the age's impulse toward iconoclasm was not only to destroy all allusion to Rome—"remove the paint of Rome and you undo her"[56]—but to replace the old idols with new ones that, because they echo them, could displace them. Keenly aware that the past accumulates in the image, Elizabethan portraiture was eager to frame her iconography with associations of earlier sanctity: Virgin and mother, chaste and fecund, mediator and protector, giver of justice and giver of mercy, Astraea, Mary, and Christ.

The infusion of sacred references into secular painting was explicitly theorized. Elizabethan portrait painters were familiar with the Mannerist treatise by Paelo Lomazzo, *Trattato dell'Arte della Pittura* (1584), in which he makes no clear distinction between the sacred and secular image: as the religious image should elicit devotion, so an image of a virtuous person should inspire emulation.[57] The first five books of this treatise appeared in a translation by Richard Haydocke in 1598, where he substitutes "civil discipline" for "divine cult." The following passage, "The further importance of this beauty and majesty of the body is seen more clearly in the *divine cult* than in anything else, for it is a marvellous thing how piety, religion, and reverence for God and the saints are increased in our minds by the majesty and beauty of sacred images" is rendered as "But if we shall enter into further consideration of this beauty, it will appear most evidently, in things appertaining to *Ciuile dicipline*."[58] With its many allusions to Mary's virginity, Elizabethan iconography tried to borrow the power of mysticism from medieval Mariology but join it to pagan embodiments of power, wealth, and empire. There were portraits of Elizabeth not only holding the globe, but planting her feet on it, spanning the starry heavens and regulating the thunderstorms, thereby projecting the order of the state onto the very cosmos—here, the state is not so much regulated by the cosmos as regulating it. The divine sphere, once mysterious, is now the Queen's territory.

The theology or kingship continues through the reign of Charles and arguably even into the Republic. James I frequently made allusion to the divinity of his kingship, stressing repeatedly, as he did in 1616 before the Star Chamber "the mysterie of the King's power."[59] By the "mystery" he meant not only state secrets, knowledge denied others to limit their power, but also the religious, indeed mystical authorization of kingship. The two, indeed, were not really separable, for the inner sanctum was forbidden to others because it was holy, and the injunction to "incroach not" on the mysteries of the present state stemmed from that ideology.[60] Official portraiture from the early years of the reigns of James I and of Charles I, engravings by Willem van de Passe, depict the respective monarch enthroned, surrounded by his angelic minstrels, in echoes of representations of the Virgin. The central panel on the ceiling of the Banqueting House, entitled, "The Apotheosis of James I," depicts the Assumption of the Virgin behind the apotheosis of James as Prince of Peace. In the effigy of James I that faces the main entrance of the Bodleian Library, on the inside of the Tower of the Five Orders, his attendants are meant to represent Fame and Oxford University, but they are direct copies of the Annunciation of the Virgin.[61] Both reigns gave ideological emphasis to the family, enshrined in Robert Filmer's Stuart treatise *Patriarcha*, in which society is an extended family wherein the natural law of the "father" commanded obedience from his "children." In painting, representations of the family increase in the seventeenth century, and still the king is depicted, without the ravages of generation, as incorruptible. In a second engraving plate by van de Passe that depicts James I and his family in the court of heaven, James, looking very much alive and kingly, holds a skull; between the first and second plate, he had died, but there he is, enthroned in splendor, as an eternal body.[62]

Similarly, equestrian paintings of Charles I take religious iconography as their starting point: *Charles I at the Hunt* is Van Dyck's adaptation of the theme of the Adoration of the Magi out of his Italian Sketchbook in which he recorded impressions of Titian, and in *Charles I on Horseback*, his design refers to Tintoretto's *Flight into Egypt* from the Scuola di San Rocco.[63] "What are we to make of how Van Dyck has taken sacred art as his starting point? Perhaps he was encouraged because of the way in which the early Stuarts identified themselves with the divine. Time and again, from the *Basilikon Doron* to the *Eikon Basilike*, that is to say from the exposition to the expiation of Stuart kingship, the reader is regaled by the analogy between God and his lieutenant."[64]

While the art historian Roy Strong concludes that "the royal portrait filled the vacuum left by the pre-Reformation image cult," perhaps that substitution was not fully successful.[65] Without the theological grounding of mystery, these images often look more like naked displays of absolute authority than icons of the sacred. Haunting the question of whether or not Elizabeth succeeds as a religious icon is the deeper one: does the material embodiment of the state point beyond itself to a transcendent authority? The confusion is palpable: when the archbishop elect of Canterbury wrote to the Queen against retaining images in her reformed English church, the Queen sanctioned the removal of images from the churches, except for the royal chapel. Apparently, she thought her people did not need the images, but she did.[66] As Louis Marin notes, the relations between power and representation are complex: on the one hand, institutions of power appropriate representation as their own; on the other, representation produces power, not only by making absent things present, by conjuring them, but also by producing its subject. Given the power of images, we should not be surprised by the extraordinary efforts Tudors and Stuarts exerted to control the royal image—to erect the very idolatry they accused the Roman church of—and we should not be surprised that these efforts failed.[67]

As Gauchet describes it, once the process of visibilizing the invisible begins, it is difficult to halt. It is in the interests of temporal power to continue this process in order to harness the invisible for its purposes. Soon, rather than offering access to the invisible, the visible itself becomes the focus, reflecting back not a transcendent Other, but the state and its grasp for power. "Visibilizing" enables control: "we conquered the Jews," says the Arch of Titus in Rome "and while this arch stands, so does our conquest"; ancient sculpture became bigger and bigger, even colossal, in order to represent the colossal power of the empire. But the claim for visibility of the once-invisible harbors an implicit tension for the social body: on the one hand, access to the divine opens the way to instrumentality, to putting the authority of divinity to the service of the state; on the other hand, such visibility means losing recourse to the protection that only a completely inaccessible transcendence can offer. If the power beyond Elizabeth were "visibilized," it could be used to sanctify her policies, but if Queen Elizabeth claimed explicitly to be coterminous with transcendent power, that is, if divinity were not separate and beyond her, how could it legitimate her? The merely human claim of absolute authority exposes itself to the fragility that someone else can always make that same claim, with no ultimate court of appeal (in the beyond) to adjudicate.

Reformers saw transubstantiation as not exceeding substance, but embodying it, and ironically, this vision—so thoroughly rejected as idolatrous—became the foundation of the state. At the time when the critique against the material claims of transubstantiation was most vociferous, ironically, the state appropriated substantialism. The logic of the Eucharist—of *embodying* the supreme value—kept coming back in different forms: a substantial body became the way to figure the monarch, the state, and the nation. The results for both early and subsequent nationalism are apparent in our lingering understanding of nationalism: we have understood nations as *substantial* entities, with territory, boundaries, production, systematized power relations, so that in many ways the cult of the nation has taken on precisely the character of the religious cult that the modern world most rejected. The risk of taking "trans" out of transubstantion is to no longer transform substance or go beyond it. Hence, the substantialist resonance grew louder than the mystical presence when Christ was no longer believed to be embodied in the mystery of the host but in the social body of the nation.

When it is stripped of its mystical sense, even the Eucharist—the *mysterion*—is no longer about faith, hope, and charity, but refers to identity, one that forges insiders, with corporate shared values, and outsiders who do not share them. The restoration of the sacramental mystery to any substantialist vision can be a vital corrective to idolatry. This is not only a question of reviving dead matter, or of resisting an impulse to instrumentalize objects of the world; it is also a question of the restoration of an ethics that exceeds the politics of identity, for it seems that modern universalist rationalism cannot defeat substantial logic alone.

## PART II

JUSTITIA MYSTICA

# Shakespeare's Tragic Mass:
# Craving Justice

Iago: The wine she drinks is made of grapes.
—*Othello*, II.1

There is something unbearable about Iago's triumph in Shake-speare's *Othello*. But where does this sense of the unbearableness of injus-tice come from? Where does the impossible expectation that it will end, or the corollary belief—that the triumph of evil must mean that the world is out of joint and that eventually it will be righted—come from? What is the source of checks upon naked self-interest, relentless self-aggrandizement, sheer grasping of power? Does it really come from some rational under-standing that our will cannot be done without compromise with the wills of others, some recognition of the necessity of essentially contractual rela-tions, whether unwritten or written? Or is its source some higher desire to make the world a good place, to secure the world through acts of justice? The experience of watching *Othello* induces a particularly painful craving for justice, in part because it is brought into relief against other justices, strict and absolute, retributive and economic, that triumph disastrously over the justice that transcends these values.

In the Bible, justice breaks into the immanent world as Revelation it-self: the gift of justice. Among many other philosophers of religion, Lev-inas and Rosenzweig understand the content of the religions of the book to be not faith in an unseeable divinity or unforeseeable end, but acts of justice in daily life. The realm of religion is "neither belief, nor dogmatics, but event, passion, and intense activity."[1] For them, "Ethics is not simply the corollary of the religious but is, of itself, the element in which religious transcendence receives its original meaning."[2] But while the source of this justice may be transcendent, justice is also markedly immanent, for it only assumes shape in the world of social relations, in and between individuals and communities. When, in Gen. 1:27, man is described as being made in the image of God, this does not mean that man is Godlike as possessor of the earth, exercising dominion over it, but man is *imago Dei* in his responsibility for keeping the created order, for tending to it, for caring for it. Each act of justice comprises a human partnership in the creation. This biblical understanding of justice veers away from possession of other beings, from dominion over them, and toward respect for the integrity and safety of others: do not kill or steal or even covet what belongs to another.

This theological understanding of ethical life could avoid the modern twin terrors of "economic" justice and "strict" justice. In economic justice, beings have a price—are owned and exchanged. The world is reduced to property. In such a worldview, retribution is translated into systematic efforts to assign adequate compensation for injury.[3] Often, when the injury is felt to be immense, these rational efforts collapse to revert to the raw motive that impels them: vengeance. And in "strict justice," that vengeance is infected by a dangerous absolute: the crime cannot be paid off, only punished to the very end—with execution, genocide, or war. But the religious tradition issues cautions. *Genesis Rabbah* draws the conclusion that strict justice is utterly destructive: "When Abraham addressed his plea to God, 'Shall not the Judge of all the earth do justly?' The meaning of his words was, 'If You desire the world to continue there cannot be strict justice; if you insist on strict justice, the world cannot endure'" (Gen. R. xxxix.6).[4] Jesus recommended that you turn the other cheek. Neither strict nor retributive, biblical justice is the command to love the neighbor, to engage in acts of goodness.[5] While Paul, on occasion, reduces ancient Israelite justice to mere legalism, to Pharisaism, Jesus typically sees the demand of justice differently. He insists that justice must be fulfilled: "Do not think that I have come to abolish the Law or the Prophets; I have not come to abolish them but to fulfill them" (Matt. 5:16–18). And he sees his own death as the means to achieve the restoration of justice, the forgiveness of sins: "And he took a cup, and when he had given thanks he gave it to them, saying, 'Drink of it, all of you; for this is my blood of the covenant, which is poured out for many for the forgiveness of sins'" (Matt. 26:27–28). In this way, from its biblical institution, the Eucharist was designed to fulfill justice.

One could argue that, in paying for human sin, Christ's death is ultimately economic: a vengeful retribution, an exaction of strict justice by the Father. Anselm's theory of atonement in *Cur Deus Homo* has been read and undoubtedly misread by many Protestant liberal theologians as just that—the execution of strict divine justice. But once men have destroyed the image of God, they have lost access to it so completely that they do not even know it. The mark of the unjust is his inability to see himself as such. It is in this context, according to the doctrine of atonement, that God took on humanity—so that mankind could have access to the image of God again as an example, to learn how to restore that image, to act justly and with love for the neighbor. This logic depends upon the ethical acts of men imitating those of Jesus, and the Eastern Fathers wanted to preserve this emphasis on the example of Christ's goodness against what they perceived as a Western overemphasis on the penal understanding of atonement. They feared that the payment model reduces atonement to "the status of a simple transaction, enacted more or less entirely on the cross, and intended solely as an appeasement of the Father's wrath against sin . . . with its unrelenting concentration of the language of penal suffering and remissions from debt."[6] But theology suggests instead that nothing can "pay off" the human failure of rejecting God. Nothing makes it right. As an infinite wrong, it would call for an infinite restitution, and man is only finite. Sin—and, for that matter, salvation—are necessarily outside of any economy. Rather than paying off a debt, the gift of justice has to be given again, and this is achieved by God becoming man, enabling man to imitate God.

If Western religious thought in contexts as various as Genesis and Paul, Anselm and Levinas, persists in imagining humanity grasping for justice, how is that preoccupation felt in cultural formations that are less explicitly theological? How is the impulse to depict justice as "satisfied" in the Eucharist, if not itself satisfied, then at least addressed? How is the moral frailty of humankind moved toward executing justice and performing acts of goodness? If this impulse moves into culture, into theater for example, how does the theater differ from the Mass? On

Saturdays, playgoers could watch a revenge tragedy like the *Duchess of Malfi*, or the afflicted conscience of Hamlet tortured by a mission delivered by his father from Purgatory, or the divestiture of divine kingship in *Richard II* or the abandonment of Lear to the raging elements by his own daughters. On Sundays, when plays could not be performed presumably because they would draw their audience from would-be churchgoers, Shakespeare and his contemporaries could attend church, a service made uniform by the *Book of Common Prayer*, a service that represented 150 years of theological conflict and ritual compromise. The theater made no claims to perform "work"; the theater was not trying to effect transformations. The theater cannot *do* anything to other humans, nor can it *offer* anything to God. But ironically, it was the Reformers' very insistence that in the Mass, the sacrifice was only *represented*, and not repeated, that brought the Mass closer to the theater. After all, it was onstage that representations of events, rather than events themselves, were performed. Perhaps it is helpful to think of the Elizabethan theater as a space where a community recalled, represented, and remembered sacrifice, but did not endure it. And if, in one sense, the Elizabethan theater competed with the Mass for an audience, in another, deeper sense, it replaced it, becoming the first truly Reformed church.[7]

With *sola fides* as its watchword, much of Reformation theology belies a deep distrust of the senses. Faith is "the evidence of things unseen, the substance of things hoped for." The invisible truth is both profoundly immanent—the inner Spirit—and transcendent—the God beyond the visible. "Lies" are very often defined as sensory illusions. When Reformers accused priests of creating illusions that they wanted to be taken as reality, they were accusing them of fraud. For instance, Cranmer complained of the Catholic Mass: "is not in the ministration of the holy communion an illusion of our sense, if our senses take for bread and wine what whiche is not so indeed?" And even as anti-Catholic propagandists pejoratively referred to the Mass as fraudulent, they inflicted the same charge on the theater.

Anti-theatrical prejudice found common cause with anti-popery, equating ritual with magic, magic with the theater, and all of them with lies. "In Stage Playes for a boy to put on the attyre, the gesture, the passions of a woman; for a meane person to take upon him the title of a Prince with counterfeit porte, and traine, is by outward signes to shewe themselves otherwise than they are, and so within the compasse of a lye."[8] This pseudo-Platonic equation of lies with the senses and truth with the invisible is fraught with difficulties. A less debased understanding of the sacramental, one less dependent upon crude binary distinctions between the visible and invisible, would issue in very different valuations: the Mass could provide access to truth and the theater could be a storehouse of truths. Indeed, even Reformers understood the sacraments as the "seal" of faith, and the most common Renaissance theory of drama was that it offered an image of actual life: "the purpose of playing . . . was and is to hold as 'twere a mirror up to nature."[9]

An accumulating body of criticism has also been willing to think synoptically and fruitfully about religious ritual and the theater, sensitive not only to the ritual origins of drama in ancient Greek religions and the miracle and morality plays of medieval Catholicism, but also to the complex relation between the Elizabethan stage and the English Reformation. Two poles have emerged in these speculations, stressing either that theater is virtually a religious ritual—"for Shakespeare, the carnal spectacles of the theater are better than demystifying: they are sacramental"[10]—or that ritual is mere theater—"theatrical seduction . . . is the essence of the church."[11]

According to Stephen Greenblatt, in order to demystify the Catholic practice of exorcism definitively, Samuel Harsnett felt the need to demonstrate not only why the ritual was empty but also why it was effective, "why a few miserable shifts could produce the experience of horror and wonder [in an exorcism]. . . . He needs an explanatory model, at once metaphor and analytical tool, by which all beholders will see fraud where they once saw God." Harsnett finds that explanatory model in theater, an arena that readily acknowledges its magical mechanisms, admitting arts of illusion as such. In theater he discovers magic, not miracles: divine justice does not prevail, sin is not redeemed. Greenblatt writes that in *Lear*, the "forlorn hope of an impossible redemption persists, drained of its institutional and doctrinal significance, empty and vain . . . but like the dream of exorcism eradicable."[12] This leads him to the conclusion that, at best, theater generates expectations that are disappointed. But where Greenblatt speaks of disappointed expectations in tones of lament, I celebrate the remarkable expectation itself, so that precisely where he is discouraged, I locate hope. The very frustration of redemption is the way theater performs its moral vision. And this craving for redemption is not a sign that religion is "emptied"; this craving is itself religious.

Because it was the work of propaganda to equate ritual with theater and both with lies, we might do well, for all of their affinities, to regard the equation as deeply suspect. Ritual is not "mere theater," in the sense of false, nor for its part, does theater, however deep its affinity to religion, claim the function of a sacrament.[13] While principals may dress in elaborate costumes and perform ceremonial-like acts, clearly religious ritual makes different ontological claims from the theater. A priest is not a character "personated" by a "player" (the Renaissance terms for acting and actor);[14] rather, he is the authorized and sanctified vicar of God. Ritual summons the holy, *mysterium tremendum*, and its acts are neither imitations of life nor imitations of imitations, but acts that enable the sacred to be manifest and the transcendent to irrupt into immanence. The effect of such acts on the audience—and they are not an audience, but participants—is to be conclusively altered.[15] The acts performed by the priest are not intended to inspire pity or strike terror, as Aristotle said tragedy does, or to delight or instruct, as Horace said poetry must, but to change the world.

And what is theater? If we were to heed anti-theatrical prejudice, we would learn that the theater is a seething caldron of disease, depravity, and debauchery, an immoral realm where "players" threaten the serious business of assuming real social roles. "[The theaters] maintain idlenes in such persons as have no vocation and draw apprentices and other servauntes from theire ordinary workes and all sortes of people from the resort unto sermons and other Christian exercises, to the great hindrance of traides and prophanation of religion established by her highnes within this Realm."[16] But if we were to tune our ears to the defenders of the theater, we would hear that, for them, the relation of the world of theater to the world of reality is a more deeply considered one, and the relation of the drama to ethics—including drama's moral accountability—is equally serious. Hamlet understands the play as the very instrument that allows us to discern morality: "the play's the thing wherein I'll catch the conscience of the king." Hamlet is not sure whether he should trust his senses or the restless purgatorial ghost (the very existence of Purgatory was subject to doubt), but he does trust *conscience*. Moreover, he trusts the play's ability to exhibit that arbiter. Then too, the notion of redemption is not an empty one to Hamlet: indeed, it is his aching need for justice, for redeeming the crime, that drives the play. If the theater could not fulfill the religious craving for justice, it could and did express that craving with stunning eloquence. Whether or not it was "the purpose of playing," it was the power of performance.

If by the late Middle Ages the traditional church rites had, for some, begun to lose some of their former power, one reason was that these rites were perceived to be on a collision course with ethics.[17] Whether the strains of Protestantism indebted to Luther stressed that only faith grounds morality through Christ's merit, or with Calvin, emphasized the discipline of the Church, or like Zwingli, focused on communal responsibility, all inveighed against the perceived "abuses" of clergy and liturgy—not with secular skepticism, but with the fury of moral indignation. The theater also addressed this felt need for a moral order, differently, but perhaps as effectively as the Church. At precisely the time when the theater was under attack for fostering immorality and the rituals of Catholicism were under scrutiny for their "falsity and hollowness," the theater was reaching its apex: the old Senecan version of revenge tragedy flowered into Elizabethan moral tragedy, that is, into a tragedy of injustice. Shakespeare can be understood as "religious," then, not because his actors satisfied or did not satisfy longings for magic acts, but because he repeatedly addressed, in his way, the problem that the sacrament also addressed in its way: justice.

When sacraments figured among the important resources he called upon from the stage business of life, Shakespeare turned them to an ethical purpose. For his audience, a spotted handkerchief would allude not only to a marriage bed, to virginity and fidelity, but also to a spotted altar cloth, ocular proof of Christ's miraculous gift of his broken and bleeding body in the Eucharist. Such cloths were relics in Catholic Europe, testimonies to the miracle of the bleeding host. Through lenses that empty it of this sacramental significance, the spotted cloth in *Othello* becomes a heathenish cloth in which magic, not God, was woven. But that reading does not suffice, for the handkerchief *also* becomes ocular "proof" of a betrayal that never occurred, a piece of false testimony used wrongfully to indict the innocent. So if the reference to the religious ritual has been "emptied out," Shakespeare has refilled it. If Shakespeare has "given up on religion," as C. L. Barbar depicts him, surely he has not given up on justice: it is the imaginary that has such a deep hold on his plays that they scarcely can make sense without it. How could we understand Lear as suffering? Hamlet as tormented? Macbeth as guilt-ridden? Emptied of its sacral significance, sacrifice is meaningless killing, but Shakespeare does not have meaningless deaths in his tragedy. Like the spotted handkerchief, they are not just emptied, but refilled—with moral outrage.[18]

### Sacrifice and Murder

Much of the Reformation was spent negotiating two different meanings of death, as murder and as sacrifice. Whether a death is viewed as a murder or an act of sacrifice depends entirely on how it is framed culturally, but in both cases, its definition is at the service of some idea of justice. Death framed as a sacrifice is most often understood as a gift to a deity, as appeasing his ire for our wrongdoing. "Sacrifice" compensates, pays back, pays off, recompenses, redeems. When the gift offered is pure, chaste, unadulterated, without sin, it compensates for the impure, tainted, adulterated, sinful nature of man. Divine justice is understood to be satisfied by this retribution: "Die he or justice must," as Milton's God puts it in *Paradise Lost.* Sacrifice is substitutive and metonymic: the individual dies for the community, on behalf of the community, as Christ dies for mankind. Murder is framed very differently: far from *satisfying* the demands of justice, murder *violates* them, and its object does not heroically embrace or stoically accept destruction; he is an unwilling victim. In murder, the emphasis shifts away from the community to the individual whose death does not satisfy collective justice, but whose murder threatens collective peace. Hence, a specific kind of retributive justice comes into play: not the substitutive redemption offered by sacrifice, but the collective apparatus of the law. In that system, murder does not satisfy justice; it cries out for satisfaction.

During the Reformation, as reinterpretations of the ritual of the Eucharist occurred, the relation between sacrifice and murder, as well as their relation to justice, was also revisited. When Reformers altered joining the material godhead through transubstantiation to only *representing* God, merit was conferred on undeserving man by Christ's sacrifice "as if" the communicant were also sacrificed; merit was imputed to man for something he did not suffer. In the process, the satisfaction of justice and the gift of mercy were radically redefined. The Church and its priesthood had no agency in the economy of grace for Luther. "Once the Mass has been overthrown, I say we'll have overthrown the whole of Popedom." Luther insisted that the Lord's Supper was only a promise and a testament. "God does not deal, nor has he dealt with man in any other way than by the word of his promise. So too we can never have dealing with God in any other way than by faith in that word of promise."[19] Distinguishing the Catholic Mass from the Reformed Holy Supper, Calvin explained that "here is as much difference between this sacrifice and the sacrament as there is between giving and receiving. And such is the most miserable ungratefulness of man that where he ought to have recognized and given thanks for the abundance of God's bounty, he makes God in this his debtor!"[20] Thomas Cranmer opens his "Defence of the True and Catholic Doctrine of the Sacrament" (1550) with a preface in which he takes pains to distinguish the reformed (that is, original and true) understanding of the Eucharist from the (he thinks) misguided direction it had taken in Rome:

Our Saviour Christ Jesus according to the will of his eternal Father . . . made a sacrifice and oblation of his own body upon the cross, which was a full redemption, satisfaction, and propriation, for the sins of the whole world. . . . [H]e hath ordained a perpetual memory of his said sacrifice, daily to be used in the Church to his perpetual laud and praise. . . . But the Romish Antichrist, to deface this great benefit of Christ, hath taught that his sacrifice upon the cross is not sufficient hereunto, without another sacrifice devised by him, and made by the priest, or else without indulgences, beads, pardons, pilgrimages, and such other pelfry, to supply Christ's imperfection: and that Christian people cannot apply to themselves the benefits of Christ's passion, but that the same is in the distribution of the Bishop of Rome.

His response to this assessment is not subtle: "O heinous blasphemy . . . O wicked abomination . . . O pride intolerable . . . For he that taketh upon him to supply that thing, which he pretendeth to be unperfect in Christ, must needs make himself above Christ, and so very Antichrist."[21] Only God could perform a sacrifice. Men perform a murder. If priests were accused of presuming to act as sacrificer, offering Christ at the altar, for its part, Catholicism never claimed that the priest was the sacred executioner, only that he was the means through which Christ repeated his sacrifice of himself. But Reformers, eager to reduce the power of the priesthood, claimed that the agency of the priest was, at best, irrelevant; at worst, idolatrous, for man could not offer God—only God could offer himself.

To underscore the point, Cranmer returns to what he deems this greatest of offenses at the beginning of Book V of his *Defence*: it is neither transubstantiation nor a failure to embrace double predestination; it is presuming to repeat the sacrifice. "The greatest blasphemy and injury that can be against Christ, and yet universally used through the popish kingdom, is this, that the priests make their mass a sacrifice propitiary, to remit the sins as well of themselves as of other, both quick and dead, to whom they apply the same."[22] Cranmer claimed that the doctrines of the *Defence* were reflected in the 1549 *Book of Common Prayer* and we can discern that even as it went through its contested emendations and revisions over the language of the real presence, this much—that the sacrifice occurred once and is now only commemorated in the Lord's Supper—remained unchanged: there are no offertory prayers; the Secret Prayers, offering-prayers that refer to the *munus, oblatio, sacrificium, hostia,* and *mysterium* have been eliminated. This distinction between divine and priestly agency was reflected in the careful wording of the *Book of Common Prayer* (1559): "And although we be unworthy through our manifold sins to offer unto thee any sacrifice: yet we beseech thee to accept this our bounden duty and service, not weighing our merits but pardoning our offences. . . . Amen."[23] Reading the sacramental logic unsympathetically produced a contradiction unknown to the Roman church: if the act is repeated, then the original must be incomplete, and conversely, if the original were complete, any repetition becomes superfluous.

This harsh emphasis on remembrance alone was somewhat softened, as became evident in the sacred treatment of the wine and bread. John Jewel's understanding of the Eucharist was close to Cranmer's with the exception of his regard for the elements; the bread and the wine needed to be set aside, consecrated, in order to fulfill their sacramental function: "We affirm that bread and wine are holy and heavenly mysteries of the body and blood of Christ, and that *by them* Christ himself, being the true 'bread of eternal life,' is so presently given unto us that by faith we verily receive his body and blood" (my italics).[24] Richard Hooker's "real receptionist" understanding of the Eucharist enunciated in his *Ecclesiastical Polity* kept the emphasis on sacramental participation: "The fruit of the Eucharist is the participation in the body and blood of Christ."[25] "This bread hath in it more than the substance which our eyes behold, this cup hallowed with solemn benediction availeth . . . what these elements are in themselves it skilleth not, it is enough that to me which take them they are the body and blood of Christ."[26] After the accession of James I (provoking the Millenary Petition, and the Hampton Court Conference, which ultimately issued in the King James Bible and the Canons of 1604), church doctrine inched closer to asserting the vital importance of the bread and wine—almost, but not quite, as an offering of sacrifice—reflected in the felt need to legislate, without precedent, the consecration not only of the bread and wine, but if that supply is supplemented, even the added bread and wine must be consecrated (canon 21). For all of the Reformers' rhetoric against the "grievous error" of making an offering, by 1604, they had rejected it in doctrine far more definitively than in ritual. Nonetheless, that same year, the stage could offer a clearer—more or less satisfying?—sacrifice, of Desdemona, whose name includes the daimon of sacrifice.

Reformers were not only disturbed by the problem of agency in sacrifice; they were also clearly uncomfortable with its materiality, preferring to speak of spiritual eating and drinking instead of the literal body and blood of God: "Take and eat this, in remembrance that Christ died for thee, and feed on him in thy heart by faith, with thanksgiving."[27] When they denied the material body in the Mass, to substitute a seal of the promise of faith, they were implicitly putting the meaning of that death—as sacrifice—at risk. Foreseeing the problem, Calvin was careful to claim that the sacrament's meaning depends wholly on the body of God having been sacrificed: "It must be carefully noted that the most conspicuous, indeed almost the whole power of the Sacrament resides in these words, 'which is given for you,' 'which is shed for you.' For otherwise is would be of no avail that the body and blood of the Lord should be administered, they had once for all been *sacrificed* for our redemption and salvation."[28] His anxiety is palpable. For with the sacrifice remembered rather than repeated, how can justice be effectively satisfied? What is remembered is the suffering of Christ, the suffering of a victim, but the question still presses: is this a murder victim or a sacrificial offering?

## *Othello* and Justice

I discern a crisis over the distinction between sacrifice and murder in *Othello*, and I will glean allusions to the sacrifice of the Eucharist from the play, not to assert that Shakespeare is more or less Catholic or Protestant[29] or to establish his position on the controversy that raged in his day over the Eucharist, but to demonstrate that *Othello* is a play that evokes longing for justice. Longing, that is, for some antidote to the rhetoric of devils and hell that fills the stage, some redressing of the fiendish rituals of murderous vows, blasphemous oaths, and monstrous births of plots engendered by hell and night, invocations of whores and sorcerers, and the triumph of a deadly design that unravels as relentlessly as a providential one—but is so antithetical to providence that it springs from one who inverts the divine name, turning the tetragrammaton of Exodus 3, "I am who I am," into "I am not what I am," thereby setting sin loose upon the world. In a play where the tempter embraces divinity as surely as Milton's Satan does—"divinity of hell . . . So I will turn her virtue into pitch, and out of her own goodness make the net that shall enmesh them all" (*Othello*, II.3); "If then his Providence / Out of our evil seek to bring forth good, / Our labor must be to pervert that end, / And out of good still to find means of evil" (*Paradise Lost* I.162–65)—it seems especially terrible that the other shoe does not fall, that infernal ends are not frustrated to bring good out of evil. Desdemona has precisely that intention. When Emilia has just described to her a world in which wrongdoing issues in wrongdoing—"the ills we do their ills instruct us so"—Desdemona objects, "God me such usage send, Not to pick bad from bad, but by bad mend!" Mend, amend, make amends, redemption: Desdemona has articulated her intent to turn evil to good with stunning emphasis at the end of Act IV but that is just before, disturbingly enough, we see evil triumph and Desdemona undone.

Shakespeare challenges us to rethink these differences between a sacrifice and a murder. In his tragedies, acts of violence seem to hint toward redemption, but it is not clear that Desdemona's death redeems. Can we see her death as a sacrifice? A remission of sins? A benefit to others? A satisfaction of the demands of justice? Othello himself wants to stage it that way. The murderous Othello stages his "sacrifice" of Desdemona like a priest at the altar and before he kills her, delivers the injunction to confess derived from the communion service: "If you bethink yourself of any crime, / Unreconciled as yet to heaven and grace, / Solicit for it straight" (V.2.26–28). He tries to stage a ritual death. It is marked by prayers:

> OTH.: I would not kill thy unprepared spirit, No, heaven forfend, I would
>    not kill thy soul.
> DES.: Talk you of killing?
> OTH.: Ay, I do.
> DES.: Then Lord have mercy on me.
> OTH.: Amen, with all my heart!

And, in the role of priest, he would extract her confession:

> OTH.: Therefore confess thee freely of thy sin
>    For to deny each article with oath
>    Cannot remove, nor shake the strong conceit
>    That I do groan withal: thou art to die.
> DES.: Then Lord have mercy on me.
> OTH.: I say, Amen.

But this is a perverse priest, for the final prayer that would assure Desdemona's redemption is silenced by Othello:

> DES.: Kill me tomorrow, let me live to-night . . .
>    But half an hour, but while I say one prayer.
> OTH.: Tis too late.

Othello's carefully orchestrated sacrifice quickly turns into a vengeful murder, as even he admits:

> OTH.: O perjur'd woman, thou dost stone thy heart
>    And makest me call what I intend to do
>    A murder, which I had thought a sacrifice.
>    (V.2.31–65)

He has come to her as a divine executor of justice: "vengeance is mine," saith the Lord; "it is the cause," says Othello, bearing the terrible mission of strict justice and retribution: "else she'll betray more men." The performative confusion of Desdemona crying out to the Lord and Emilia crying "My Lord" seems to lure Othello himself into confusion about his divine mission: "I that am cruel, am yet merciful," he pronounces like an old testament deity who punishes the hardened heart, but also like the new testament Father who demands the life of his Son. But wait: he is murdering all the while, stifling Desdemona's breath *even as* he invokes mercy. Is this sacrifice or murder? If sacrifice, it should redeem, and indeed Othello alludes to the eclipse and earthquake that marked Christ's death. But none happen. He expects to see cloven hoofs on the devil Iago, but has to admit it is only a myth. And so his pretensions to being divine judge soon collapse and he assumes another role: the betrayer of divinity. No longer God the Father demanding retribution for sin, Othello becomes the Judas who betrays his master.

Amidst his confused assertions of justice, Othello virtually confesses that he has sold her:

OTH.:                         nay, had she been true,
    If heaven would make me such another world
    Of one entire and perfect chrysolite,
    I'd not have sold her for it.
    (V.2.139–42)

Like Judas, Othello brought false evidence against the blessed one, and like Judas, he kissed before he killed.

Now the traitor had arranged a signal with them: "The one I kiss" he had said, "he is the man." So when the traitor came he went straight up to Jesus and said, "Rabbi," and kissed him and then he turned him over to his death ... The chief priests and the whole Sanhedron were looking for evidence against Jesus on which they might pass the death-sentence. But they could not find any. Several, indeed, brought false evidence against him. But the evidence was conflicting. (Mark 14: 44–56)

False evidence violates justice but Othello's court of justice does not hesitate to admit it.

In the communion service in the *Book of Common Prayer*, after the recital of the Lord's prayer, it calls for the rehearsal of the Ten Commandments, with the communicant praying that each of the sins he has committed be forgiven and that grace help him ward off transgression in the future. It is little wonder that this play incites hunger for some vision of redemption, for in it, each of the commandments is broken. The name of the Lord is used in vain repeatedly; "s'blood" (Christ's blood) is the first word out of Iago's cursing mouth and "zounds" (Christ's wounds), "by the mass" are blasphemous invocations of the sacrifice. The Sabbath day is not kept holy—it sees a brawl; a father is not honored—his daughter flees him in the night and disobeys him; what belongs to the neighbor is coveted—Iago covets Cassio's position; false witness is made—Iago uses the handkerchief; and murder is committed: all of the "thou shalt nots" are violated. The only command of the decalogue that is conspicuously not broken is adultery, and it becomes, in this perverse covenant with a God who-is-not-what-he-is, the provocation of wrath. Othello succumbs to a perversion of the violence of monotheism: "For I am a jealous God, you shall have none but me."

With this old covenant broken, we may well long for a new one, written on the heart, like that of the prophets, not like the covenant broken when Israel disobeyed the law, but a Logos incarnated. And the breaking of the old law given in blood may well demand a new gift given in blood, a sacrifice, like that of Jesus. These allusions hover tantalizingly around Desdemona, who does her part in tempting us into seeing her own death as a sacrifice. She calls out in her moment of death, "O Lord Lord Lord" as Christ had, "Eli Eli." And she withstands her version of the temptation offered to Christ in the wilderness, the gift of all the kingdoms of the world: "all this dominion will I give to you and the glory that goes with it." Just as Jesus need only do homage to Satan to gain the whole world, so in Emilia's test, Desdemona could have the whole world for one infelicity.

DES.:   Wouldst thou do such a deed, for all the world?

EMIL.:   Why, would not you?

DES.:   No, by this heavenly light!

EMIL.:   Nor I neither, by this heavenly light. I might do it as well in the dark.

DES.:   Wouldst thou do such a thing for all the world?

EMIL.:   The world is a huge thing, it is a great price, For a small vice.

DES.:   Good troth, I think thou wouldst not.

EMIL.:   By my troth, I think I should, and undo't when I had done it; marry, I would not do such a thing for a joint-ring; nor for measures of lawn, nor for gowns, or petticoats, nor caps, nor any such exhibition; but for the whole world? Why, who would not make

her husband a cuckold, to make him a monarch? I should venture
purgatory for it.

DES.: Beshrew me, if I would so such a wrong for the whole world.

(IV.3.62–78)

The communion service begins with the recitation of the Lord's
Prayer, eking out its Eucharistic significance: "give us this day our daily bread
and forgive us our trespasses as we forgive those who trespass against us. And
lead us not into temptation but deliver us from evil." Desdemona is not led to
temptation, and her dying words suggest that she forgives Othello's trespass:
"Commend me to my kind Lord, O farewell!" But is she delivered from evil
or to evil? She is the soul of purity who kneels and prays before her murder.
Her prayer is drawn from the general confession of the communion service
of the *Book of Common Prayer:* "We [ac]knowledge and bewail our manifold
sinnes and wickedness, which we from time to time most grievously have
committed, by thoughts, word, and deeds, against thy divine majestie."

DES.:                    Here I kneel:
 If e'er my will did trespass 'gainst his love
 Either in discourse of thought or actual deed,

 .  .  .  .  .  .  .  .  .  .  .  .

 Comfort forswear me.
 (IV.2.153–61)

How can Desdemona's death be figured as a redemptive sacrifice
when Othello so resembles a perverse priest or even a sorcerer at a Black
Mass? At the opening of the play, he is arraigned and tried in what is virtually a witch-trial scene, "I therefore apprehend and do attach thee, For
an abuser of the world, a practiser of arts inhibited and out of warrant"
(I.2.77–79), one whose foul charms, drugs, or minerals, have bound her in
his chains of magic. But his acquittal by the Venetian Senate in this scene
does not put an end to the suggestion of dark arts in this play. He calls
Desdemona to the same court, demanding ocular proof of her fidelity—
the spotted handkerchief he had given to her—but "ocular proof" was the
technical term in witch trials for the mark on the body of the witch, the
"witch's teat," as it was so misogynistically called. To demand ocular proof
is to demand evidence of sorcery. From at least one of the (perverse) per-

spectives that reigns in the play, she is indicted: according to Iago, Braban-
tio, and Roderigo, she *has* had sexual congress with the devil.

According to historians' accounts of witchcraft beliefs, the devil himself presided at the sorcerer's mass as a big black-bearded man, or as a stink-
ing goat or occasionally as a great toad, and an infernal Eucharist took place
at the witch's sabbath where the blood of the devil is drunk instead of the
blood of God. In that context, Cassio drinks a cup that holds the devil in it
at an infernal marriage celebration: "O thou invisible spirit of wine, if thou
hast no name to be known by, let us call thee devil!" (II.3.277–79). This
seems compatible with a Reformer's version of the Mass as the work of the
devil, a Black Mass, in their rejection of transubstantiation for the invisible
spirit. Cassio will even invoke transubstantiation, not upward of man into
god, but downward, of man into beast. "I remember a mass of things," he
laments with remorse—and we can be sure the pun on Mass was not lost to
the audience—"but none distinctly, a quarrel but nothing wherefore. O
God, that men should put an enemy in their mouths, to steal away their
brains; that we should with joy, revel, pleasure, and applause, transform
ourselves into beasts! . . . To be now a sensible man, by and by a fool, and
presently a beast! Every inordinate cup is unblessed and the ingredient is
the devil" (II.3.284–303). This is the Eucharist from hell.

By means of all these perversions and inversions—all the while calling to mind doctrinal Christian solutions even as they are withheld—
Shakespeare is teasing us over and over with the possibility of redemption:
an aborted Mass ministered by a demented priest; a communion cup
turned into a vessel of drunken disorderliness and bestiality; a prayer
("Lord, have mercy on me") that is really a plea for life from the hands of
a murderer; a vow that is really a curse; a sacrifice that is really a murder; a
death that does not make the earth quake or the sun stand still; a light that,
once put out, will not rekindle. Shakespeare even assigns the most explicit
articulation in the play of that yearning for salvation to a drunk: "there be
souls must be saved, and there be souls must not be saved," slurs Cassio.
Again, Shakespeare is only teasing us with the idea of redemption, for
Cassio's high but drunken talk of salvation reduces to ludicrous pettiness:

CASSIO.: For mine own part, no offense to the general, nor any man of
quality, I hope to be saved.

IAGO.: And so do I Lieutenant.

CASSIO.: Ay, but by your leave, not before me; the lieutenant is to be saved before the ancient.

(II.3.102–6)

This tease about the idea of redemption is sustained from the beginning of the play to the end: an "old black ram"—it was a ram caught in the thicket that substituted for the sacrifice of Isaac, the typological prefiguration of the sacrifice of Christ—"tupping your white Ewe," the Lamb of God. But is there a sacrifice? Othello takes by the throat the circumcised dog—circumcision, the mark of the old covenant—and smote him thus—with the sign of the new covenant? That is, is Othello's suicide a sacrifice? Does it offer, in his self-murder of the self-defined infidel / idolater a restoration of justice, one confirmed by the legal restitution of order? Or rather, are we left aching for justice in the face of the triumph of evil? I would argue that this unmet craving for justice, so carefully incited and sustained throughout the play, is both the source of the play's tragedy and its "conscience," pointing beyond the terrors of plot and experience to another vision of human possibility.

All of this is certainly not to say that *Othello* is merely a Christian allegory; of course it plumbs the depths of all-too-human passions (as do powerful religious myths, for that matter). Nor would I want to suggest, despite the frequent dating of the play to 1604, the very year Convocation was assembled to further emend the *Prayer Book* in a period fraught with controversy over the Eucharist, that the play became Shakespeare's covert expression of what had been censured on the stage—his stand on the religious controversy.[30] The evidence is conflicting: on the one hand, a deranged Othello imagines himself a priest at a sacrifice as he performs a murder; on the other, an innocent victim, falsely accused but faithful to the last, cries out to the Lord at her death by a deranged killer, invoking prayers that did precede the Anglican communion service but do not save or redeem her.[31] These do not add up tidily to an argument that Shakespeare is either critiquing or embracing the doctrine of the sacrifice of the Mass. Rather, in a play preoccupied with the problem of evil and the problem of justice, I discern Shakespeare needing to invoke the Mass—not only the Catholic Mass, but also its infernal parody—because it addressed the problem of justice so forcefully with its promise of the remission of sins through the sacrifice.[32]

Surely something profound was lost when Reformers attenuated the

sacrifice of the Eucharist, or, to be more precise, turned it into a commemoration of a sacrifice rather than a re-enactment, a commemoration of
a moment in the distant past rather than a sacrifice that occurs at the very
moment when the communicant ingests the host, a moment when suffering is redeemed, a mysterious moment when our depravity is absolved.
Gabriel Biel was one of the most widely read authorities on the Mass at the
time of the Reformation—seven editions of his *Exposition of the Sacred
Canon of the Mass* were printed between 1488 and 1547; even Luther said it
was the best Catholics possessed on the subject—and he summarizes well
what was at stake in the loss.

In this sacrifice there is the commemoration of and calling on that unique and
perfect sacrifice by which heaven was opened, grace is given, through which alone
our works can be meritorious, through which alone all the sins of men are remit-
ted, and heavenly glory, lost by our sin, is restored.[33]

For most of Christian history, the work of redemption was able to occur
during the Mass because it is theologically grounded in a ritual temporal-
ity that is not simply or strictly linear: the sacrifice of Christ was both then
and now. Although Christ was offered but once in the natural appearance
of his flesh, nevertheless, he is offered daily on the altar, veiled under the
appearances of bread and wine. This offering of him does not, of course,
entail any suffering, for Christ is not wounded, does not suffer and die
each day, a distinction that came to be known as the bloody and unbloody
sacrifices of the Lord. As Biel summarizes, consecration and reception of
the Eucharist is called a sacrifice and an oblation both to commemorate
and to re-enact: "first, because it represents that true sacrifice and holy im-
molation made once upon the cross, and is its memorial; secondly, because
it is a *cause* through which similar *effects* are produced."[34]

Having dispelled the *opus operatum*, Reformers threatened to dispel
the sacramental organ of salvation, the means for incarnating Christ
within each communicant to effect his redemption. How frail the mantra
of their movement, "faith," must have felt before the power of the sacrifice
of the God-man that had successfully satisfied justice from the time of the
gospels to Luther.[35] With the English Church's reluctance to offer sacramental deterrence and remission of sins—that is, sacramental justice—the
scene shifted to the theater where justice was taken on imaginatively. With
its change from sacrifice to remembrance, from transformation to repre-

sentation, the Church had embraced less the power of ritual than (ironically, given its opposition to theater) the catharsis of spectacle. When communion offers a memory of a past and a promise of a future event but no redemption in the present, then redemption becomes the object of longing—in memory and in hope. Not only because Reformers foregrounded representation were they were unwittingly closer to the theater they so severely critiqued, but also because the theater too evinced the moral outrage—the longing for justice rather than its satisfaction—that became the deep structure of the Reformed ritual. On the one hand, the theater can invite its audience to long for a grace it cannot give through a faith it cannot confer. On the other, when the wine only signifies blood and does not become the blood, the Church's communion risks the slippery slope toward disillusionment: "the wine she drinks is made of grapes." And if there is no wine that is blood—not even Desdemona's—then perhaps there is no redemption, and this may well be the matter for tragedy and tears, after all, and not for the transformations of religious ritual.

That the theater should flower during the chill of Protestantism's heyday is no mystery. With bodies strewn all over the stage, the theater became a truly protestant church, where a community convened and remembered sacrifice—without the *operatum* of the Church—and where each individual was challenged privately to try to distinguish sacrifice from murder—*the* question for faith—and to crave for a justice no longer satisfied by the sacrament. Othello's distorted oath, "My life upon her faith" hauntingly suggests theater's distinct performative symbiosis of sacrifice and faith in a world that craves for both, for either, for anything but "what you know you know" as an answer to why our demi-devils ensnare our souls.

# 4

## Milton's Cosmic Body: Doing Justice

Shakespeare evinces our mysterious craving for justice. Milton takes on the mystery of doing justice. In his vision, the world was a just place once upon a time, with all created things expressing the will of God. Not only did all participate in the All; in effect, all of creation was continually transubstantiating into God. Iago's sneer against Desdemona's perfection—"the wine she drinks is made of grapes" rather than the blood of Christ—offers a chilling window onto his cynical vision of the world. In contrast, when Milton dares to imagine an unfallen world, he depicts the sun supping at evening with the ocean, receiving its "alimental recompense in humid exhalations" (*Paradise Lost* V. 425–26). There, where all ingests All, he offers an ideal natural Eucharist, and with it, an idealized vision of universal justice. This paradisal vision also inspires craving, a "real hunger" for a perfect world that is expressed, less by portraying the horrors of human nature, as in Shakespearean tragedy, than by drawing a vision of what *could be* in contrast to what is. Paradise is lost, after all.[1]

### Paradisal Communion

Milton does not mince words about the doctrine of transubstantiation: "Consubstantiation and particularly transubstantiation and papal anthropophagy or cannibalism are utterly alien to reason, common sense and human behavior. What is more, consubstantiation and transubstantiation are irreconcilable . . . with the normal use of words!"[2] Against the doctrine of transubstantiation, he hurls the accusations of cannibalism, of profaning the body of Christ by chewing, digesting, and defecating it along with charges of idolatry, of worshipping a wafer. Milton is certain that Christ is present in faith, in spirit, and not in the flesh: "The Papists hold that it is Christ's actual flesh which is eaten by all in the Mass. But if this were so, even the most wicked of the communicants, not to mention the mice and worms which often eat the Eucharist, would attain eternal life by virtue of the heavenly bread." A physical Mass brings down Christ's holy body from its supreme exaltation at the right hand of God. "It drags it back to the earth, though it has suffered every pain and hardship already, to a state of humiliation even more wretched and degrading than before: to be broken once more and crushed and ground, even by the fangs of brutes. Then, when it has been driven through all the stomach's filthy channels, it shoots it out—one shudders even to mention it—into the latrine." His rant is colorful, if conventional among his peers.

And yet (and I invoke the Miltonic *yet* with its full force of contradiction), Milton gives the communion pride of place in *Paradise Lost*. Startlingly, he embraces transubstantiation with gusto in his epic, framing the meal Adam and Raphael partake in the Garden, a meal that forms the centerpiece of *Paradise Lost*, as a communion.

> So down they sat
> And to their viands fell, nor seemingly
> The angel, nor in mist, the common gloss
> Of theologians, but with keen dispatch
> Of *real hunger*, and concoctive heat
> To *transubstantiate*;
> (V. 433–38; my italics)

What is Milton doing calling to mind theologians, real presence—which has here become, notably, "real hunger"—and why this explicit invoking of *transubstantiate* when it is such an overloaded term? Why does he allude to long intricate doctrinal debates for such a simple luncheon on the grass? The angel compares their meal to heaven's high feasts, where "Tables are set . . . and piled with Angel's food, . . . Fruit of delicious vines, the growth of heaven," and where the angels "eat, drink, and in communion sweet quaff immortality and joy" (632–38), echoing Jesus's own words at his last supper that allude to the heavenly communion: "I tell you, I will not drink of this fruit of the vine from now on until that day when I drink it anew with you in my Father's kingdom." But we anticipate, for Milton is describing paradise here—the earthly, not the heavenly kingdom. So, in the *earthly* paradise in *Paradise Lost,* what kind of communion is this? First, it takes place on a table and not an altar.

> Raised of grassy turf
> Their table was, and mossy seats had round,
> And on her ample square from side to side
> All autumn piled, though spring and autumn here
> Danced hand in hand.
> (391–95)

Secondly, the communion is not ministered by a priest in vestments, but by a naked woman.

> Meanwhile at Table Eve
> Ministered naked and their flowing cups
> With pleasant liquors crowned
> (443–45)

And this minister, the narrator assures, does not inspire distracting libidinous thoughts in her communicants. Eve crushes grapes for their drink. And the bountiful fruits of Paradise really are digested by the angel—materially, "nor in mist, the common gloss of Theologians" (435–36). Instead of the words of institution or a sermon, there is instead a conversation with the angel—a conversation whose subject is, of all things, the nature of transubstantiation. Adam and the heavenly guest converse for a third of the epic, and elsewhere Milton even defines marriage partners as "fit conversing Souls."[3] George Herbert is not alone in exalting conversation.

Adam feels himself to be inferior to his guest and protests that Raphael's "high Power so far exceed[s] human," that he must find his humble human diet offensive. Raphael corrects him, offering the hope of human elevation: "time may come when men with angels may participate; their bodies may at last turn all to spirit" (493–95). And he explains that this hope is grounded in the very nature of the universe:

> one Almighty is, from whom
> All things proceed, and up to him return,

> If not depraved from good, created all
> Such to perfection, one first matter all,
> Indu'd with various forms various degrees
> Of substance, . . .
> But more refined, more spiritous and pure
> As nearer to him placed or nearer tending
> (469–76)

Then the Angel offers the metaphor of the plant to illustrate the process of continual change into higher substance:

> So from the root
> Springs lighter the green stalk, from thence the leaves
> More aery, last the bright consummate flower
> Spirits odorous breathes: flowers and their fruit
> Man's nourishment, by gradual scale sublimed
> To vital spirits aspire . . .
> Differing but in degree, of kind the same.
> (479–90)

After the analogy, the angel offers a demonstration of this transubstantiation: he eats. Then he offers further explanation of how this wondrous digestion works,

> Wonder not then, what God for you saw good
> If I refuse not, but convert, as you
> To proper substance;
> (491–93)

And finally, he explains to Adam what this whole process is really about: it is not about the wafer turning into the body of Christ or the wine turning into the blood of Christ; it is about man turning into God—but is that not the heart of the traditional doctrine? Is that not what eating the body of God is about? And is that not what Raphael and Adam are discussing, after all? Given that the Eucharist commemorates the redemption of man's fall by Christ's death, it is quite an imaginative feat to place the communion in Paradise, with the unfallen Adam![4]

We soon learn that the whole universe is engaged in this cosmic digestive process, but with an important difference from the traditional doctrine of transubstantiation: changes are not effected by priests. They just happen naturally. The universe is a body that is engaged in ceaseless transformation, feeding and excreting, a material, digesting, concocting, assimilating body that perpetually and naturally turns matter into spirit.

> For know, whatever was created, needs
> To be sustained and fed; of Elements
> The grosser feeds the purer, Earth the Sea,
> Earth and Sea feed Air, . . .
> Nor doth the Moon no nourishment exhale
> From her moist continent to higher orbs.
> The sun that light imparts to all
> Receives from all his alimental recompense
> In humid exhalations
> And at Even Sups with Ocean
> (414–26)

In his vituperative prose, Milton described transubstantiation as a cannibalistic doctrine, but in *Paradise Lost,* he has delineated an entire vision of a transubstantiating universe.[5] And that vision of a naturally transubstantiating lost paradise implicitly critiques his theological and ecclesiastical context far more than any explicit satire would.

We can see this implicit critique by noting what Raphael's discourse on digestion and transubstantiation does *not* include. (In the heated political and theological context of *Paradise Lost,* absences are as meaningful as assertions.) He does not explain the nature of real presence; that is, he does not discuss whether the wine and wafer are only symbolic of Christ's real presence or if they translate into his very substance. He does not opine on priestly authority, on whether the Eucharist should be taken in both kinds (although his "communicants" do drink of the cup too). He does not discuss whether the Eucharist is a re-enactment of the sacrifice or a commemoration of it. He does not discuss the position of the communion table in the Garden (or whether it is an altar). He does not discuss whether the communicant must kneel when he receives it, how often to receive it, or what to do with the leftover. He does not even discuss whether it is a remedy for sin. Like Calvin, the Angel is not interested in taking up the fine points of the mystery, however much they may have preoccupied others (one supposes that in the garden, these are matters indifferent). Instead, Milton's Angel is quite focused on the one point the disputing Reformers could all agree upon—even when Luther, Calvin, Oecolampadius, and Melanchthon kept everything else about eucharistic theology under contention. In Raphael's version, like theirs, a substance does not turn into another substance. It turns into spirit—or so it seems.

Unlike those theologians, for the Miltonic Angel, spirit is only another substance, "differing but in degree, of kind the same." As one critic has shown in an insightful study of Milton in the context of the period's philosophy, spirit and matter are "two modes of the same substance: spirit is rarefied matter, and matter is dense spirit. All things, from insensate objects through souls, are manifestations of this one substance."[6] The character of Milton's universe, of the body of God, is both material and spiritual, for these are not distinct. Angels eat (and make love) without embarrassment. With his belief in the corporeality of the universe, Milton makes his contribution to the vexed controversy over the character of the Real Presence in the Eucharist: the entire digesting universe is not only tending toward God; that universe also constitutes the body of God. The longer we dwell on this vision offered by Raphael in light of the Reformers' efforts to attenuate—or reject altogether—the materiality of Christ's body in the Eucharist, the more astonishing it becomes. Even Milton inveighed against that materiality in his prose. But in the sense that the body of God is present everywhere, then, it would surely be in the wafer and the wine too—if, that is, Milton were interested in talking about them, which he pointedly is not.

To illustrate just how innovative Milton is when he sets the communion in the Garden of Eden, we can turn to both extremes of the spectrum on the eucharistic debate and still discern that, whatever else communion may suggest, it always signifies the death of Christ. First, John Eck, the chief among the Catholic apologists of the Roman Mass:

In the celebration of Mass there is sacrifice: and not only because in it the passion of Christ is represented by commemoration. The holy Catholic Church not only administers the Eucharist in commemoration of the passion, she also represents the offering of Christ's passion by the whole liturgical action of gestures, words, ritual and vestments. . . . The faithful members of the Church are in consequence made sharers in the manifold fruits of the Lord's passion. For just as the grace and merits of the Saviour are applied to the faithful through the application of the sacraments, so the merits and fruits of the Lord's sacrifice are applied to the faithful.[7]

Next, John Hales, who, in his "On the Sacrament of the Lord's Supper" adopts the opposite position: "Jesus Christ is eaten at the Communion Table in no sense, neither spiritually by virtue of anything done there nor really, neither metaphorically nor literally. Indeed that which is eaten (I mean the bread) is called Christ *by a metaphor*, but it is eaten truly and properly. The spiritual eating of Christ is common to all places as well as the Lord's Table."[8] Hales next reminds us that the communion has two purposes: to testify to our union with Christ and one another, and to commemorate the *death of Christ*. That is, both extremes of the theological spectrum include an emphasis on redemption from sin through the death of Christ. But in the garden, mankind has not yet sinned, so Christ does not yet die to redeem that sin.

Milton's Eucharist does not even call to mind the sacrifice. The body and blood of Christ are not a bleeding body, but a breathing body, indeed, a giant living pulsing universe, one whose breath joins the very breath of angels to become the spirit of God. In his imaginative flight, Milton has depicted a sinless man in the garden, with no need for the redemption signaled by the communion, engaging in communion. And readers are thereby challenged to conceive a wondrous thing: what is a sinless Eucharist? What is the radical Milton radically offering us in his radical communion? Needless to say, the repast in the garden is not a "traditional" Eucharist: man has not sinned, Christ has not been sacrificed, there is no institutional church, no church liturgy, and so such a Eucharist is impossible. Nonetheless, Milton is determined to bring *transubstantiation* to mind in the midst of a discussion of the process of the entire universe engaged in eating and digestion, determined to transform it from the popish cannibalistic rite he inveighs against in his polemic prose into a new conceptual possibility: the entire universe is ceaselessly transforming into God. In light of this perpetual cosmic communion with God—"All in All"—how minimal the Church rite must have seemed to Milton.[9]

Elsewhere, Milton's emphasis on redemption through the sacrifice is strong. In Book III of *Paradise Lost*, he depicts the Son volunteering for the Father's challenge to become mortal to redeem man's mortal crime:

> Behold me then, me for him, life for life
> I offer, on me let thine anger fall;
> Account me man; I for his sake will leave
> Thy bosom, and this glory next to thee
> Freely put off, and for him lastly die
> Well pleased,
> (III. 236–41)

And yet, even here, where the Son's "account me man" promises to be accountable and pay the debt for man, Milton has constructed the scene to make the emphasis less on the Son's sacrifice than on his choice, on the Son's *decision* to die for man, for his words are made to follow the immense silence that reigned in heaven after the Father's dreadful question—which of ye will be mortal to redeem / Man's mortal crime? (III. 214–15). We are invited, I take it, to understand that silence as signaling not any cowardice or ambivalence from the Son, but as affording responsible decision-making. Here, too, in this account of the sacrifice, Death is only given short shrift (one line) before it is vanquished:

> on me let Death wreak all his rage;
> Under his gloomy power I shall not long
> Lie vanquished;
> (III. 241–43)

We know that Milton was uncomfortable writing about the death of his God. He left his only lyric on "The Passion" unfinished; and perhaps even more remarkably, when he does rise to the challenge of writing about regaining the lost paradise, it is not regained by the passion of Christ or even his resurrection, but by the *choice* of Christ.[10] Milton is only consistent here—the moment of choice has been the center of all his major poetry—but the implications are fraught: to choose wrongly is to deny ourselves participation in the natural transformation of matter toward divinity. Our inevitable perfectibility has been corrupted, so that now we "transubstantiate down" toward death instead of eternal life.

As we have seen, the Reformers had already changed the nature of the eucharistic allusion to sacrifice: it was to be *remembered* at the communion, not *repeated.* The altar became a table; Calvary was to be called to mind, not re-enacted. Since the twelfth century, communion had been conducted separately and rather mysteriously in the Church of Rome. Only the priest could utter the words of institution and it was customary for him to elevate the host high above his head immediately afterward. With the altar physically distant, communicants could not always hear the words of institution, and with a rood screen blocking their view, they could not readily see the elevation of the host. Cranmer satirizes these practices in his charge of idolatry:

What made the people to run from their seats to the altar, and from altar to altar, and from sacring (as they called it) to sacring, peeping, tooting and gazing at that thing which the priest held up in his hands, if they thought not to honour the thing which they saw? What moved the priests to lift up the sacrament so high over their heads? Or the people to say to the priest "Hold up! Hold up!" What was the cause of all these, and that as well the priest and the people so devoutly did knock and kneel at every sight of the sacrament, but that they worshipped that visible thing which they saw with their eyes and took it for very God?"[11]

Cranmer also draws a firm distinction between a communion table and an altar. "The use of an altar is to make a sacrifice upon it: the use of a table is to serve for men to eat upon. Now when we come to the Lord's board, what do we come for? To sacrifice Christ again, and to crucify him again, or to feed upon him that was once only crucified and offered up for us?" *Altar* was so offensive a word to Reformers' ears that they struck it out of the *Prayer Book* when it was revised in 1552. As for the "table," to have a table in their midst gave communicants more access to the ritual even as it diminished the role of the priest / minister. When Calvin stressed the importance of the communal involvement in the ritual, he turned to the early church for authorization:

the Supper was to have been distributed in the public assembly of the church to teach us of the communion by which we all cleave together in Christ Jesus. . . . *The sacrifice of the Mass dissolves and tears apart this community.* For after the error prevailed that there ought to be priests to perform sacrifice on the people's behalf, as if the Supper had been turned over to them, it ceased to be communicated to the believer's church according to the Lord's commandment. An opening was made for private masses, which would seem to suggest an excommunication rather than the communion / community established by the Lord. (my italics)

In a rhetorical inversion, Calvin, who so well understood the terror of ex-communication, saw the separation of the altar as excommunicating the congregation from God. When he pursues the trope, he even sees the priest as excommunicating himself: "For the petty sacrificer, about to de-vour his victim by himself, separates himself from all believing folk."[12] Apparently, the position of the altar was a visible marker of a mighty power struggle.[13] When the bishops claimed the power to redeem, they moved the altar to the east end; and when the presbyters wrested that power away from them, they moved it back to the center. Of course, there was more than the table at stake: material or spiritual presence, sacrifice or a commemoration, hierarchical priesthood or community of saints? Like the wine and the bread, the position of the table came to symbolize all of these and more: how to achieve redemption.[14]

It was in this wider context that Milton attacked, in his prose, the ritual innovations made by Archbishop Laud. He inveighed against the moving of the communion table, claiming that

> the Table of Communion now become a Table of separation stands like an exalted platforme upon the bow of the quire, fortifi'd with bulwark and barricado, to keep off the profane touch of the Laicks, whilst the obscene, and surfeted Priest scruples not to paw, and mammock the sacramentall bread, as familiarly as his Tavern Bisket. . . . And thus the people vilifi'd and rejected by them, give over the earnest study of vertue: and godlinesse as a thing of greater purity then they need, and the search of divine knowledge as a mystery too high for their capacity's, and only for Churchmen to meddle with, which is what the Prelates desire, that when they have brought us back to Popish blindnesse we might commit to their dispose the whole managing of our salvation.[15]

In his *De Doctrina Christiana*, he is similarly impatient with the prerogative of the priesthood, and he makes the Bible the adjudicator: "There is nothing in the Bible about the Lord's Supper being administered. . . . Does it seem probable, then, that since the distribution of the Lord's Supper is assigned to no one in particular, we are right to restrict it only to ministers?"[16] Now we can better understand the force of having the mother of mankind "minister naked . . . crowning their flowing cups" at a table of grassy turf.

What are the implications of imagining a Eucharist without the death of Christ? When Milton dares to describe a Eucharist without sacrifice, he is imagining materiality without hierarchy and without violence. This absence of authority accords with the vision put forth by the Son who relinquishes his scepter at the end of time, when all shall be God:

> Sceptre and Power, thy giving, I assume,
> And gladlier shall resign, when in the end
> Thou shalt be All in All, and I in thee
> For ever, and in mee all whom thou lov'st;
> (VI. 730–33)

But in the garden, salvation is neither a memory nor a promise: the process of all turning into God is the very order of the universe. When Milton tackles the difficult problem of how to embrace rather than revile matter, without embracing authority, he achieves much. He defends freedom on two fronts, refusing to cede authority to works or to predestination. Alchemy, atomism, vitalism, the new science—each in its own way thrived in response to this problem, in response to the hunger left when people no longer fed on God's body.[17] Milton offered a different response: his vision of Paradise. In that vision, the key to salvation is not works, nor is it faith in the promise of redemption, nor is it election. It is, quite simply and sparely, obedience to the law of God.[18]

> And from these corporal nutriments perhaps
> Your bodies may at last turn all to spirit,
> Improv'd by tract of time, and wing'd ascend
> Ethereal, as we, or may at choice
> Here or in Heav'nly Paradises dwell;
> If ye be found obedient
> (V. 496–501)

In *Paradise Lost*, Milton places the cosmic communion in the lost paradise, and it will only be recovered at the end of time. In between, the body is broken or lost. The body of truth is dismembered in *Areopagitica*;[19] it is violated by the monsters of the deep in *Lycidas*, a poem engaged in a search for a longed-for, but forever lost, body. As such, *Lycidas* comprises a lament for the living Eucharist. And as one critic has shown so compellingly, Milton often imagines the dismemberment of his own body, dreading that his corpse will be so violated.[20] But in *Paradise Lost*, the body of God is figured otherwise, not as broken, dismembered, but as the body of the universe, ceaselessly digesting, or "subliming" its elements into God.

In *Paradise Lost*, Milton is also thinking about not only his communion, but ours, that is, our participation as readers in that innocent communion in the garden, and he invites us to share that magical natural repast, to taste its joy—only to bar us from it in the end. With the disobedient Adam, we are exiled from the paradisal communion. The ideal vision of union with all matter, with each other, with the universe, and with God is a repast offered to Tantalus, dangling our desire like the "various fruits of the Trees of God that heep Adam's table" when he is denied access to it. In Milton's paradisal sinless Eucharist, the emphasis falls on desire, but not on a historically achieved redemption or one forever repeatable in ritual. He thereby replaces a long tradition of reflection about the Real Presence with one of Real Hunger.

And yet, while Milton may fall silent before the mystery of redemption, he waxes eloquent on paradise. Paradise *is* his vision of a redeemed world, this lost world, this way of being in the world. And paradise is not wholly lost as long as he can imagine it and we can imagine it with him. This vision of an original goodness at the beginning of the story, instead of achieved as the goal at the end, makes it perpetually present in language, and hence, not only possible, but in language, actual. After all, this long-ago and far-away, long before any historical memory, far from any polity we know, shapes the aspirations and judgments we make about the here and now. "The excess of the immemorial and the unhoped for over our present, in so far as they tear it apart from one end to the other, is what gives to the present its precariousness and its splendid luster."[21] When we see the present world through the lenses of this paradise, we know it should not be like this; it should be otherwise. "A past more ancient than all memory and a future beyond all expectation," as Jean-Louis Chrétien writes, "confronts us each time we take speech. . . . it makes no sense to specify what there is when we no longer are, or not yet are, unless it is to transport ourselves there, by speech itself, as fictive witnesses, and thus to act as if we are already there, or still are there."[22] Paradise impinges upon the present with its vision of a world that God inhabits fully, not one from which he has departed. In such a world, to return to the imagery from *Othello,* the wine we drink is never made of *mere* grapes, for all grapes, like all things, are bursting with the glory of the Lord. That Milton is blind, defeated, and punished does not remove that garden from his vision, nor does our exile from paradise remove God from the garden. God walks in the cool of the day in paradise forever. To speak a paradise so full of God, to inhabit that space imaginatively, is perhaps the most sacramental gesture we can make.

## Unspeakable Salvation

Milton also addresses this craving for a lost paradisal communion by writing an epic about regaining paradise. In his "brief epic," Milton explicitly takes up the problem of the meaning of redemption; here, salvation means something other than the satisfaction, reparation, punishment, and suffering of Christ that have dominated the tradition. Instead of invoking the biblical scenes of the passion or exaltation for his poem, Milton turns to the biblical narratives of Christ's temptations by Satan in the wilderness, seeking to learn there "how the mighty work he might begin of savior of mankind." Milton's understanding of salvation is not drawn from any of the Christian options available to him: neither the suffering, the crucifixion, the resurrection of Christ, nor the afterlife of an eschatological paradise. Instead, in his thinking, justice can reign and paradise be regained through choice—the right choice. All of his major works are preoccupied with choosing the good when confronted by the temptation to choose evil. The role of reason in this process is considerable, so considerable that it is difficult to ascribe any mystery to it. Indeed, of all of England's Reformation poets, Milton seems, at first glance, to be the least "mystical." Jesus offers rational explanations, discursively, to Satan when he is tempted in the wilderness in *Paradise Regained*. "Reason is but choosing," Milton declares in *Areopagitica* (2.527.11). Humans are entrusted "with the gift of reason to be our own chooser" (2.514.2). But we should understand that this reason is, in Benjamin Whichcote's phrase, "the candle of the Lord," or in Milton's phrase, "the Umpire conscience" planted in man by God to enable "right reason." As God the Father says of man in *Paradise Lost*:

> I will place within them as a guide
> My umpire conscience, whom if they will hear,
> Light after light well used they shall attain,
> And to the end persisting, safe arrive.
> (III. 194–97)

Then too, in *Paradise Regained*, the temptation withstood by Jesus, which we are invited to imitate, occurs in secret, according to the narrator, and it concludes in secret. It is not the stuff of a discourse emerging from a community, politics, or the Church. The individual is tried alone, and alone, he must struggle against received wisdom in order to discover the will of God. That will—to choose good—is the work of salvation in Miltonic theology. Of all of Milton's many heresies—Arianism and Socinianism, among others—this one may be the most radical.[23] For

Milton, when Christ refuses to succumb to the temptations of pride, ambition, wealth, success, and learning, his work of salvation has already begun, in secret.

Satan's first temptation to Christ is extended explicitly as the most obvious way to save both himself and mankind: he proposes that saving is feeding.

> But if thou be the Son of God, command
> That out of these hard stones be made thee bread;
> So shalt thou save thyself and us relieve
> With food, whereof we wretched seldom taste.
> (*Paradise Regained*, I. 342–45)

Milton's Satan is not original to understand salvation as feeding.[24] Not only did Joseph save his brothers, the tribes of Israel, by feeding them, so also Boaz sustained Ruth, and hence the Davidic line, with grain. When the ancient Israelites begged for food in the wilderness, they also understood feeding as saving. Then too, Yhwh understood salvation that way when he responded by raining food from the heavens miraculously, enough to feed everyone. In the New Testament, Jesus multiplies loaves and fishes to feed his flock, and in both Testaments, the Promised Land, whether the earthly or heavenly paradise, is repeatedly described as the place where milk and honey flow. Before Christ's suffering begins, he asks that his broken body be remembered by eating the bread, instituting the ritual understood as the saving work of the Eucharist. But Milton's Jesus adamantly refuses to think of salvation as feeding: "thinkst thou such [saving] force in bread?" Jesus dares to reject the option of miraculous feeding so frequently offered in the scripture, echoing the sentiment in Deuteronomy, "He . . . fed thee with manna . . . that he might make thee know that man doth not live by bread only, but by every word that proceedeth out of the mouth of the Lord" (8:3).

The seemingly contradictory biblical precedents on feeding require interpreting, and by some principle. Elsewhere I have argued for the interpretive lens of charity: for Milton, the scripture does not say anything that would run counter to charity.[25] Here, in *Paradise Regained*, because his interlocutor is uncharitable—Jesus likes not the giver—his offers are not genuine gifts; hence, they are not real charity. Rejecting the giver, Jesus must reject the gift: "thereafter as I like the giver" (II. 321–22).

Anticipating recent gift theory, Milton understood that both the giver and the receiver are part and parcel of what constitutes "the gift." When they are false, the gift is false: "thy pompous delicacies I contemn / And count thy specious gifts no gifts but guiles" (II. 390–91).[26] Jesus distinguishes between the false gift falsely offered (demanding, as it does, the worship of the devil), and the true gift of redemption—no "thing" that is offered with an expectation of return, but a state of grace. He plumbs the doctrine of "things indifferent," showing Satan his error, for even according to that doctrine's loosening of Levitical prohibitions, all meats are still not allowed. The meats that had been reserved for idolatry are still forbidden. Satan is just such an idol, making these idolatrous foods unclean, even under the doctrine of things indifferent. Hence Jesus asks Satan, "with my hunger what hast thou to do?" The entire banquet scene dramatizes the succinct verse from I Corinthians: "Ye cannot drink the cup of the Lord and the cup of devils: ye cannot be partakers of the Lord's table and the table of devils."

Jesus interprets the manna story, not to signal salvation through bread, but to demonstrate that salvation depends solely on obedience to the word of God. In doing so, he follows not only Deuteronomy 8 but also the spirit of Exodus, for when God rains bread from the heavens, he asks the receivers to count on that sustenance, to have faith that each will have his needs met.

"That," said Moses to them, "is the bread Yhwh gives you to eat. This is Yhwh's command: Everyone must gather enough of it for his needs." . . . When they measured in an omer of what they had gathered, the man who had gathered more had not too much, the man who had gathered less had not too little. Each found he had gathered what he needed. (Exod. 16:15–18)

The hungry Israelites fail to follow their Giver's will. Distrusting providence, they hoard manna: "Moses said to them, 'No one must keep any of it for tomorrow.' But some would not listen and kept part of it for the following day, and it bred maggots and smelt foul; and Moses was angry with them" (Exod. 16:19–20).[27] Later, when the murmuring Israelites complain of manna, again doubting providence, Yhwh answers their demand for meat with a plague of quail:

The Lord said to Moses, "Tell the people, 'Now the Lord will give you meat, and you will eat it. You will not eat it for just one day, or two days, or five, ten or twenty days, but for a whole month—until it comes out of your nostrils and you loathe it—because you have rejected the Lord who is among you, and have wailed before him, "Why did we ever leave Egypt?'" (11:18–20)

Jesus concurs on the saving power of obedience, not of bread or meat (I. 351). He hungers only to do his father's will (II. 259). "My meat is to do the will of him that sent me" (John 4:34). If, in Milton's unfallen Paradise, the material world need only be obedient to aspire to God, here, at the temptation of the Redeemer, obedience is contrasted to fallen materiality. No food suffices for heeding the divine will, ritual or otherwise. A relentless Satan returns to the manna story to suggest that although God took care of the others in the wilderness—the ancient Israelites, Elijah, John—he does not feed Jesus. Uninfected by this effort to inspire envy, Jesus responds with his own consistent principle of obedience: if God has not fed him, then he must not need feeding (II. 318).

Still, Satan does not give up. Renewing his efforts to tempt Jesus with food, he sets a sumptuous banquet table before him, punctuating his temptation three times with the familiar phrase, "sit and eat." One of the phrase's biblical sources is Exodus 24, where the elders sit and eat in a covenant with God. Like Satan's earlier offer of bread, this scriptural allusion has redemptive overtones: God is saving the Israelites from bondage and delivering them through his covenant to an earthly paradise. "Sit and eat" has another allusion, to Thomas Tallis's hymn in the *Book of Common Prayer*, one of the sources for George Herbert's conclusion to "Love": "so I did sit and eat."

> behold
> Nature ashamed, or better to express,
> Troubled that thou shouldst hunger, hath purveyed
> From all the elements her choicest store
> To treat thee as beseems, and as he Lord
> With honour, only deign to sit and eat.
>     He spake no dream, for as his words had end,
> Our Saviour lifting up his eyes, beheld
> In ample space under the broadest shade
> A table richly spread, in regal mode,
> With dishes piled, and meats of noblest sort . . .
>     What doubts the Son of God to sit and eat?
> These are not fruits forbidden, no interdict

Defends the touching of these viands pure,
Their taste no knowledge works, at least of evil,
But life preserves, destroys life's enemy,
Hunger, with sweet restorative delight . . .
What doubt'st thou Son of God? Sit down and eat.
(*Paradise Regained*, II. 331–77)

The theology of salvation has included "satisfaction," indebted to both Roman public law where satisfaction meant punishment, and to private law where it meant paying back or satisfying justice. Under the doctrine of satisfaction, man's sin must be paid for, and Christ assumes this debt through his suffering and death. But Milton understands this willingness on Christ's part as a radical passivity. It is achieved only by refusing to take on other roles in salvation: feeding the hungry, ruling a nation, securing an empire, gaining all wisdom. Christ can *do* nothing. He must *suffer* everything. And this passivity deepens when we understand that he cannot even choose what he suffers. His Father has appointed his persecutors, has permitted their violence, and has designed the saving work of his Son to be their victim. Jesus waits, obeys another's will, another's time, and paradoxically, in that waiting, he acts, fulfilling his destiny as the obedient suffering servant.[28]

From Irenaeus on, the suffering, passion, and exaltation of Christ have been understood as the work of redemption, not to the exclusion of his life-work, but certainly receiving greater emphasis. For Irenaeus, Christ not only recapitulated each stage of human life, but the obedience of his passion brought salvation by undoing the sin of the tree of disobedience on the tree of the cross.[29] Tertullian added the notion of satisfaction, elaborated by Hilary who saw the death of Christ as paying satisfaction for the sins of mankind and by Anselm's doctrine of atonement in which Christ, as God-man, had assumed human nature of his own free will so that he could voluntarily pay the satisfaction owed by humanity and make that salvation available to them. With Maximus, the concept of Christ the victor was elaborated: in his death, Christ overthrew the dominion of Satan. His victory over sin and death was signaled by the resurrection. Christ "by his suffering, destroyed death and error, corruptibility and ignorance, and he endowed believers with incorruption."[30] To the imagery for salvation of sacrifice, satisfaction, and crucifixion were added, especially in the liturgy of the Eastern Church, the images of battle and victory. Needless to say, understanding salvation as achieved through the *suffering* of Christ was given renewed emphasis during the Reformation by Luther's elaborate theology of the cross. The "wondrous duel" between Christ and the enemies who enthralled mankind issued in the victory over sin and death at the cross where God was revealed while remaining hidden. Because speculative reasoning cannot discern him, the only access to God is through his suffering.[31] On the redemptive suffering of Christ, Calvin concurred, as well as on the hiddenness of divine justice; indeed, so hidden is his justice that the temptation of Job and David, for Calvin, is that they will believe that God has abandoned them along with human history.[32]

Where does Milton locate himself among these options? Seeing the Savior as victor? As offering ransom? As paying the satisfaction? Enduring the suffering of the cross? Achieving the exaltation of the resurrection?[33] Not in *Paradise Regained*. Here, Milton has greatly simplified the long intricate story of redemption in the history of Christianity (far more intricate than my summary expresses) along with the further complications presented by changing Christologies, paring it all down to what he believes is the simple essence: obedience.

Obedience is the "victor" in Irenaeus: "He [Christ] fought and was victorious; for he was man doing battle for the fathers, and by *his obedience utterly abolishing disobedience*. For he bound the strong man, liberated the weak, and by destroying sin endowed his creation with salvation."[34] If we needed a patristic explanation for Milton's choice to portray redemption as "the will to obey" in Jesus, we could not invent a more perfect one. Writing in the second century against the Gnostics, Irenaeus was especially eager to counter their dualism, to demonstrate that Satan does not share the governance of the cosmos. Satan does not own the kingdoms of the earth, leaving the heavenly kingdoms to another power: "As therefore the devil lied at the beginning, so he did also in the end, when he said: 'All these are delivered unto me, and to whomsoever I will I give them'" (Matt. 4:9). Only God distributes the kingdoms of the world. "This also the Lord confirmed when he did not do what he was tempted to by the devil."[35] "So *the Word was made flesh*, in order that sin, destroyed by means of that same flesh through which it had gained the mastery and taken hold and lorded it, should no longer be in us; and therefore our Lord took up the same first formation for an Incarnation, that so He might join battle on behalf of His forefathers, and overcome through Adam what had stricken us through

Adam."[36] Because Christ recapitulated Adam's temptations, he saves, and because Christians recapitulate Christ's temptations, they are saved.

Nevertheless, as one historian of theology summarizes, "while the relation of Jesus Christ to God and the relation of the human and the divine within his person became the subject for doctrinal controversy and doctrinal definition, the *saving* work of Christ remained dogmatically undefined."[37] And frankly, beyond Milton's affinities for the logic of recapitulation that allows his obedience before temptation to be our example, in Milton's epic devoted to salvation, the concept of salvation itself ultimately remains radically undefined. When Satan shifts from the option, if only momentarily, of salvation as ruling (whether from Jerusalem or Rome), he suggests the philosopher's solution to redemption: wisdom. Taking Jesus from Rome to Athens, Satan offers him another solution to the problem of salvation: he can conduct his "mighty work" with the instruments of classical learning, reason, and persuasion. His offer of all knowledge goes farther than scriptural learning to include the learning of the gentiles.

Given that the dialogue in *Paradise Regained* between Satan and Christ is proceeding on these very terms—relying, as it does, on both scriptural and classical learning, and conducted by reason and persuasion—Milton's Satan is now striking close to Milton's home. "*Milton* cannot really be attacking learning," Miltonists have not hesitated to apologize. But his Jesus *is* rejecting learning as tantamount to salvation. As Irene Samuel discerned long ago,[38] to grant limits to learning is nothing new: in *Paradise Lost*, one angel cautions the curious Adam to "be lowly wise" in his paradise (VIII. 173) and another gives his parting advice to the exiled couple to cling only to the wisdom "that to obey is best" (XII. 561):

> Th'Angel last repli'd:
> This having learnt, thou hast attained'd the sum
> Of wisdom; hope no higher, though all the Stars
> Thou knew'st by name, and all th'ethereal Powers
> All secrets of the deep, all Nature's works,
> Or works of God in Heav'n, Air, Earth, or Sea,
> (XII. 574–86)

"To obey is best": the first Adam's last words in *Paradise Lost* succinctly contain the proscription the second Adam embraces in *Paradise*

*Regained.* Still, the temptation of learning causes scholars unease for good reason. Making wisdom the offer of the devil, regarding philosophy and poetry, ideas and arts, as idolatrous solutions to the problem of salvation, seems difficult to square with the remarkably learned Milton.

Nonetheless, as the apophatic tradition and its recent revival in philosophy suggest, the idolatry of "the concept," as the slyest of idolatries, is the worst. Renouncing the external achievements of worldly power, philosophers have long claimed the superiority of defining the good (Plato), virtue (Aristotle), and how to live the good life (the Stoics). But in the end, these rest upon the rational idols of metaphysics. Like Satan's options for redemption, they must be refused in order for the incomprehensibility of God to be "manifest" and the ineffability of God to be "expressed." Food, power, learning: all of these temptations are still categories of the concept of being that has so strangled both theology and metaphysics. In *Paradise Regained,* Milton moves beyond these.[39] Instead of re-inscribing the idolatry of being, in effect, his Jesus suggests that we need to unsay what has been said.[40]

"Unsaying" is one way to characterize the dialogue between Satan and Jesus. As Northrop Frye noted, it is a dialogue like none other:

None of the ordinary literary categories apply to it; its poetic predecessors are nothing like it, and it has left no descendants . . . its closest affinities are with the debate and with the dialectical colloquy of Plato and Boethius, to which most of the Book of Job also belongs. But these forms usually either incorporate one argument into another dialectically or build up two different cases rhetorically; Milton's feat of constructing a double argument on the same words, each highly plausible and yet as different as light from darkness, is, so far as I know, unique in English Literature.[41]

In his argument, Jesus does far more than contradict Satan's evidence or quarrel with his reasoning; he pulls the ground out from each of Satan's presuppositions, rendering him literally speechless and also bereft of further options. When Jesus completes his argument, Satan has nowhere else to take his reasoning. His idols have been silenced, as they were by the Incarnation in Milton's youthful Nativity Ode. Having silenced the idolatrous concepts of salvation that Satan offers, Jesus does not propose new ones. Having rejected the Satanic options for redemption, he does not offer divine ones.[42] While his adversary falls silent, Jesus stands silent—silent because he has submitted himself to the mystery of divine will, to the mystery of divine grace, and to the mystery of redemption.[43]

While Milton is no "mystic" in the sense of one who has an unmediated ecstatic apprehension of God, he does invoke the negative language of mystical theology, a way not to speak about or to predicate a God whose unthinkable goodness language cannot describe. The poet who implored that the "celestial light shine inward" to reveal "things invisible to mortal sight" would surely have resonated to the *Mystical Theology,* where Pseudo-Dionysius writes, "If only we lacked sight and knowledge so as to see, so as to know, unseeing and unknowing, that which lies beyond all vision and knowledge. For this would be really to see and to know: to praise the Transcendent One in a transcending way, namely through the denial of all beings."[44] In *Paradise Regained,* it is Satan who offers what we can know and what we can think about redemption. When he is refuted, we enter a realm beyond knowing and beyond speech. "The fact is that the more we take flight upward, the more our words are confined to the ideas we are capable of forming; so that now as we plunge into that darkness which is beyond intellect, we shall find ourselves not simply running short of words but actually speechless and unknowing. . . . the more [my argument] climbs, the more language falters, and when it has passed up and beyond the ascent, it will turn silent completely, since it will finally be at one with him who is indescribable."[45] To know God would be to join God.

To read the denials of Jesus to Satan in the context of the building denials of *Mystical Theology* allows us to be attuned to the renunciation of the mystical traditions of speaking about God, goodness, and even redemption:

It cannot be spoken of and it cannot be grasped by understanding. It is not number or order, greatness or smallness, equality or inequality, similarity or dissimilarity. It is not immovable, moving or at rest. It has no power, it is not power, nor is it light. It does not live nor is it life. It is not a substance, nor is it eternity or time . . . it is neither knowledge nor truth. It is not kingship, it is not wisdom. It is neither one nor oneness, divinity nor goodness . . . it is not sonship or fatherhood and it is nothing known to us or to any other being. It falls neither within the predicate of nonbeing nor of being. . . . Darkness and light, error and truth—it is none of these.[46]

Finally, *Mystical Theology* concludes with a negation of the negations: "It is beyond assertion and denial."[47]

How do we reconcile Milton the epic poet, the loquacious prose writer, the man who spoke so eloquently and frequently of God, even here in *Paradise Regained*, with speechlessness? In Pseudo-Dionysius the *via negativa* is never separated from the *via affirmativa*; apophatic or negative theology is never isolated from kataphatic or positive theology, so we would violate him to tear the negative way out of the context of divine naming, a naming that proliferates endlessly, for all of creation can name God in praise. This constant praise fills the air in the world of *Paradise Lost*; so much that it is possible to read the entire epic as a great paean to creation.[48] The aubade sung daily by Adam and Eve urges all created things, stars, sun, moon, mists, winds, pines, and plants, to praise:

> On Earth join all ye Creatures to extol
> Him first, him last, him midst, and without end . . .
> Join voices all ye living souls, ye birds,
> That singing up to heaven gate ascend,
> Bear on your wings and in your notes his praise;
> Ye that in waters glide, and ye that walk
> The earth, and stately tread, or lowly creep;
> Witness if I be silent, morn or even
> To hill, or valley fountain, or fresh shade
> Made vocal by my song, and taught his praise.
> (V. 164–208)

"When all talk about God has been exhausted, the rest is silence."[49] Another way this has been helpfully phrased is that "the *via negativa* is not the way simply of saying nothing about God, but the encounter with the failure of what we *must* say about God to represent God adequately."[50] In short, Milton *earns* the silence that concludes *Paradise Regained* only after all of his exquisite verbal rendering of paradise in *Paradise Lost*. Ironically, where paradise is presented, it is lost, and where it is unrepresentable, it is regained.

When Satan resorts to his last option to tempt Jesus, he offers him a miracle. Specifically, he distorts Christianity's understanding of salvation as the resurrection. Satan's offer seems as miraculous as the defeat of death by Christ: jump from the pinnacle, defy nature, as it was prophesied in scripture (Ps. 9:11–12) that

> He will give command
> Concerning thee to his angels, in their hands
> They shall uplift thee, lest at any time
> Thou chance to dash thy foot against a stone.
> (IV. 556–59)

Jesus says no even to this offer of defeating death miraculously. It is not the "mighty work" of redeeming, although indeed, Jesus will die and be lifted up. But he will not select the time or the conditions by which he defeats death, nor will he accept those conditions from the devil to test his father's will to resurrect him. Quoting Deuteronomy 6:16, "Do not put the Lord God to the test," Jesus refuses to satisfy Satan's curiosity:

> Of gaining David's throne no man knows when,
> For both the when and how is nowhere told,
> Thou shalt be what thou art ordained, no doubt;
> For angels have proclaimed it, but concealing
> The time and the means:
> (IV. 471–75)

Here, as ever, he only hungers to do his father's will. Instead of performing a miracle in order to redeem mankind, Jesus will submit to his Father. He "stands fast": the central phrase in *Paradise Lost,* the final warning in Deuteronomy, and the ringing admonition given to Adam, to obey. The first Adam's failure to stand is undone by the second Adam's standing here: "now thou hast avenged / Supplanted Adam, and by vanquishing temptation, hast regained lost Paradise" (IV. 606–8). Satan falls, foiled in his efforts to grasp the nature, seize the moment, and define the means of redemption. Satan falls in *Paradise Lost*—unable to comprehend the obeisance of redemption, he is unable to achieve it—and in *Paradise Regained,* he falls again, silenced and doubly lost.

When Milton chooses the gospel narratives of the *temptation* in the wilderness, instead of the narrative of the *passion,* for his epic on regaining paradise, he makes a strong move: he makes redemption depend on the drama of refusal rather than the more familiar drama of acceptance. Milton is well aware of their interconnection—that to refuse the devil is to accept God—and he relies on his reader's awareness of the way the temptations in the wilderness foreshadow the temptation in Gethsemane to let this cup pass. Still, he makes the focus of a poem about "salvation" the *temptations*, and we would do well to restore the sense of surprise that such a move induces. For Milton, redemption is Jesus saying "no." We know he will say "yes" to his death, but not yet, and not here.

Here, he will return "private" to his mother's house, having ventured out to make his public career. Private renunciation of the wrong options, more than the public activity of preaching and miracle working, more, perhaps, than even the suffering of Jesus, regains paradise for mankind. And Milton expresses this, not coincidentally, at the end of his own public career, transvaluing what may look like political impotence during the Restoration of a monarchy that he fought to destroy into something far more heroic: refusal.[51] Milton offers no active mission for his Savior, no positive definition of salvation. Only negations. Milton may have felt, having been defeated in his struggle for a republic, that no earthly solution to salvation was within reach.[52] No nation, no empire, no wealth, and no wisdom could redeem man.

But this did not give way to hopelessness. Despite—or because—he endured blindness, isolation, poverty, and defeat, he wrote of redemption; and when he did, he understood it as refusal to succumb to the temptations that so many of his contemporaries had. In refusal, his example is no less than Jesus's; the stakes are no less than redemption. For the blind poet, "to follow the Savior is to participate in salvation, and to follow the light is to perceive the light."[53]

Although the problem of the divinity of Jesus has become largely a curiosity in the history of theology, the problem of redemption is not.[54] The problem of redemption is the ever urgent problem of justice. At the end of a career devoted fully to forging justice in any way he could—by articulating visions of a just republic, a just marriage, and a just church with copious arguments—Milton seems to have found himself at a complete loss to define justice. Like his Jesus, he had no historical precedent from ancient Israel, Greece, Rome, the early church, and certainly not from the history of England. There was no paradise on earth; worse still, there was no way that this most imaginative of political and religious thinkers, who had bequeathed to posterity his exquisite vision of an earthly paradise in his major epic, could now imagine one. Ultimately this is why *Paradise Regained* is about renunciation—not because of Milton's theological forebears, whom he only marshaled (as always) to lend credence to his own vision. This is why the work ends in silence.

According to Thomas Ellwood's account, when he suggested to Milton that he had written of paradise lost but not of its being regained, Milton initially fell silent. Later, he gave Ellwood *Paradise Regained*. We can now discern that these two responses, Milton's initial instinctive silence before the subject of redemption and his later gift of the manuscript of this epic, were, after all, one in the same. When he portrays Satan before his last desperate attempt, he depicts him summarizing all of the options for saving that Jesus has denied:

> Since neither wealth, nor honour, arms nor arts,
> Kingdom nor empire pleases thee, nor aught
> By me proposed in life contemplative,
> Or active, tended on by glory, or fame,
> What dost thou in this world?
> (IV. 368–73)

"What dost thou in this world?" is *the* question that moral philosophy and religious ethics poses to every one, and even the perfect man cannot answer it. The question goes unanswered.

This inability to imagine and articulate the restoration of justice is also, I believe, why he appended *Samson Agonistes* to *Paradise Regained,* wanting them to be read synoptically. The impossibility of achieving or imagining justice gives way to two responses. One has tragic, despairing tones: while Milton could not fathom the suffering and death of his God, he could write of the agony of the less perfect Samson. Perhaps he dare not even implicitly compare his own paltry suffering to the supreme pain of Jesus, who bore all human suffering.

> Blind among enemies, O worse than chains,
> Dungeon, or beggary, or decrepit age!
> Light the prime work of God to me is extinct,
> And all her various objects of delight
> Annulled, which might in part my grief have eased;
> Inferior to the vilest now become
> Of man or worm; the vilest here excel me,
> They creep, yet see; I dark in light exposed

> To daily fraud, contempt, abuse and wrong . . .
> O dark, dark, dark, amid the blaze of noon
> Irrecoverably dark, total eclipse
> Without all hope of day!
> . . . why was the sight
> To such a tender ball as to the eye confined?
> (*Samson Agonistes*, 68–94)

Another response to the failure to achieve paradise on earth is hopeful: this is the hope that emanates from that poet who claims to see inwardly *because* he is blind. Here, the inability to see and the inability to speak signal no failure, but rather, complete capitulation to the will of an unknowable, unsayable God. Redemption is only achieved, paradise is only regained, when we give up seeking it, says the poet who always sought it, and instead throw ourselves upon the mystery of that final goodness. Fully aware that the public career of Christ was devoted to reform and that what Christ spoke of so insistently and consistently was justice, Milton surely derived his strength and his hope from *his* example. And like the hearers of Jesus, some hearts among Milton's contemporaries were hardened, but others were opened. Poised between the examples of Samson and Jesus, Milton looks toward his future with dread and hope, with excruciating pain that we have failed to make the earth a just place, that we have lost paradise because of the guile of misguided devils and our own weakness, and with the undying hope that somehow somewhere justice will prevail, the hope that is the wellspring of messianism—like the first man and woman leaving paradise, weeping and wiping their tears, like everyman, poised between dread and hope.

## PART III

AMOR MYSTICUS

# 5

## Donne in Love: Communion
## of the Flesh

While John Milton takes the Eucharist to the cosmos, John Donne takes it to the bedroom. Between their imaginations, communion is stretched to the limits of the universe and contracted to the space of most exquisite intimacy. Even Donne's seduction lyrics can allude to communion. He dares to inject the imagery of the Eucharist into a conventional "flea poem," to tell the lady that in a mere flea "our two bloods mingled be."

> Thou know'st that this cannot be said
> A sin, or shame, or loss of maidenhead,
> Yet this enjoys before it woo,
> And pampered swells with one blood made of two,
> And this, alas, is more than we would do.
> ("The Flea")

The seducer marshals the imagery of the Incarnation and the Trinity, "Oh stay, three lives in one flea spare," to accuse the lady of the "sacrilege of three sins in killing three." He also invokes the sanctity of marriage—"This flea is you and I, and this / Our marriage bed, and marriage temple is"—and even the passion—"Cruel and sudden, hast thou since / Purpled thy nail, in blood of innocence?" Such high religious rhetoric over a flea achieves amusing ironic contrast: if the lady yields to his seduction, any honor lost by her is like the loss of a flea. And yet, despite how satiric it may be to juxtapose the sacrifice of Christ to the smashing of a flea, something serious hovers as a remainder. Physical love is sanctified, even if comically. The entire trope requires the leap that lovemaking is communion.

Without recourse to what he regarded as the logic-splitting of the doctrine of transubstantiation, Donne explored the mystery of the sacrament that is based upon the Incarnation, passion, and resurrection—turning all into the mystery of making love. In sexual love and the resurrection of the body Donne expresses the same longing: for the union of bodies and souls. This longing is not for a miracle wrought by the Church but by desire—for love, the lover, and Lover. That miracle enables the lover to live both in another body and beyond death: "We die and rise the same and prove / mysterious by this love" ("The Canonization," ll.26–27).

The poetry of Donne does not mourn a lost paradise where to behold the face of God was Adam's "highth of happiness" (*Paradise Lost,* X. 724); rather, it typically looks for the face of God in the face of the lover. The irony is palpable in light of Donne's preoccupation with cosmology and Milton's emphasis on sexuality in Eden. Along with the sexual inuendo in "The Good Morrow," Donne's poem suggests that full love, fully given, achieves a kind of resurrection, hence, a kind of redemption.

> My face in thine eye, thine in mine appears,
> And true plain hearts do in the faces rest,
> Where can we find two better hemispheres
> Without sharp north, without declining west?
> Whatever dies, was not mixed equally;
> If our two loves be one, or, thou and I
> Love so alike, that none do slacken, none can die.
> ("The Good Morrow," 15–21)

Donne's sustained attention to the Incarnation, the Passion, and the Resurrection (along with his frequently noted attention to alchemy and cosmology), and, throughout all, to love, are all part and parcel of his larger project of grasping the full life of the immanent material world. In one of his sermons, he says that the angels should envy us for having bodies, rather than we them: "Man cannot deliberately wish himself an angel, because he should lose by that wish, and lack that glory, which he shall have in his body. *We shall be like the angels* (Mark 12:25), . . . in the exalting and refining of the faculties of our souls; But they shall never attain to be like us in our glorified bodies."[1] In another sermon, Donne suggests that the "Kingdom of Heaven hath not all that it must have to a consummate perfection, till it have bodies too . . . they thought not their glory so perfect, but that it might receive an addition from creatures; and therefore they made a world, a material world, a corporeal world; they would have bodies." As God made the bodies of the sun and moon and placed them in the Firmament, "so also the Heaven of Heavens, the Presence Chamber of God himself, expects the presence of our bodies."[2] This means that he differs from Milton, for whom communion was an achievement before the world as we know it, a feature of paradise. And he differs from Herbert, for whom communion is achieved beyond this world, in an apocalyptic afterlife. For John Donne, communion—between body and soul, man and God, and human lovers—is achievable in *this* world and in *this* time. Again, what is remarkable is that he does not pursue this quasi-mystical project by transcending the world through asceticism. Rather, fully embracing materiality, sexuality, and desire, he makes them the very medium of his transvaluation. Immanence is not transcended so much as it is transubstantiated.[3] While Donne's subject longs to leave the mundane world of limited time and space to enter that of eternity and infinity, he does not simply reject one world for another; rather, he tries to break through the separation of these two worlds, to translate "here and now" into "everywhere and always." In this, he anticipates Blake's ambition "To see a World in a grain of sand . . . / And Eternity in an hour." His goal is to join time and eternity, the physical and the spiritual, the immanent and the transcendent. After all, this is what the Incarnation does, wherein God became man, and what the Eucharist does, wherein man combines with God. His method is Love.

Rather than recover Donne's many explicit allusions to holy communion, I want to heed his investment in the physical body to argue that for him, physical lovemaking recapitulates the union of God and man. So redemptive is lovemaking for Donne that he even imagines making love beyond the grave. In the introduction to *John Donne's Religious Imagination*, the editor observes, "What makes love a religious experience for Donne . . . is that the intensely private nature of the love experience allows transcendence of worldly, everyday concerns, launching the lovers out of the world of prosperity and display, in which men struggle to improve their estate or mind, into a realm of transcendent meaning." But this does not mean transcending the flesh. If "love, for Donne, is a cohering experience capable of making one little room an everywhere," it may be worthwhile to further interrogate the nature of this "experience," and to ask how love is related to religious experience.[4] It would also be helpful to substitute a term that is both more precise and more accommodating—*communion*—not only in the sense of *holy communion*, but also in the senses of *communication* and *combining*. The speakers in Donne's poetry often seek such communion with the lover and with God in all of these senses, but they also express a painful awareness of how difficult this is to achieve, how transitory its moments are, how much the lover fails to apprehend his beloved due to his own self-absorption, and how much the would-be lover fails to love due to his worldly preoccupations.

As we would expect of one of England's foremost Anglican preachers, Donne critiques the doctrine of transubstantiation.[5] Like many clergy, Donne was eager to avoid questions about the manner by which God is made present in the Eucharist: "But for the manner, how the body and blood of Christ is there, wait his leisure, if he have not yet manifested that to thee: Grieve not at that, wonder not at that, press not for that; for he hath not manifested that, not the way, not the manner of his presence in the Sacrament, to the Church." But he does more than steer clear of controversies about how God is made present in the sacrament; he also advocates tolerance toward any doctrine concerning it. Intolerance, for him, is against the very spirit of communion. "A peremptory prejudice upon other men's opinions, that no opinion but thine can be true, in the doctrine of the Sacrament, and an uncharitable condemning of other men, or other Churches that may be of another persuasion than thou art, in the matter of the Sacrament, may frustrate and disappoint thee of all that benefit."[6] Nonetheless, even after urging toleration, he cannot resist offering his own reservations about transubstantiation. It is the contradictions that Donne objects to:

There cannot be a deeper atheism, than to impute contradictions to God; neither doth any one thing so overcharge God with contradictions, as the transubstantiation of the Roman Church. There must be a body there, and yet nowhere; in no place, and yet in every place, where there is a consecration. The bread and the wine must nourish the body, nay, the bread and the wine may poison a body, and yet there is no bread, nor wine there. They multiply miracles, and they give not over, till they make God unable to do a miracle, till they make him a contradictory, that is, an impotent God.[7]

The real sacrifice of God by God cannot be compromised by miraculous changes of substance or accidents. Mocking transubstantiation, he suggests priests should also engage in "trans-accidentiation" and change the bread too. And yet Donne clings to the physical presence, objecting that symbols alone threaten to annihilate that very bodily presence of God—"there are other dissolutions of Jesus, when men will . . . mold him up in a wafer Cake, or a peece of bread; there are other annihilations of Jesus when Men will make him, and his Sacraments, to be nothing but bare signes."[8]

In his seduction poetry, nonetheless, Donne alludes to the *mystery* and *miracle* of the Eucharist frequently—in "The Ecstasy," "Love's mysteries in souls do grow, / But yet the body is his book"—the sacrament is contrasted to the Bible. In "Love's Alchemy," the speaker confesses, "I have loved, and got, and told, / But should I love, get, tell, till I were old, / I should not find that hidden *mystery*." In "Twickenham Gardens," love even "*transubstantiates* all / And can convert manna to gall"—that is, love does not simply transform welcome nourishment into an unwelcome one, but more specifically, the manna that typologically foreshadows the Eucharist can be transubstantiated by love into the vinegar-wine given to Christ on the cross—thereby alluding not only to pain and sacrifice but also to redemption.[9] In his biography of Donne, John Carey points out what should be obvious: "Donne's opinions upon such furiously controverted issues as original sin, election, resurrection and the state of the soul after death were generated by recognizably the same imagination as the poems about love and women."[10] And he goes on to note some striking correspondences:

"Love's Progress" depicts the womb and "Centrique part" of the girl whom Donne is about to delve into as a gold mine. A sermon of 1624 shows the Almighty taking the girl's place. "Centricall Gold, viscerall Gold, gremiall Gold," Donne informs his congregation, is "in the Matrice and womb of God." The same sermon makes God into the "Eastern hemisphere" of spices as well as the "Western hemisphere" of gold—"both the Indias of spice and Myne" as Donne's sweet golden girl had been in "The Sunne Rising." The bringing together of East and West—an idea Donne endlessly nags at—is, we see, like mountains, sphere, gold, and wombs, adaptable to God or girls indiscriminately.[11]

It is not just the same "fancy" that enables Donne to substitute a divine womb for a woman's womb and divine hemispheres for the lovers; it is also a theology with a long and rich tradition from the biblical Song of Songs through Bernard to Donne's contemporaries, one that reads the lover in the Song of Songs as both God and woman and that frames desire for and from God as erotic. It is less surprising that religion and love are thought of together by a scholar of Donne's learning when we heed the theological context in which they were intertwined so explicitly and so creatively for so long. I certainly would not argue that this theological context is the *only* resource for Donne's thinking about desire. Explorations of Donne's Petrarchanism have already been richly rewarding.[12] Not only do Petrarchan and divine lovers coalesce in Donne's work, but he could also lean on the tradition of Renaissance love treatises: Ficino, Pico, Leone, Bembo, Speroni, Betussi, and Tullia of Aragon were concerned with cosmological and religious love, the love between God and his world as well as between God and man.[13] Equicola's *Libro di natura d'amore* (Venice, 1536) succinctly encodes the high Renaissance union of the physical and spiritual:

love is of both the soul and the senses. . . . And whoever speaks of loving only the soul of a beautiful, wise lady is far from the truth, and even further from it is he who speaks of loving only her bodily beauty. We conclude in all cases that to love truly is to love body and soul together, necessarily to love vigorously both the one and the other; and I affirm that in such love one may not be separated from the other. The lover seeks both sensual enjoyment, and to be loved in return. Therefore the lover wants two things: from his lady's soul, love; and from her body, the fruit of love, which fruit, if given by a soul which hates us, makes us angrier than sexual deprivation, for such a sexual consummation destroys our hope for mutual love."[14]

The story of the Christian soul has often been told as a love story—a story of desire, of frustration, of anticipation, and sometimes, of consummation. This emphasis on eros is not a secondary tradition, rather the rhetoric of eros is the rhetoric of Augustine and Gregory, of Bernard of Clairvaux and William of Saint Thierry, it is the language of Hadewijch and Mechtild of Magdeburg, of St. Francis and Bonaventura, of Eckhart and the Rhineland School, of Jean Gerson and Denys the Carthusian, Nicholas of Cusa and Catherine of Genoa. Beyond the Middle Ages, it pervades the work of Luis de Leon, of John of the Cross and of Teresa of

Avila.[15] In that tradition, love is characterized as both immanent and transcendent desire, consummated in physical and spiritual union—a union of mortals that grants access to union with the immortal. It is no competition between lowly carnal love and higher spiritual love; rather, it is a commingling of them both to produce the fruit of human and religious love.[16] The Christian theological discourse on the relation between human and divine love is multiple and complex, but I read Donne as steering a course through that tradition toward not just "apprehending our relation with God" but more: Donne's God is ultimately related to man as his Lover. To love another, for Donne, is to love God and to be loved by God.[17]

To ground his "doctrine" of human love as the expression of divine love, Donne had a wide assortment of theological models to draw upon, from human analogy to the divine to participation in the divine, from man created as *imago Dei* to living a life of *imitatio Christi*. Holy Sonnet XV begins by asking, "Wilt thou love God, as he thee?" and concludes with the God / man analogy, " 'Twas much, that man was made like God before, / But, that God should be made like man, much more." Here the speaker invokes at once the *imago Dei* tradition and the Incarnation, and does more: by invoking Anne More, his wife, in what is otherwise his allusion to the Incarnation, he makes her analogous to the incarnation of God. Far from understanding the love of Anne More as provoking conflict with the love of God, she becomes the very vocabulary by which he expresses God becoming human. In an Easter sermon, Donne writes "Woman, as well as man, was made after the image of God, in the Creation; and in the Resurrection, when we shall rise such as we were here, her sex shall not diminish her glory."[18] As divine love makes human love possible, so human love grants access to the divine. Only such a presupposition can make sense of his rhetoric of divine lovemaking, where the supplicant begs to be ravished to find freedom in God: "Take me to you, imprison me, for I, / Except you enthral me, never shall be free, / Nor ever chaste, except you ravish me" (Holy Sonnet XIV, 12–14).[19] And when Donne's speaker anguishes that he is not the fortunate recipient of love, as he so often does, it is this divine / human love that he is longing for: "Or I shall soon despair, when I do see / That thou lov'st mankind well, yet wilt not choose me" (Holy Sonnet II, 12–14).

Such an understanding of human love challenges us to rethink idolatry: when love of man or woman leads *to* God instead of away from God, it cannot be idolatrous.[20] Instead of finding passion dangerous, Donne's speakers confront another threat, one more disturbing because it is more difficult to discern: the idolatry of false love. False love includes inauthentic worship and false valuation. Both "The Canonization" and "The Relic" mock the efforts of later imagined worshippers to create saints and even gods of the lovers:

> And if unfit for tombs and hearse
> Our legend be, it will be fit for verse;
> And if no piece of chronicle we prove,
> We'll build in sonnets pretty rooms;
> As well a well wrought urn becomes
> The greatest ashes, as half-acre tombs,
> And by these hymns, all shall approve
> Us *canonized* for Love.
> ("The Canonization," 29–36; my italics)

> Then, he that digs us up, will bring
> Us, to the Bishop, and the King
> To make us relics; then
> Thou shalt be a Mary Magdalen, and I
> A something else thereby,
> All women shall adore us, and some men . . .
> ("The Relic," 14–19)

But even through their light mockery, both lyrics also suggest that if there is something worthy of worship in our fallen world, it is indeed love: "The Canonization" concludes, "beg from above / A pattern of your love!" and the jeering tone is dropped at the conclusion of "The Relic": "All measure, and all language, I should pass, / Should I tell what a miracle she was."

Several sonnets from the Westmoreland manuscript address the concern of idolatry explicitly. In one, Holy Sonnet XVII, because the speaker's wife is a stream from the fountainhead of God, his love for her leads naturally enough to the water's source: "Here the admiring her my mind did whet / To seek thee, God; so streams do show the head." And because her soul is "early into heaven ravished, / Wholly in heavenly things," his mind is set: to focus on her is to focus on heaven. And yet, the speaker doubts:

But why should I beg more love, when as thou
Dost woo my soul, for hers off'ring all thine:
And dost not only fear lest I allow
My love to saints and angels, things divine,
But in thy tender jealousy dost doubt
Lest the world, flesh, yea devil put Thee out.
(8–14)

Here, where Donne's speaker imagines the possibility of infidelity to God, it is not with his wife, but with "saints and angels, things divine" or with the "world, flesh, yea devil." Loving Anne offers no temptation from loving God; human love is not the devil. Instead, he worries about another tempter. Sonnet XVIII ventures to describe what idolatry would be with more specificity. Following through the trope of the Church as the bride of Christ, it suggests that the mistake is embracing one Church: loving one institution instead of God is idolatrous. The bride of Christ could be "richly painted" on "the other shore"—the Church of Spain—or "robbed and tore / Laments and mourns in Germany and here"—the Protestant Church—or she could be on Mount Moriah or on the seven hills of Rome. But these are partial: the bride of Christ knows no single place, but all places.

Betray kind husband thy spouse to our sights,
And let mine amorous soul court thy mild dove,
Who is most true, and pleasing to thee, then
When she is embraced and open to most men.
(11–14)

The bride of Christ pleases God most when she gives to most; in this sense, "betrayal" is completely transvalued to become liberality. At her best, the bride of Christ is promiscuous, the sonnet says provocatively. No one church has exclusive possession of the faithful; conversely, they come from all churches: "from the *Eastern* Church, and from the *Western* Church too, from the *Greek* Church, and from the Latine too, and, (by Gods grace) from them that *pray not in Latine too*." Embracing eros as divine takes the speaker to the logical conclusion that the more love the better.[21] Dangers do not lurk from love, but from its lack, from not enough love, partial love, false love, and above all, no love: this is the devil. God offers himself to all, fully and freely; man's challenge is to receive that love and to reciprocate. "But though I have found Thee, and Thou my thirst has fed, A holy thirsty dropsy melts me yet. But why should I beg more love?"[22] Desire, insatiable love, more love and love of More coalesce. Over and over, the theological ground of eros informs Donne's approach to human love as surely as his theology informs his life-world.

Donne's love poetry has vexed critics most when it seems most "rakish." How can the speaker be now the suffering Petrarchan lover and now the Ovidian game-player: how could he play the devoted lover in some lyrics and the indiscriminate libertine in others? A lyric like "The Indifferent" seems to challenge the conclusion that Donne embraces human desire as the path to divinity.

> I can love both fair and brown,
> Her whom abundance melts, and her whom want betrays,
> Her who loves loneness best, and her who masks and plays,
> Her whom the country formed, and whom the town,
>
> .  .  .  .  .  .  .  .  .  .  .  .  .  .  .  .  .
>
> I can love her, and her, and you and you,
> I can love any, so she be not true.
> ("The Indifferent," 1–9)

Oddly, many of the same critics who are willing to argue that there is no secular Donne distinguishable from the religious thinker reject their own presupposition, for they reinscribe erotic dualism when they claim that Donne writes profane as well as sacred love lyrics. But for the "one-thinker" contention to hold, we must rise to the challenge of understanding lyrics like "The Indifferent" within a sacred framework.[23] The seemingly secular poems must be also "divine" on another register.

> Let me, and do you, twenty know.
> Rob me, but bind me not, and let me go.
> Must I, who came to travel thorough you,
> Grow your fixed subject, because you are true?
>
> Venus heard me sigh this song,
> And by love's sweetest part, variety, she swore,
> She heard not this till now; and that it should be so no more.
> She went, examined, and returned ere long,
> And said, "Alas, some two or three
> Poor heretics in love there be,
> Which think to 'stablish dangerous constancy.

But I have told them, 'Since you will be true,
You shall be true to them, who are false to you.' "
("The Indifferent," 15–27)

While we should not turn a deaf ear to the playfulness of this lyric, it makes a point that Donne endorses elsewhere with high seriousness: there can be too little love, not too much.

The title puns on the doctrine of *adiaphora*, or "things indifferent"— the idea often invoked in the Reformation that some things are neither commanded nor forbidden, neither good nor bad. Indifferent, wrote Jerome to Augustine, is that which is neither good or bad, so that, whether you do it or not, you are neither just nor unjust. Much was at stake in this doctrine for Reformers, for it offered them the defense they needed for faith alone over against the Roman Church's ritual traditions. As Melancthon argued in the Augsburg Confession (1530), it is mistaken to believe that

the differences of Meats, and such like human traditions, are works available to merit grace, and are satisfactions for sins. And that the world thus thought is apparent by this—that new ceremonies, new orders, new holidays, and new fasts, were appointed; and the teachers in the churches did exact these works as a service necessary to deserve grace; and they did greatly terrify men's consciences, if ought were omitted. Of this persuasion concerning traditions many disadvantages have followed in the Church.[24]

Taken together, the biblical prooftexts distinguish faith from the religious traditions that legislate ritual. They include: "Do not let anyone judge you by what you eat or drink, or with regard to a religious festival, a New Moon celebration or a Sabbath day. These are a shadow of the things that were to come; the reality, however, is found in Christ" (Col. 2:16–17).

Does Donne's lyric—which seems to celebrate a promiscuous lover with light mockery—register this serious Reformation theological context? The speaker of the poem distinguishes the "indifferent" not from what is commanded or forbidden; he places what is indifferent in another context: "true" or "false." This unsettles the category, for while some things may be neither good nor bad in themselves, people are either faithful (true) or unfaithful (false). Furthermore, statements are either honest (true) or dishonest (false). "True" and "false" do not sit comfortably in a doctrine about things indifferent, for there is no zone of indifference between these states.

Furthermore, far from being "neither commanded nor forbidden," both infidelity and lying are explicitly forbidden in the Decalogue, and those commandments are never attenuated in the New Testament. On the contrary, amid the injunctions delivered in Acts 15:29 as appropriate substitutes for the Pharisaical demand of circumcision (the earliest of the "Church's works") is to abstain from food polluted by idols and from sexual immorality—these are *not* indifferent. "Things indifferent" alluded to ritual requirements that Reformers thought were arbitrary; it never encompassed infidelity or falsehood. Throughout biblical and theological discourse—as a reader with Donne's sensitivity well knew—infidelity is an analogy for idolatry. They are frequently interchangeable, as in Jeremiah's inveighing against Israel for "committing adultery with lumps of stone and pieces of wood." When Donne's speaker confesses himself as unfaithful, is he not also defining himself as an idolator? "I can love you and you and you and you"—this is not indifferent in the theological context; it is *sin,* and the speaker does eventually acknowledge himself a sinner who is worshipping a false god, Venus, whose doctrine is variety, a false doctrine.

But this is not all, for Donne does not only use "false" to convey infidelity and lack of faith. He also invokes its meaning as dishonest. His speaker's Venus utters a doctrine that resounds with punning:

> Venus heard me sigh this song,
> And by love's sweetest part, variety, she swore,
> She heard not this till now; and that it should be so no more.

[By her doctrine of variety, she demands "no more constancy," as well as "no More"—Anne More, his wife.]

> She went, examined, and returned ere long,
> And said, "Alas, some two or three
> Poor heretics in love there be,
> Which think to 'stablish dangerous constancy.
> But I have told them, 'Since you will be true,
> You shall be true to them who are false to you.'"
> ("The Indiffent," 19–27)

Critics have acknowledged one meaning: that if a woman is faithful (and there are only two or three such women), she will be devoted to one who is unfaithful. But another meaning that may offer a key to reading the entire lyric has been curiously neglected: if she is honest, she is honest to one who is dishonest and hence he is dishonest also about depicting himself as promiscuous. If you are true to one who is false to you, and who asserts his promiscuity falsely, then he is really true, in the sense of faithful. Donne has offered the reader another hint of his speaker being "true," this one structural: ending his other two stanzas with "true" he invites the reader to expect the final stanza to conform: that expectation interacts with his explicit statement of the opposite, making the echo of "true" challenge his assertion of falsity. He has been posing as unfaithful throughout, but is genuinely faithful, and he thereby redefines the "indifferent" not as the unfaithful, but as the faithful. This is precisely the deep emphasis of the doctrine of things indifferent for Reformers. Faith, faithfulness, fidelity, and only faith—not only rituals—must be embraced.

The soul of Donne's "wit" is to offer different and often contradictory meanings that interplay. On the one hand, the speaking subject of "The Indifferent" is false about his fidelity; but perhaps on the other, if he *is* indiscriminate in his love, he is like the bride of Christ in the lyric "betray, kinde husband, thy spouse to all our sights," who loves all. In that reading, the god of Love would indeed regard the limitation of love to one alone as heresy. But this has also a theological dimension in the embrace of generosity and liberality, that Donne demonstrates in a sermon: "All the good things that we can consider, Light, Sight, Gold, all are accompanied with a liberality of themselves, and are so far good, as they are dispensed and communicated to others; for their goodness is in their use."[25] Perhaps the challenge is to hold both the priorities of faithfulness and liberality, in the sense of generosity, in creative tension, to embrace the one love—the Creator—and thereby to allow that love to overflow onto all of the creation.

Does this mean that *every* Donne lyric that seems licentious is, upon closer scrutiny, endorsing fidelity? Surely the drive to universalize such a complex, playful poet would be suspect; nonetheless, we should be alert. For instance, in "Twickenham Gardens," where the speaker carries on histrionically with Petrarchan tropes: "Blasted with sighs, and surrounded with tears," daring other lovers to compare their mistress's tears to his, for "all are false that taste not just like mine," here, it is the lady's *fidelity* (to another, her husband), not her falsehood, that is the cause of his despair:[26] "O perverse sex, where none is true but she, / Who's therefore true, because her truth kills me" ("Twickenham Gardens," 26–27).

While the biblical texts concerning "the indifferent" focus on the prohibition of certain meats (and that became the section heading in the Augsburg Confession of 1530), they are also part of a larger nexus that includes not only distinguishing between meats, but also determining who can marry and the grounds of forbidding adultery. In his *Doctrine of Discipline of Divorce,* Milton also inveighs against prohibiting "things indifferent," and for him, two of those "things indifferent" are separation and divorce.

The greatest burden in the world is superstition; not onely of Ceremonies in the Church, but of imaginary and scarcrow sins at home. What greater weakning, what more suttle strategem against our Christian warfare, when besides the grosse body of real transgressions to encounter; wee shall bee terrify'd by a vain and shadowy menacing of faults that are not: When *things indifferent* shall be set to over-front us, under the banners of sin, what wonder if wee bee routed, and by this art of our Adversary, fall into the subjection of worst and deadliest offences. The superstition of the Papist is, *touch not, taste not,* when God bids both: and ours is, *part not, separat not,* when God and charity both permits and commands.[27]

Charity trumps prohibitions for Milton as surely as faith trumps deeds for Donne.[28]

Seizing on this homology of food and sexuality, Donne plays with it further in his lyric, "The Community," a term alluding to common, a social group, and communion.

> Good we must love, and must hate ill,
> For ill is ill and good good still,
> But there are things indifferent,
> Which we may neither hate, nor love,
> But one, and then another prove,
> As we shall find our fancy bent.

The speaker proceeds to define women as things indifferent and therefore as available for use:

> But since she [Nature] did them so create,
> That we may neither love, nor hate,
> Only this rests: All, all may use.

This speaker seems less concerned with his stance of libertinism than with the nature of women and whether they can be good or bad. Good ones are betrayed to all eyes, and in that way, presumably, rendered bad. Bad ones "waste" and so do not remain bad, but disappear. So both are indifferent, he argues, neither good nor bad. But for all its playfulness, the poem becomes, in the final stanza, not only sexually but also theologically charged.

> But they are ours as fruits are ours,
> He that but tastes, he that devours,
> And he that leaves all, doth as well:

If "they are ours as fruits are ours" whether, tasted, devoured, or left, then again, it is the *use* to which the fruit is put and not the thing itself that causes sin. But its strong allusion to the original sin, wherein the fruit was expressly forbidden by God, suggests that perhaps to taste and devour are not at all indifferent. In that context, in which women are as expressly forbidden as the forbidden fruit, they are not indifferent. And if "changed loves are but changed sorts of meat," then the doctrines that no meats are forbidden (for all are indifferent) is invoked again, wherein what we ingest is in itself neither clean nor unclean; those categories describe our souls. But because Donne works inside a theological context that forbade meat used in the service of idolatry—"you are to abstain from food sacrificed to idols" (Acts 15:29)—that prohibition can render the vision of all women being used by all men as idolatry.

The final couplet is as sexually outrageous as it is theologically conventional:

> Changed loves are but changed sorts of meat,
> And when he hath the kernel eat,
> Who doth not fling away the shell?

The offensive implication that having had the favors of a woman (her kernel) the man would fling her away conforms to the stance of the speaker as a libertine. But the language of kernel and shell also permeated Reformation discourse on the Eucharist, where the kernel signaled the substance and the shell the accidents. In that sense, the final couplet suggests, when you have the substance, why worry about the accidents? When you have taken in the true Christ, why worry about the status of the bread and the wine? "Community," then, means not only the community of the women and men who have one another sexually; it also alludes to communion.

And the "changed loves" are not only new women, but the change in Christ. No transubstantiation is needed for his doctrine of community. The All (of Christ) gives to all (the congregation). Having taken in Christ (the kernel), the shell (the bread and the wine) are unnecessary.[29] In the end, the theological argument helps us make sense of the sexual one: asking who needs the shell when he has the kernel, the speaker has suggested that he does not need "all" these women because he has All in having his one true love. In his poem "Community," communion and community are once again imagined together through sexuality.

Donne would doubtless be loath to subscribe to the distinction Raphael makes between lust and love in *Paradise Lost*. There, the Angel cautions Adam to understand that while passion is bestial, love is human.

> In loving thou dost well, in passion not,
> Wherein true Love consists not; love refines
> The thoughts, and heart enlarges, hath his seat
> In Reason, and is judicious, is the scale
> By which to heav'nly Love thou may'st ascend,
> Not sunk in carnal pleasure, for which cause
> Among the Beasts no Mate for thee was found.
> (*Paradise Lost*, VIII. 588–94)

Human love enables one to ascend the scale to heavenly love for Donne too, but this is made possible *by* (not despite) erotic desire. Passion is the very motor that drives love. In Donne's work, love is not only contemplative, spiritual, and abstract. It is "elemented," material, and active.

> Love's not so pure, and abstract, as they use
> To say, which have no mistress but their Muse,
> But as *all* else, being elemented too,
> Love sometimes would contemplate, sometimes do.
> ("Love's Growth," 11–14; my italics)

Donne's *all* is not only the apocalyptic folding into the Deity at the end of time when "all shall be in All." He also uses the stock theological phrase rather heretically—to signal the woman. She,

> Who being here filled with grace, yet strove to be,
> Both where more grace, and more capacity
> At once is given: she to Heaven is gone,

> Who made this world in some proportion
> A heaven, and here, became unto us *all*,
> Joy (as our joys admit) *essential.*
> ("Second Anniversary," 465–70; my italics)

Here, it seems that the woman, like Christ, is essence of all, ascends and descends, full of grace, making this world a heaven. The woman, like Christ, becomes us all, and turns us into the essence of all, the all of being—joy.[30]

Donne's debt to Pseudo-Dionysius is extensive in his sermons—in references to the liberality of God's creation, to God creating out of His desire to disseminate goodness, and in repeated emphasis on human communion with the divine. Among his lyrics, that debt may be most explicit in "Negative Love," where he relies on the Dionysian distinction between kataphatic (positive) theology and apophatic (negative) theology. Again, the first approaches God with what can be said about Him; the second approaches God with what cannot be said. Within the context of the *via negativa,* the following lines become an apt description of divine love:

> If that be simply perfectest
> Which can by no way be expressed
> But negatives, my love is so.
> ("Negative Love," 10–12)

Then, the poem takes its complicating turn:

> To all, which all love, I say no.
> If any who decipher best,
> What we know not, ourselves, can know,
> Let him teach me that nothing; this
> As yet my ease, and comfort is:
> Though I speed not, I cannot miss.
> ("Negative Love," 13–18)

Here, "all" points both to the divine All as well as to all women. And saying no to this All is both a negative love of God and remaining faithful to one woman. Fidelity and faith are expressed together, as "nothing." (In addition to referring to God, "nothing" alludes to a woman's genitals in early modern slang.) The speaker claims that while he does nothing to succeed, he cannot fail to attain his goal: but "cannot miss" is also can not-miss, the negative of woman, suggesting, even when he speaks of attainment, that something about the woman will elude him.[31]

In "Air and Angels," the "lovely glorious nothing" that the speaker would approach but cannot find assumes "lip, eye and brow." As the child of love, the soul assumes a body.

> But since my soul, whose child love is,
> Takes limbs of flesh, and else could nothing do,
> More subtle than the parent is
> Love must not be, but take a body too;
> ("Air and Angels," 7–10)

In theological terms, his love is the purview of negative theology, wherein God is unseeable, unknowable, unnamable, without predication—as in Exodus where "no one can see the face of God and live," and Moses asks God for his name, only to be told "I am who I am." "Twice or thrice had I loved thee, / Before I knew thy face or name." The poem is packed with allusions to the negative theophany of Exodus—where God appears but does not appear as a burning bush, "so in a shapeless flame / Angels affect us oft, and worshipped be"; and to the mystery of the Trinity, where Christ is the embodied God while the Spirit is not embodied. The speaker hedges: "Twice or thrice had I loved thee." But embodied, the beloved becomes what Jean-Luc Marion has termed a "saturated phenomenon": too much to comprehend, too much to encounter, dazzling, overwhelming.[32] Her physical beauty is dazzling, so dazzling that the lover is unable to approach love. She is inaccessible, not in her absence, but in her overwhelming presence. The vessel of love is "overfraught." And yet, it is in this seeming paradox that, by means of materiality, man's soul achieves some measure of union with the ineffable God.

In a sermon Donne expresses wonder that the entire creation is made from nothing: "a cloud is as nobly born as the sun in the heavens; and a beggar, as nobly, as the King upon earth; if we consider the great-grandfather of them all, to be nothing: to produce light of darkness thus, is a Revelation, a manifestation of that, which, till then, was not: . . . A Leviathan, a whale, from a grain of spawn; an oak from a buried acorn, is a great; but a great world from nothing, is a strange improvement."[33] As the creation begins, remarkably, from nothing, so the revelation at the end is also of nothing. "St John's is a Revelation too: a manifestation of that state, which shall be, and be for ever, after all those which were produced of nothing, shall be returned and resolved to nothing again . . ."[34] In another sermon Donne speaks of man's soul as made in the image of God in the sense "that this soul is made of nothing, proceeds of nothing. . . . Now, not to be made at all is to be God himself: Only God himself was never made. But to be made of nothing; to have no other parent but God, no other element but the breath of God, no other instrument but the purpose of God, this is to be the image of God. For this is nearest to God himself, who was never made at all, to be made of nothing."[35] Donne does not shirk the consequences for our knowledge: "The less any thing is, the less we know it: how invisible, how unintelligible a thing then, is this nothing!" Knowing is grasping the unknowability of the nothing.[36]

Origen, Augustine, Gregory the Great—all described the workings of the inner soul, its craving for God, in sensual terms, drawing upon the example of the Song of Songs. The Christian theological tradition of interpreting the Song of Songs as the marriage of the Church to the bride of Christ began with Origen, who wrote in the prologue to his commentary, "This book seems to me an epithalamium, that is, a wedding song, written by Solomon in the form of a play, which he recited in the character of a bride who was being married and burned with heavenly love for her bridegroom, who is the Word of God." He offers two allegorical senses for the bride: "Whether she is the soul made after His image or the Church, she has fallen deeply in love with Him."[37] It reached its finest flowering in the twelfth century when Bernard of Clairvaux produced his "Sermons on the Song of Songs." For him, "There are only two evils—or two chief evils—which war against the soul: an empty love of the world and too much self-love" (Sermon 1:1.2.11). "And when we have put these evils from us, we can then feed on another discourse, the Song of Songs."[38]

Not only is Donne's emphasis on erotic and spiritual yearning drawn from the Christian mystical tradition, but also many of Donne's rhetorical devices are indebted to its language of "spiritual sense": his resort to paradoxes and punning, to synaesthesia, and over and above the combination of senses, the joining of affect to intellect. The fusion of feeling and knowing was captured in the well-known phrase from medieval Latin Christianity, *amor ipse intellectus est.*[39] The rhetoric of Christian mysticism translates external sensory language into a language of interiority. Origen explains this coincidence of exterior and interior in his analysis of the

Song of Songs: "The divine scriptures make use of homonyms, that is to say, they use identical terms of describing different things . . . so that you will find the names of the members of the body transferred to those of the soul; or rather the faculties and powers of the soul are to be called its members." And when he approaches the question inspired by the Song of Songs (2:5): "What does scripture mean when it says I am wounded with love?" he combines feeling and thought, the senses and intellect. "If there is anyone who has ever been pierced with the loving spear of his knowledge so that he yearns and longs for him by day and night, can speak of nothing but him, can hear of nothing but him, can think of nothing else, and cannot desire nor long nor hope for anything save him, that soul then truly says, 'I have been wounded by love.' "[40] To this Augustine adds the synaesthesia that combines vision, feeling, and thought to attempt to describe inner experience. But while Origen, Gregory of Nyssa, Augustine, and Gregory the Great all maintain some distinction between external sensory experience and the inner spiritual senses, these are blurred by Bernard of Clairvaux, whose "book of experience" (*liber experientiae*) encompasses both.[41] Can it be a surprise that many centuries later the hallmark of Donne's work is discerned to be his yoking together of thought and feeling?

The classic guide for those who follow the path of love in Christian spirituality is Bernard. Hence, Dante chose Bernard as his spiritual guide at the climax of *The Divine Comedy*. And for this reason, Donne quotes the twelfth-century Cistercian's works so frequently in his sermons. "In a century that was unique in Western history for the cultivation of love, Bernard towered above his contemporaries," writes one theologian appreciatively: "In his eulogies of human love, he echoed the troubadours, trouvères, and the writers of romance; but unlike his secular counterparts, he saw this love as a symbol of the soul's love for Christ, and he charted a journey through love to union with God."[42] Bernard speaks of "likeness" between self-knowledge and knowledge of God (*iam in aliquo similes*) in Sermon 30, seeing this likeness portrayed in the Song of Songs as the creature who retains its resemblance to God, desiring to return to the being who made divine likeness. He also refers to the Song of Songs as "bread," thereby lending the text all the allusions of feeding and the eucharistic meal: "O most Kind, break your bread for those who are hungering for it; by my hands, if you will allow, but by your own power. Tell us, I beg, by whom, about whom, and to whom is said 'Let him kiss me with the kiss of his mouth'?"[43]

Bernard's ensuing theological argument is constructed from a literary close reading of the Song of Songs, one that culminates in his understanding that all of sacred history comes down to erotic consummation. God joins to man in the Incarnation and in turn, Christ offers the kiss that joins mankind to God. Bernard asks insistently,

Why this sudden and abrupt beginning in the middle of a speech? For he breaks into words as if he had mentioned a speaker in the text, to whom this speaker is replying as she demands a kiss. Then again, if she asks for or demands a kiss from someone, why does she clearly and specifically say "with his mouth," as if lovers were in the habit of kissing with anything but the mouth, or with mouths which are not their own? Yet she does not say, "let him kiss me with his mouth" but, more intimately, "with the kiss of his mouth."[44]

He will argue in his second sermon that the kiss is the Mediator between God and man. As an attentive literary critic, he pauses to analyze the prefatory material; the title says not simply "song" but song *of songs*. Israel sang a song to the Lord (Exod. 15:1–19), Deborah sang (Judg. 5:1), Judith sang (Jth. 16:1), the mother of Samuel sang (I Sam. 2:1), and some of the prophets sang too (Isa. 5:1–2, 26:1–10), and none of them is said to have called his song the "song of songs."[45] Among all of Israel's many songs to the Lord, only here is "expressed the longing of the holy soul, its wedding song; and exulting in the Spirit, he composed a joyful song."[46]

Let those who have experienced it enjoy it; let those who have not, burn with desire, not so much to know it as to *experience* it. It is not a noise made aloud, but the very music of the heart. It is not a sound from lips but a stirring of joy, not a harmony of voices but of wills. It is not heard outwardly. . . . Only he who sings it hears it, and he to whom it is sung—the Bride and the Bridegroom. It is a wedding song indeed, expressing . . . the concord of their lives and the mutual exchange of their love. (my italics)[47]

Each experiences the joy of God in a different way, with him varying the joys he bestows, but desire is paramount: love is "constantly on the watch" and "whoever drinks of this water will thirst again" (John 4:13). "The soul no longer sees the Bridegroom as King, but as Beloved. . . . The soul welcomes the Bridegroom in wonder and thanksgiving that grow stronger as he gives himself to the spouse even more. This mutual praise produces a kind of intoxication of the soul."[48] "Suddenly its flame grows and, with the sudden burst of unaccustomed ardor, the presence of God is recognized. 'It burns with sweetness'" (57:7). "He does not appear; he enters the soul. He touches and excites the heart, communicating his love without saying much" (31:6).

The joining of lover and beloved, of man and God, are theologically inscribed in the Incarnation, communion, marriage, and resurrection, which helps to explain why these so often flow into one another in Donne's thought. It is difficult to discern which of these theological themes governs his thinking, so intertwined are they, but we can suggest plausibly that marriage is the governing trope. "GOD is *Love*, and the *Holy Ghost* is amorous in his *Metaphors*; everie where his *Scriptures* abound with the notions of *Love*, of *Spouse*, and *Husband*, and *Marriadge Songs*, and *Marriadge Supper*, and *Marriadge-Bedde*."[49] In his sermons, marriage not only "describes" the creation and incarnation, it even suggests the union of mortality to immortality in the resurrection.

In thy first work, the Creation, the last seale of thy whole work was a Mariage. In thy Sonnes great work, the Redemption, the first seale of that whole work, was a miracle at a Mariage. In the work of thy blessed Spirit, our sanctification, he refreshes to us, that promise in one Prophet, that thou wilt mary thy selfe to us for ever: and more in another, That thou hast maryed thy selfe unto us from the beginning . . . And as thou hast maryed in us two natures, mortall and immortall, mary in us also, the knowledge, and the practise of all duties belonging to both conditions.[50]

These unions of mortal to immortal and the allusion to a life of love beyond death are full of eucharistic sensibility. It is not too much to say that metaphorically, Donne puts marriage in the place of the Eucharist as the "sacrament" or mystery of union.

Because baptism and the Eucharist were the only two sacraments that the Anglican church retained from Catholicism, eliminating the others, including marriage, for lacking biblical grounding, it is all the more surprising that Donne casts marriage as the sacrament of union. For him, marriage unites man to woman and both to God, it unites them physically as well as spiritually, and it unites them eternally—like the Eucharist:

for that *union* with God, which is also our salvation, (as this *vision* is) when we shall be so united, as that we shall *follow the Lambe whither soever he goes*, though that union be unexpresible here, yet here, there is a union with God, which represents *that* too. Such an union, as that the *Church* of which we are parts, is his *spouse* and that's *Eadem caro*, the same body with him; and such an union, as that the obedient *children* of the Church are *Idem spiritus cum Domino*, we are the same *body*, and *the same spirit*: So united, as that by being sowed in the visible Church, we are *Semen Dei*, the seed of God, and by growing up there in godlinesse, and holinese, we are *participes Divinae naturae*, partakers of the divine Nature it selfe. Now these two unions, which represent our eternall union with God (that is, the union of the *Church* to him, and the union of *every good soule* in the Church to him) is the subject of the Song of Songs, this heavenly *Poeme*, of *Solomons*; and our *baptisme*, at our entrance into this world, is a Seale of the union; our *marige*, in the passage of this world, is a *Sacrament of this union*; and that which seems to be our dissolution, (our death) is the strongest *band* of this union, when we are so united, as nothing can disunite us more. (my italics)[51]

It is difficult to imagine a more eloquent paean to the union of body and soul, and both with God. It is doubtless the beauty of this bond that makes Donne able to express such yearning for it.[52]

Bernard writes, "Alternating throughout life between union with and separation from its Spouse, the soul knows both the joy of his coming and the sadness of his going away. The suffering is that much greater for having tasted such sweetness."[53] "The 'perception of God' for Gregory of Nyssa is "a paradoxical state in which every enjoyment of God is also at one and the same time the kindling of a more intense and unfulfilled desire, and in which every knowing of God is also a grasping of his transcendental unknowability."[54] The pursuit of God is endless (*epektasis*). This fervent desire for God, this longing for union and the agony of separation—this sweetness and suffering—preoccupy Donne. He returns again and again to this longing for union:

From the beginning God intimated a detestation, a dislike of *singularity*, of beeing *Alone*. The first time that God himselfe is named in the Bible, in the first vers- of *Genesis*, hee is named *Plurally, Creavit Dii, Gods*, Gods in the plural, Created Heaven and Earth. God, which is but *one*, would not appeare nor bee presented so *alone*, but that hee would also manifest more persons. As the *Creator* was not *singular*, so neither were the *creatures*; First he created *heaven* and *earth*; both together; which were to be the generall parents, and out of which were to bee produced all other creatures; and then, he made all those other creatures plurally too; *male and female created hee them*; And when he came to make *him*, for whose sake (next to his own glory) he made the whole world, *Adam*, he left not *Adam alone*, but joyned an *Eve* to him; Now, when they were married we know, but wee know not when they were *divorced*, we heare when *Eve* was made, but not when shee *dyed* . . . So much detestation hath God himselfe, and so little memory would hee have kept of any singularity, of being alone. *The union of Christ to the whole Church is not expressed by any metaphore, by any figure, so oft in the scripture, as by this of Marriadge, and there in that union with Christ to the whole Church, neither husband, nor wife can ever die.*"[55]

Donne concedes that Christ excludes marriage in the afterlife, because there is no need of it in heaven; "(because they need no physick, no mutuall help, no supply of children)" but he still insists, remarkably, that lovemaking is not expressly ruled out: "yet he excludes not our *knowing* [carnally], or our *loving of one another* upon former knowledge in this world, in the next; Christ does not say expressely we *shall* yet neither does he say, that we *shall not know one another* there. Neither can we say, we *shall not*, because we know not how we *should*."[56] Donne is so committed to this vision of sexual consummation after death that he even projects it back to paradise where, "After all, the first man Adam awoke from his slumber, like our death, to find Eve, bone of his bone, and he knew her."[57]

## Resurrecting Love

In Donne's work, the body not only makes love, it also suffers fevers and tortures; it dies and is resurrected, it is disassembled and reassembled.[58] His work depends so completely on embodiment that it is difficult to imagine how he could express love, agony, or salvation without it.[59] The author whose poem envisions the torn flesh of Christ does not shy away from reminding his congregations "that Jesus wrought redemption through pouring out his blood" in his sermons. Donne dwells insistently upon the meaning of the sacrament of sacrifice. Allusions to the passion, the bodily presence of God, as well as the communicant's material union with God, abound. And while Donne may have accepted the doctrinal line against transubstantiation, his fascination with both the sacrifice and the resurrection of the body suggest that the body of God was central for his theology. For Donne, the real and tangible body of Christ—and not just the spirit—stars in this drama of love, suffering, and redemption. As Bernard put it to Abelard, both redemption and forgiveness come "through his blood."[60] Just as Donne displaces the impulses of union from the Eucharist onto marriage, so he defers the physical presence of God from the Eucharist to the resurrection; and in this, he has both liturgical and theological precedent. In the Liturgy of the Eucharist of Basil, Christ had "come by the cross into Hades, in order that he might fulfill in himself the pangs of death, and by arising on the third day, open the way for all flesh to the resurrection of the dead."[61] Moreover, in the Liturgy of Basil, the words of institution themselves were amplified to include the resurrection: "for as often as you eat this bread and drink this cup, you proclaim my death and you confess my resurrection." Putting the words of Paul from I Corinthians 11:26 into the mouth of Christ, the confession of resurrection is added to the very heart of the Eucharist.

The resurrection and physical love are bound together in Donne's lyric, "The Ecstasy," with the entire seduction depending on the conceit of the resurrection of the body. The speaker describes the separation of the lovers' souls from their bodies—their souls are sent out of their bodies to negotiate—and then their souls combine, with an "abler soul" forming from the interanimation of the two souls. "We" is now defined, not as the new soul, but as the two bodies left behind.

> As 'twixt two equal armies, Fate
> Suspends uncertain victory,
> Our souls, (which to advance their state,
> Were gone out), hung 'twixt her, and me.
> And whilst our souls negotiate there,
> We like sepulchral statues lay . . .
> ("The Ecstasy," 13–18)

Their motionless bodies are like the images of the dead, and their souls hover between two armies—not only the two speakers (presumably faced off in an argument about having sex), but they also hover between physical and nonphysical love. Two victories are at stake: the resurrection's victory over death, but also the victory of physical love. With these separated souls hovering, the solution to the implied challenge, "do you only love my body?" becomes clear.

> This ecstasy doth unperplex
> (We said) and tell us what we love,
> We see by this, it was not sex,
> We see, we saw not what did move:
>
> .  .  .  .  .  .  .  .  .  .  .
>
> When love, with one another so
> Interanimates two souls,
> That abler soul, which thence doth flow,
> Defects of loneliness controls.
> We then, who are this new soul, know,
> Of what we are composed, and made,
> For, th'atomies of which we grow,
> Are souls, whom no change can invade.
> (29–48)

Their combined soul seems superior for it is incorruptible and eternal, and this should contrast with the corruptibility of the body. Instead, the poem embraces their bodies, denying the "change" of corruptibility and asserting that their bodies are equally immortal: "small change, when we're to bodies gone." That "small change" also offers the sexual innuendo of an erection. The mortal and immortal, corruptible and incorruptible, sexual and religious are indissociable here. What ensues is a paean to the body that resonates with eucharistic language and sensibility: "We owe them *thanks*" (in Greek, *eucharistia*), and "Love's *mysteries* in souls do grow" (again, the Greek for *sacramentum* was *mysticum*), and the imagery moves from body to blood (lines 70–71).

> But O alas, so long, so far
> Our bodies why do we forbear?
> They are ours, though they are not we, we are
> The intelligences, they the sphere.
> We owe them thanks, because they thus,
> Did us, to us, at first convey,
> Yielded their forces, sense, to us,
> Nor are dross to us, but allay.
> (49–56)

Here, the bodies are "they" and the souls "we." And Donne calls upon his rich resources for images of the body—from astronomy to alchemy—to depict manifestations of the physical universe from the cosmos to atoms.

> On man heaven's influence works not so,
> But that it first imprints the air,
> So soul into the soul may flow,
> Though it to body first repair.
>
> . . . . . . . . . .
>
> So must pure lovers' souls descend
> T'affections, and to faculties,
> Which sense may reach and apprehend,
> Else a great prince in prison lies.
> (57–68)

The soul descends into the sensible body as Christ descends into a sensible body, but the allusion to the Platonic image of the body as prison house of the soul is put to an opposite purpose from the Platonic one, to ratify the senses, not the soul. The phallic overtones of the imprisoned "great prince" contrast with the "love revealed."

> To our bodies turn we then, that so
> Weak men on love revealed may look;
> Love's mysteries in souls do grow,
> But yet the body is his book.
> (69–72)

Because we are weak, we need assurances, revelations. He alludes to two kinds of revelation: the sacrament, the *mysticum* of the soul, and the Bible, but the body is the *book*.

> And if some lover, such as we,
> Have heard this dialogue of one,
> Let him still mark us, he shall see
> Small change, when we'are to bodies gone.
> (73–76)

In the end, they will still interanimate one another as physical lovers, as their souls did spiritually—as God raises man's body with his soul, giving him life beyond death. As the body and soul of lovers are united in "The

Ecstasy," so the body is resurrected to join the soul for eternity. Further-more, the "little death," orgasm, is not so much the end of life, as its con-dition. That is, the condition of ecstasy is not just the soul leaving the body, ex-stasus, but reentering to recombine with it. Donne's lyric probes the mystery of love: its ecstasy wherein one leaves the body only to reen-ter it and combine with another, body and soul. And it probes the mys-tery of a body divinized through material combining, one whose death is followed by eternal life with its eternal union of body and soul, man and God.

Among the many times that Donne argues for the resurrection of the body with the soul are three sermons that he gave (in 1626) on I Corinthi-ans 15:29: "Now if there is no resurrection, what will those do who are baptized for the dead? If the dead are not raised at all, why are people baptized for them?" In them he argues repeatedly,

> We are assured then of a Resurrection, . . . But of what? Of all, Body and soule too; For *Quod cadit, resurgit*, says S. *Hierome*, All that is falne, receives a resurrec-tion; and that is . . . the person, the whole man, not taken in pieces, soule alone, or body alone, but both. . . . A man is not saved, a sinner is not redeemd, *I am not re-ceived into heaven, if my body be left out*; The soule and the body concurred to the making of a sinner; and body and soule must concur to the making of a Saint."[62]

In his sermons, the separation, dissolution, and dispersion are all suffered by the body prior to its reunion, reformation, and recollection with the soul.

> In naturall death, there is *Casus in separationem*, The man, the person falls into a separation, a divorce of body and soul; and the resurrection from this fall is by Re-union, the soule and body are re-united at the last day. A second fall in natu-rall death is *Casus in dissolutionem*, The dead body falls by putrification into a dissolution, into atoms and graines of dust; and the resurrection from this fall, is by Re-efformation: God shall re-compact and re-compile those atoms and graines of dust, into that Body, which was before: And then a third fall in naturall death, is *Casus in Disperionem*, This man being falne into a divorce of body and soule, this body being falne into a dissolution of dust, this dust falls into a dispersion, and is scattered unsensibly, undiscernibly upon the face of the earth; and the res-urrection from this death, is by way of Re-collection; God shall recall and re-collect all these Atoms, and grains of dust, and re-compact that body, and re-unite that soule, and so that resurrection is accomplished: And these three falls, Into a Divorce, into a Separation, into a Dispersion; And these three Resurrections, By

Re-union, by Re-efformation, by Re-collecting, we shall also finde in our present state, The spirituall death of the soule by sinne.[63]

Donne's description of the materiality of the resurrection is remarkably graphic, vividly imagining the corrosions, dismemberments, and putrefactions that the fleshly body will endure before it is resurrected miraculously into a whole, when splintered bones will be fused, body parts that have been separated by continents will be rejoined, humors that have suffered different fates will be reassembled, and every speck of dust that has been scattered over earth, air, fire, and water will be gathered into a body at the right hand of God.

Where be all the splinters of that Bone, which a shot hath shivered and scattered in the Ayre? Where be all the Atoms of that flesh, which a *Corrasive* hath eat away, or a *Consumption* hath breath'd and exhal'd away from our arms and other Limbs? In what wrinkle, in what furrow, in what bowel on the earth, ly all the graines of the ashes of a body burnt a thousand years since? In what *corner*, in what ventricle of the sea, lies all the jelly of a Body drowned in the *generall flood*? What cohaerence, what sympathy, what dependence maintaines any relation, any correspondence, between that arm that was lost in Europe, and that legge that was lost in Afrique or Asia, scores of yeers between? One humour of our dead body produces worms, and those worms suck and exhaust all other humour, and then all dies, and all dries, and molders into dust, and that dust is blowen into the River, and that puddled water tumbled into the sea, and that ebs and flows in infinite revolutions, and still, still God knows in what *Cabinet* every *seed-Pearle* lies, in what part of the world every graine of every mans dust lies; and, *sibilat populum suum* (as his Prophet speaks in another case) he whispers, he hisses, he beckens for the bodies of his Saints, and in the twinckling of an eye, that body that was scattered over all the elements, is sate down at the right hand of God, in a glorious resurrection. A Dropsie hath extended me to an enomous corpulency and unwieldinesse; a Consumption hath attenuated me to a feeble macilency and leannesse, and God raises me a body, such as it should have been, if these infirmities had not interven'd and deformed it.[64]

"We die and rise the same / And prove mysterious by this love" ("The Canonization," 26–27).

But if Donne's preoccupation with death and with love are of a piece, his lovers do not only imitate the love, death, and resurrection of Christ in their union. They are also, conveniently, part and parcel of another tradition he draws upon deeply: the romantic lover is in love with devotion and it is a devotion unto death. This love knows no obstacles. And for a love without limit, even the limitation of life must be overcome. "If romantic love is indeed a passion that surpasses all worldly bounds, then it is not surprising that death, as a release from the world, is its logical out-come."[65] Denis de Rougemont believes "the dark secret of romantic love is that it is really in love with death rather than life." The otherworldliness of romantic love is so strong that self-annihilation may be the only prospect powerful enough to prove the totality of the lover's devotion. The not-so-dark and not-so-secret truth of Christianity may be that, beyond death, it is really in love with love.[66] In the sacrifice of the Eucharist the man / god gives his life and suffers for love of mankind, and the communicant loves his god so much that he would join him in that sacrifice.

# 6

## Herbert's Praise: Communion in Conversation

> All things long for it. The intelligent long for it by way of knowledge, the lower strata by way of perception, the remainder by way of the stirrings of being alive—and it is praised by every name.
> —Pseudo-Dionysius

### Mystical Poetry and Theology

Along with mystery, the liturgy of the Eucharist is insistent in its emphasis on gratitude. The Greek *eucharistia* is generally translated as "thanksgiving," but in contemporary parlance, thanksgiving has largely come to signify gratitude for a favor, for some *thing* received, while *eucharistia* suggests thanks-giving, or praise, without reference to an object. In fact, the biblical psalms of thanksgiving have been distinguished, in just this way, from the psalms of praise: thanks for a particular favor is contrasted to a generalized celebration.[1] The earliest sense of *eucharistia* may have been, like the Hebraic *berakah*, a proclamation, a celebration of the *mirabilia Dei*, an expression of wonder. Such praise is not caught up in an economy of exchange, of thanks in return for a specific gift, but it is a response—a response to revelation. As Hans Urs von Balthasar describes, "God's revelation is not an object to be looked at: it is his action in and upon the world, and the world can only respond, and hence 'understand,' through action on *its* part."[2] Theologically, responses to revelation are in kind: when the focus of the revelation is the Passion, the response is the

Eucharist—God gives his body so that it may be given; when it is the Word, the response is words—God gives the scripture so that creatures can send up their psalms of praise. In this way, humankind's most precious gift, praise, is indeed not theirs: it is God's gift.[3] Furthermore, how this gift and response occur is a mystery.

In the Christian tradition, the Eucharist expresses this mystery, as we have seen, in manifold ways, for in it, mysteriously, the present is united to the past, the material is joined to the spiritual, remembering and repeating know no difference, the subject knows no separation from the object of worship, transcendence is manifest in immanence, and the individual is not separable from the community. Chrysostom spoke of the Eucharist as a mystery, Eusebius described the Eucharist as a "mystical liturgy," Gregory of Nyssa called it a mystical action, and Gregory of Nazianzus called the altar a "mystical table." In the Apostolic Constitutions, the Eucharist is described as the "mystical sacrifice of the body and blood of Christ." The term was also used to describe the "discovery by faith of the mystery of Christ as the key to the scriptures." Gregory of Nazianzus writes,

I must be buried with Christ, rise again with him and inherit heaven with him, become God's son, become God! . . . That is for us the great mystery. That is what it means to us that God became incarnate, a poor man, for us. He came to raise up the flesh, to save his own image, to put men together again. He came to make us perfectly one in Christ who came to be perfectly one of us, to bestow on us all that he is.[4]

Mysteriously, Christ came to bestow, not all that he *has,* but all that he *is* upon man.

Surely, if any poetry can evoke this mystery, the lyrics that comprise George Herbert's anthology, *The Temple,* do. While *The Temple* is regarded by both early modern and postmodern readers as a triumph of literary imagination, in its own time it was also perceived as a source of religious inspiration and even a model for practical devotion. The seventeenth-century Anglican pastor was called the "blessed Herbert" by a mid-century Puritan, the "divine" Herbert by a late-century Presbyterian, and he was even regarded as a saint by a Cambridge divine during the Restoration. One recent scholar said that it is "hardly too much" to call the work's main section, "The Church," "a book of seventeenth-century psalmody."[5] Another writes that "Herbert seems to have conceived his book of lyrics as a book of Christian psalms, and his speaker as a new David, a Christian Psalmist."[6]

While word and sacrament, scripture and Eucharist, were always connected as modes of praise, the Reformers stressed their connection polemically, with both Luther and Calvin describing the sacraments as the "seal of the word." With the Reformation's focus on scripture reading, its scripture translations, and its proliferation of translations of the psalms in particular (with Sir Philip Sidney and John Milton making their own contributions in English), and with church choirs and organs largely replaced by psalm singing, biblical liturgy was a key part of the cultural context that forged the period's devotional verse. It is a poetry constituted by hymns of praise that are deeply indebted to the Bible in vocabulary and form.[7] George Herbert grew up in a household that, according to John Donne's account, sang psalms every Sunday evening, and as a pastor at the rural village in Bemerton, he repeated that practice. While his contribution to English verse is already acknowledged to be biblical, I want to add that his understanding of language is, ironically in an age when the sacraments were undergoing intense critique, also sacramental.[8] I will add that this was not felt as a contradiction (not a conflict of works and faith) for, after all the debates, it was the *mystery* of the sacrament more than its materiality that was so attractive to Reformation poets like Herbert. Amid all the doctrinal and ceremonial crossfire over the sacrament, that mystery was never in doubt.

While theologians argued about the status of signs in the Eucharist— for Luther, Christ was "in, with and under" the elements, for Calvin there was a "distinction without division" between Christ and the elements, and for Zwingli, the elements were metaphors only—the *mysteries* of the Eucharist gave Reformation *poets* little difficulty. Rejecting the ontological questions—how the accidents could stay the same and the substance change—they asked instead how the signifier, the word, which is the word of God, could point to the mystery of man joining God. They asked, not *what* does this word stand for, but *how* does this verse evoke mystery? Similarly, for all their doctrinal and stylistic differences, Milton, Donne, and Herbert share the ambition to evoke the holy. Again, an understanding of language emerges from these writers—a poetics, even a language theory, that is virtually "sacramental,"[9] in which poetry is called upon to carry the performative power of liturgy—and this includes the evocation of mystery.

While debates over the sacraments by the magisterial Reformers were already a century old in seventeenth-century England, a series of bitter, divisive doctrinal and liturgical battles continued to be waged. Notably, the battle continued between those who advocated the return to the "beauty of holiness," ceremonialism, and sacramentalism, and those who had more iconoclastic tendencies and so were offended by such so-called popish practices. The temptation to search the devotional verse of the period to ascertain the correct doctrinal label for each poet has not been resisted by critics; in fact, the old battles over liturgy and doctrine have continued to be waged in literary studies where the discussion has been dominated by the question of whether these poems are the products of a "Protestant poetics" or betray a doctrinal and even ceremonial debt to the Roman church. A session at the Modern Language Association convention where critics squared off over "George Herbert's Theology: Nearer Geneva or Rome?" is symptomatic.[10] But it might be more productive to focus on the writers' claims for their poetry rather than to continue to worry over confessional labels—after all, they are writing poetry and not systematic theologies.[11] With Reformation theology insisting that the sacrifice be remembered rather than re-enacted in the communion, these poets are all asking, albeit in different ways, that their *poetry* carry the mystical force of the sacramental re-enactment; hence, we discover the irony that Reformation poetry becomes the new site of transubstantiation of the Word.

To trace the theological roots of their language theory deeper, we need to take a detour through Calvin's understanding of signs and his way of reading Augustine; to the extent that anything about religious thought and practice in Reformation England can be generalized, the understanding of signs informing the English church was, generally speaking, indebted to Calvin and to his forebear, Augustine. For Calvin, signs do not contain God, but can lift you up to God; they are the very vehicle by which man is enabled to participate in Christ. He wants to steer between the two dangers Augustine warns against: one, that signs would be empty (the Zwinglian way that harbored the threat of nihilism for Calvin, much as postmodern sign theory does for some); the other, that signs would be too full (that signs contain the thing itself, the Roman way, as Calvin saw it). Toward the first, the empty sign, he believed that it is wrong to think that signs are given in vain, to disparage or diminish their signification, and thereby to exclude ourselves from the benefits that we ought to derive from them. Conversely, he warns that signs must not be taken for idols, mistaken for the Spirit. Signs are only effective because they are the gift *by* the Spirit, given to signal the gift *of* the Spirit. "If we do not elevate our minds beyond the visible sign, we transfer to the sacraments the praise of those benefits which are only conferred upon us by Christ alone, and that by the agency of the Holy Spirit, who makes us partakers of Christ himself." External signs, language, invite us beyond themselves, to God.[12]

Calvin is careful to stress the mystery of this process of signifying along with the mystery of communion. Speaking of "communion with Christ" in a letter to Peter Martyr, he wrote that "in no other way does he reconcile us to God by the sacrifice of his death but as he is ours and we are one with him. . . . How that is done, I confess, is very far above the comprehension of my understanding. I rather humbly admire, than labour to comprehend this mystery."[13] Calvin's etymology for sacrament also takes him immediately to mystery: "For whenever the author of . . . the New Testament wanted to render the Greek word, mystery, [*musterion*] into Latin, especially where it related to Divine things, he used the word *sacramentum.*" Examples follow of Calvin quoting the use of *musterion* in the epistle to the Ephesians (I:9, 3:3), the Epistle to the Colossians (I:26, 27) and Timothy (3:16). "In all of these places," he continues, "where the word *musterion* is used, the author of that version has rendered it sacrament. He would not say *arcanum,* or secret, lest he should appear to degrade the majesty of the subject. Therefore he used the word sacrament for a sacred or Divine secret. . . . And it is well known, that baptism and the Lord's Supper, which the Latins denominate Sacraments, are called mysteries by the Greeks" (Inst. 4:14:2). In stressing the mystery of the Eucharist, he is also stressing the mystery of signification.

What enables the sacramental union of *signum* and *res*, sign and thing, is the mystery of Christ's gift, the mystery of faith conferred by the Spirit through the gospel, a mystery grounded in the Word. Without that mystery, the sign is not effective, it is empty—a "vain and useless figure" in Augustine's phrase. If God "had impressed memorials . . . on the sun, the stars, the earth, and stones they would all have been to us as sacraments. For why is the shapeless and the coined silver not of the same value seeing they are the same metal? Just because the former has nothing but its own nature, whereas the latter, impressed with the public stamp, becomes money and receives a new value. And shall not the Lord be able to stamp His creatures with His word, that things which were formerly bare elements may become sacraments? (Inst. 4:14:18)" For Calvin, a sacrament is an *act* of God that "makes . . . divine mysteries lurk under things that are in themselves quite abject" (Inst. 4:19:2). What would make poetry sacramental, according to this logic, would be no less than the agency of the Spirit—a mystery indeed—and the Reformation poets do invoke just such agency.

When George Herbert opens *The Temple* with an invocation of the mystery of the sacrifice, he thereby frames the ensuing poems as an offering, an offering of praise—"singing the Name" as he says—with gifts he can give only because they were given to him, "for from thee they came."[14]

> Lord, my first fruits present themselves to thee:
> Yet not mine neither: for from thee they came,
> And must return. Accept of them, and me,
> And make us strive, who shall sing best thy Name.
> ("The Dedication")

The lyric echoes the biblical liturgy for the offering of the first fruits of the harvest (Deut. 26:1–10), which concludes with "And now behold, I have brought the first fruits of the land, which thou, O Lord, hast given me." Elsewhere, the fruits of the land become the "fruit of our lips, giving thanks to his Name" (Heb. 13:15), and Paul even refers to Christ as the "first fruits" (I Cor. 15:20–23): "Christ has been raised from the dead, the first fruits of those who have fallen asleep. . . . For as in Adam all die, so also in Christ shall all be made alive. But each in his own order: Christ the first fruits, then at his coming those who belong to Christ." Here, the first fruits are turned into Herbert's hymns of praise. Before we even enter the Temple, his entire collection of poems is framed thereby as an offering.

Once we enter, he takes us first through the Church-porch where precepts are offered in verse: "a verse may finde him, who a sermon flies, / And turn delight into a sacrifice." And then to the heading before entering the Church proper: "Thou, whom the former precepts have / Sprinkled and taught, how to behave / Thy self in church; approach, and taste / The churches *mysticall* repast" (my italics). And then we encounter the first poem of the main section: "The Altar." It is little wonder that the Eucharist has been called the very "marrow of Herbert's sensibility." In "The Altar," he repeats that he is offering his praise, his language itself, as a sacrifice, and he makes the explicit request that his verse be sanctified.

> A broken ALTAR, Lord, thy servant reares,
> Made of a heart, and cemented with teares:
> Whose parts are as thy hand did frame;
> No workmans tool hath touch'd the same.
> A HEART alone
> Is such a stone,
> As nothing but
> Thy pow'r doth cut.
> Wherefore each part
> Of my hard heart
> Meets in this frame,
> To praise thy Name:
> That, if I chance to hold my peace,
> These stones to praise thee may not cease.
> O let thy blessed SACRIFICE be mine,
> And sanctifie this ALTAR to be thine.

While the stones of the altar are the speaker's heart, they are also his words, arranged in the shape of an altar. In Augustine's language, the sacrament includes both the Word and the visible word. The offering signals both divine grace and human gratitude. And this insistent allusion to sacrifice—so explicitly deleted from the Anglican Eucharist—is no anomaly in Herbert's *Temple*; rather, the explicit offering of sacrifice recurs in another verse, "Providence," in which Man, "the world's high priest," presents "the sacrifice for all"—a sacrifice of praise.[15] How can we speak of *praise* as the sacrifice at the altar?

Why does Herbert frame *The Temple* with the mystical repast? In the Eucharist, the bread points beyond itself to an agent beyond itself by means of an agency beyond itself. The Eucharist straddles a critical divide between understanding signification as a revelation, as presence, and as lack, as absence. Something is suggested that is more than the sign, and yet it is suggested by the sign. Meaning both participates in the sign (God in the bread and wine) and is wholly other than it (God is not merely bread and wine). The substance of the signs is changed, and this is achieved by a mystery beyond their self-propelled activity. Whether the explanation relies on semiotics or divine gift—and in the early modern period there was little dispute that divinity invests language with meaning—language exceeds the embeddedness of its utterance. It relies on inspiration—the notion, evident by its etymology, that the very breath of language itself is a gift. If the idolator will hope to make the divine available, and by doing so, distort it, the work of art makes no such claim to the availability of the divine. Instead, it "opens in its depths upon an invisibility whose distance it does not abolish but reveals."[16]

The crafted poem does not deceive its maker any more than the idol deceives its worshipper: "to the contrary, he knows he is the artisan who has worked with metal, wood, stones or words to fashion the image. He may hope the divine will invest in this, but in the end it is the best he, the artist, can conceive. It is not Other than him. It has no external source. . . . For that, we move toward another concept of language, not the prowess of the artist, the best he can write, but inspiration, something given to him, and that gift from beyond is both source and signification."[17] This iconicity of language, in contrast to its idolatry, informs the mystery of how language means, how language cannot altogether contain what it nevertheless points to, which is beyond itself, and how this is made possible by forces of meaning beyond words.[18]

This is why critics have argued for the "extinction" of the poet or at least of poetic artifice in Herbert and for the "correcting motion" of his poetry by the word of God.[19] Hence, the speaker in Praise (I) describes his verse as amplified and multiplied by the Lord's help, which enables the writer's words to "mount unto the skie." "A True Hymn" also addresses just this problem. The speaker asks what would constitute a genuine offering of praise, a "true hymn." "The finenesse which a hymne or psalme affords, / Is, when the soul unto the lines accords." There is some congruence between the soul and the verse, but how is this possible? In the third stanza, the speaker says that when a poet wants "all mind, soul, strength and time" to be offered in a poem, he is justifiably disappointed if all he produces is a rhyme; and he offers just such a stanza—second-rate verse that rhymes.

> He who craves all the minde,
> And all the soul, and strength, and time,
> If the words onely ryme,
> Justly complains, that somewhat is behinde
> To make his verse, or write a hymne in kinde.

Instead of banal rhyming verse, the poet offers another possibility, negatively. What he cannot say points to what he would say. The speaker repeats "somewhat"—"somewhat it fain would say," "somewhat is behind," "somewhat scant"—as if words were failing him, for no category of being suffices as he gropes to describe the true hymn; "somewhat" is not even "some thing." The hymn is not contained in this verse. This "somewhat" echoes Pseudo-Dionysius when he speaks of the impossibility of naming the divine, for it is beyond all names. As it says in *The Divine Names*, "The sacred writers lift up a hymn of praise to this Good. They call it beautiful, beauty, love, and beloved. They give it the names which would convey that it is the source of loveliness and the flowering of grace."[20] But it is called beauty not because it *possesses* beauty, but because it *bestows* it, confers it. Similarly, the verse does not contain praise, it confers it. Simply put, it praises what it cannot even name.

The biblical texts echoed in "A True Hymn" are Deuteronomy 6:5, "Thou shalt love the Lord thy God, with all thy heart, with all thy soul and with all thy might," and Luke 10:27, which changes it to "all thy heart, soul, strength, and mind." Herbert's poem speaks of mind, soul, strength, and *time*, substituting poetic meter for heart.[21] No wonder the poet is dissatisfied; meter and rhyme are no substitute for the heart. But if the heart is missing in this stanza, it appears twice in the final one:

> Whereas if th' heart be moved,
> Although the verse be somewhat scant,
> God doth supplie the want.
> As when th' heart sayes (sighing to be approved)
> *O, could I love!* and stops: God writeth, *Loved.*

If the verse is lacking, God supplies the want. What it cannot say is said by an Other. If the meter does not scan, God will complete it. And the verse demonstrates this in the last couplet, which does not scan without the addition of *Loved*. The lyric is co-authored, by a human and a divine writer, and in this way becomes a "true hymn."

One obvious logical answer to the cry, "O, could I love" would be "you *can* love," but the request is granted in a different way: "you *are* loved." This is not only God's word in the lyric, but it is also the divine logic explained in scripture, "We love him because he first loved us" (1 John 4:19). Pseudo-Dionysius writes of the Unnamable with all Names, "they especially call it loving toward humanity, because in one of its persons it accepted a true share of what it is we are, and thereby issued a call to man's lowly state to rise up to it."[22] The human effort is partial, unfinished, pointing to the need for intervention from Outside. If only the speaker acknowledges that need with yearning for more, that is, if his heart calls, "O, could I love," then it is answered: *Loved*. The mystery of divine love not only informs sacramental agency; it also makes a hymn "true" and a verse work.

Herbert makes the connection between verse and negative theology explicit in "The Quidditee." In scholastic philosophy, the quiddity was the nature or essence of a thing. Rather than describing the essence of verse or trying to grasp it, here the speaker can only approach it through negations, as Milton approaches the mystery of salvation in *Paradise Regained*.

> My God, a verse is not a crown,
> No point of honour, or gay suit,
> No hawk, or banquet, or renown,
> Nor a good sword, nor yet a lute:
> It cannot vault, or dance, or play;
> It never was in *France* or *Spain*;

After all these negations that include courtly love poetry, heroic verse, Homeric epic, and Virgilian pastoral, he offers his affirmation of what verse is. Significantly, it has no predicate:

> But it is that which while I use
> I am with thee,

"That which while I use": verse is not nameable as a thing; rather, it is a vehicle that takes him beyond. If a "quiddity" is reached here in the defining process, it is a negative one. The final lines echo Anselm's famous definition of God: "that which nothing greater can be thought."[23]

## The Theology of Conversation

From the perspective of sacramental poetics, it is wholly appropriate that Pseudo-Dionysius's *Mystical Theology* begins with a poem. That poem depicts an alternative revelation to the one at Sinai—not thunder and lightning, but silence and darkness, not words graven on stone tablets soon dashed to pieces, but a mystic scripture whose words need not be cut or broken for they "lie simple" in the brilliant darkness of a hidden silence. To approach them, we too must be silent and blind: revelation only occurs when our senses and our understanding are left behind so that our sightless minds can be filled with treasures beyond—beyond being, divinity, goodness, and all beauty. This poem, this hymn of praise, is both a supplication and a celebration. The supplication—"lead us up beyond unknowing and light to the farthest peak"—indicates that we are not there yet. Everything in the poem points beyond itself—from the invocation of the first line, "Higher than any being," to the revelation conferred in the last, "treasures beyond all beauty." This feature of signifying is described in Herbert's "Providence":

> Each thing that is, although in use and name
> It go for one, hath many wayes in store
> To honour thee; and so each hymne thy fame
> Extolleth many wayes, yet this one more.

Not simply a recommendation for multiplicity, he observes that a sign cannot point only to one thing, but to more, and that excess is impelled by the desire to praise, "to extol many ways," for all things are impelled to praise. This resistance to containing, this pointing beyond, this grasping and yearning and desiring more—more than the language can say, more than the humn can express—is, as we have seen, a key feature of sacramental poetics.

Not only did Pseudo-Dionysius enjoy a resurgence of interest in seventeenth-century England, England had its own mystical tradition, including the *Cloud of Unknowing*, and this, combined with the influence of Calvin's Augustinian sign theory, including his understanding of the mystery of the sacrament as an act of God, "which makes divine mysteries lurk under things that are in themselves quite abject" (Inst. 4:19:2), helped to shape England's sacramental poetics. Furthermore, Herbert's friend, Nicholas Ferrar, translated Juan de Valdés's mystical work, *The Hundred and Ten Considerations*, with Herbert's explicit endorsement: "I wish you by all meanes to publish it, for . . . God in the midst of Popery should open the eyes of one to understand and expresse so clearly and excellently the intent of the Gospell . . . and observation of Gods Kingdome within us, and the working thereof."[24] For Herbert, this internal, mystical, kingdom was attained by submitting the human will to divine will.[25]

In this context, a closer look at Pseudo-Dionysius's opening poem in *Mystical Theology* should be helpful: "Trinity!! Higher than any being, any divinity, any goodness! . . . Lead us up!" says the prayer / poem, simultaneously praising and desiring. How can gratitude be expressed when the request is not yet granted? Lead us up, says Pseudo-Dionysius, amidst his praise, but we are not yet led up, so why be grateful? Grateful for what? For desire, for what is given *is* this desire; hence, to feel desire is to feel gratitude, and when we express gratitude, we also express desire: this paradox is at the heart of mystical liturgical language. The theologian Henri de Lubac explains that the longing for the beyond that informs mystical theology is a symptom that humanity is called; the desire for God is the human response to the call. "God is not governed by our desire," writes de Lubac, "the relation is precisely the other way around—it is the giver who awakens desire . . . it remains true that once such a desire exists in the creature it becomes the sign, not merely of a possible gift from God, but of a certain gift. It is the evidence of a promise, inscribed and recognized in the being's very self."[26] This is precisely the (theo)logic of Herbert's "The Altar," where each part of the poet's heart, cut by God, is inscribed with want and desires only to praise, and so the poem is visibly shaped, not only like an altar, but to form the shape of the pronoun "I"—in the end, the subject is the offering made at the altar.[27]

If mystical theology invites us to think of praise as a gift that has been made to us and as an offering we return, as a pure expression of desire and as a ceaseless activity, praise can also take the form, in a seeming paradox, of lament. For in the very act of lamenting, one is implicitly celebrating what she already has: someone to hear. Apart from whether a request is honored, when it is made, it is with the presupposition of responsiveness.[28] Confidence that one is heard is apparent in many biblical psalms. "I will tell of thy name to my brethren; in the midst of the congregation I will praise thee: You who fear the Lord, praise him! . . . For he has not despised or abhorred the affliction of the afflicted; and he has not hid his face from him, but has heard, when he cried to him" (Ps. 22:22–24). While scholars have separated psalms of lamentation from psalms of praise for convenience, they admit that the distinction does not hold liturgically. Even as the biblical speaker laments, he demonstrates his confidence that God will not fail him. And conversely, in the very act of praising God, the speaker expresses his longing for him in lament. Furthermore, the vow contained in the psalms of lamentation indicates to biblical scholars that they were probably offered in a cultic setting, especially when some distress had been overcome, as a song of thanksgiving.[29] The *todha,* or thanksgiving psalm, had two functions: to offer testimony to the saving work of God, and to thank God for that salvation. It begins with praise, such as "I will extol thee, Yhwh, for thou hast lifted me up" (Ps. 30:1) and proceeds to an account of affliction, and then, salvation: "On the very day I cried unto thee Thou answered me at once" (Ps. 138:3). To cry is to be heard; to hear is to answer; to answer is to save.

The verb *hvdh,* generally translated as "to praise," properly means "to confess" or "to accept," so that praising also includes a confession of unworthiness and acceptance of the judgment for that unworthiness. The biblical scholar Gerhard von Rad points to the "avowal" component of praise: "in accepting a justly imposed judgment, the man confesses his transgression, and he clothes what he says in the mantle of an avowal, giving God the glory."[30] This is praise from the depths, like the praise of Jonah from the belly of the whale, or the praise of the afflicted Job. Of such praise, the Bible says hauntingly, "God gives these songs in the night" (Job 35:10). It is the praise of Christ from the cross: "My God, my God, why have you forsaken me?" he says, quoting Psalm 22, a psalm that begins in lament but ends in praise:

> Why art thou so far from helping me,
> from the words of my groaning?
> My God, I cry by day, but thou dost not answer;
> and by night, but find no rest.
> Yet thou art holy,
> enthroned on the praises of Israel.
> In thee our fathers trusted;
> they trusted, and thou didst
> deliver them.
> To thee they cried, and were saved;
> in thee they trusted, and were not disappointed.

Herbert's brief lyric, "Bitter-sweet" compresses both understandings of praise that we find in the psalms, as gratitude and lament, fullness and lack, love and desire. This compression begins with the hyphenated title, one word that combines the bitterness of affliction and sweetness of praise: "Bitter-sweet."

> *Bitter-sweet*
> Ah my deare angrie Lord
> Since thou dost love, yet strike;
> Cast down, yet help afford;
> Sure I will do the like.
> I will complain, yet praise;
> I will bewail, approve:
> And all my sowre-sweet dayes
> I will lament, and love.

Psalm 126:6 expresses a similar sentiment, if more succinctly: "They that sow in tears shall reap in joy."

The "true hymn," for Herbert, is a call and an answer: "*O, could I love!* . . . God writeth, *Loved.*" It is not an unheard lament, but a conversation, even if short and very much to the point. We see this call and response expressed dramatically in "The Collar" whose title puns on choler as anger, collar as a yoke, and finally, the caller, the One who calls. Initially, the speaker is angry, frustrated, unable to find fulfillment, lamenting his condition when suddenly a voice breaks in:

> But as I rav'd and grew more fierce and wilde
> At every word,
> Me thoughts I heard one calling, *Child*!
> And I reply'd, *My Lord.*

"Since the unknowing of what is beyond being is something above and beyond speech, mind, or being itself, one should ascribe to it an understanding beyond being . . . ," explains Pseudo-Dionysius, "For . . . the things of God are revealed to each mind in proportion to its capacities; and the divine goodness is such that, out of concern for our salvation, it deals out the immeasurable and infinite in limited measures."[31] We could understand these "limited measures" in two ways: the immeasurable is made proportionate to man in the Incarnation, but the immeasurable is also given "limited measure" in the measures of poetry, another kind of incarnation, the Word made words. Hence, what follows in *Mystical Theology* could be an apt description of the metaphors in Herbert's poetry: "the Transcendent [comes to us] clothed in the terms of being, with shape

and form on things which have neither, and numerous symbols are em-
ployed to convey the varied attributes of what is an imageless and supra-
natural simplicity. . . . We now grasp these things in the best way we can,
and as they come to us, wrapped in the sacred veils of that love toward humanity with which scripture and traditions cover the truths of the mind
with things derived from the realm of the senses." But if God offers revelation proportionate to man's capacities, how could man respond? Herbert's answer: with a hymn of praise awakened by the desire that invites us
beyond ourselves.

The character of this interchange is a conversation—not a thunder-
ous clap from the beyond that flattens the listener into shock. A conversation, not a devastation, and not the kind of overwhelming ravishing that
crushes, like Donne depicts in the "Batter my Heart" sonnet, where the
speaker says to God that he can never be "chaste unless you ravish me."
Clearly, this conversation has deep theological roots—not a human call that
echoes in a cavern, a lonely call that is unanswered, only deferred endlessly
until it fades away. The mystery of this conversation "according to our proportion" is like the mystery of the incarnation and the Eucharist, and that
mystery is called *Love* by both Pseudo-Dionysius and by George Herbert.
For Pseudo-Dionysius: "The sacred writers lift up a hymn of praise to this
Good. They call it beautiful, beauty, love, and beloved. They give it the
names which would convey that it is the source of loveliness and is the flowering of grace." It is called beauty, he goes on to say, not because it possesses
beauty, but because it bestows it. It is called love, not because it is loved, but
because it loves: "And there it is ahead of All as Goal, as the Beloved."[32]

## "Love III"

Herbert's final poem in *The Temple*, the lyric sequence that, as we have seen,
begins wih the Eucharistic sacrifice in "The Altar," concludes with partaking
the Eucharist.[33] The altar gives way to the table. In "The Altar," the speaker
asks to be sanctified so that he may receive the sacrifice and offer it in return.
In the final poem, "Love," the speaker *is* asked. Here, reciprocity is depicted
as a conversation; the poem itself is a dialogue. While the guest feels unworthy of the host, in the course of their conversation, the host lifts the guest up
to her level, qualifying the guest to dine, to "taste her meat."

The feast of love to which God has invited man alludes to both the earthly communion with the implied pun on "host" and to the heavenly marriage banquet it anticipates.[34] The Book of Common Prayer makes that very association, invoking the parables of the marriage feast and the wedding garment in the communion service. The *Prayer Book* exhorts those who are "negligent to come to the holy Communion," using the parable of the great supper:

Ye know how grievous and unkind a thing it is, when a man hath prepared a rich feast, decked his table with all kind of provision, so that there lacketh nothing but the guests to sit downe, and yet they which be called (without any cause) most unthankfuly refuse to come. . . . If any man say, I am a grievous sinner, and therefore am afraide to come: wherefore then doe you not repent and amend? When God calleth you, be you not ashamed to say "yee will not come"?[35]

Like all of Herbert's poetry, "Love" is also dense with biblical allusion. As he explains in his poem on the Scriptures, one allusion points to the next in patterns that form a virtual constellation of "stars" or biblical passages.

> Oh that I knew how all thy lights combine,
> And the configurations of their glorie!
> Seeing not onely how each verse doth shine,
> But all the constellations of the storie.
> This verse marks that, and both do make a motion
> Unto a third, that ten leaves off doth lie:
> ("H. Scriptures II")

While Herbert speaks Scripture in his poetry, he does so in his own voice. It is as if Herbert has ingested it, like Ezekiel who had eaten the Scripture and found it tasted like honey. This is, in fact, the allusion Herbert invokes to open his other poem on the Bible: "Oh Book! infinite sweetnesse! let my heart/Suck ev'ry letter."[36] Accordingly, "Love" derives much of its resonance from the echoes of many biblical passages that describe God inviting man to a feast. Song of Songs 2:4, "He brought me to the banqueting house, and his banner over me was love"; the 23rd Psalm where God is a gracious host; Matthew 26:29, "I tell you I shall not drink again of this fruit of the vine until that day when I drink it new with you in my Father's kingdom"; Luke 12:37, where the master comes and serves his servants; Revelation 3:20, the promised messianic banquet: "Behold I stand at the door and knock; if any one hears my voice and opens the door, I will come in to him and eat with him, and he with me"; Matthew 22:1–10 and Luke 14:7–24, the parables of the great supper. Luke 14:7–11 is especially apt:

Now he told a parable to those who were invited, when he marked how they chose the places of honor, saying to them, "When you are invited by any one to a marriage feast, do not sit down in a place of honor, lest a more eminent man than you be invited by him; and he who invited you both will come and say to you, "Give place to this man" and then you will begin with shame to take the lowest place. [The setting of Herbert's poem could follow logically.] But when you are invited, go and sit in the lowest place, so that when your host comes, he may say to you, "Friend, go up higher" then you will be honored in the presence of all who sit at table with you. For every one who exalts himself will be humbled and he who humbles himself will be exalted."

Herbert's unworthy guest alludes directly to Matthew's version of the parable: "the king said to his servants, 'The wedding is ready, but those invited were not worthy'" (Matt. 22:8). But Herbert has changed the plot. Luke 14:16–24 says,

A man once gave a great banquet, and invited many; and at the time for the banquet he sent his servant to say to those who had been invited, "Come; for all is now ready." But they all alike began to make excuses. The first said to him, "I have bought a field, and I must go out and see it; I pray you, have me excused." And another said, "I have bought five yoke of oxen, and I go to examine them; I pray you, have me excused." And another said, "I have married a wife, and therefore I cannot come." So the servant came and reported this to his master. Then the householder in anger said to his servant, "Go out quickly to the streets and lanes of the city, and bring in the poor and maimed and blind and lame." And the servant said, "Sir, what you commanded has been done, and still there is room." And the master said to the servant, "Go out to the highways and hedges, and compel people to come in, that my house may be filled. For I tell you, none of those men who were invited shall taste of my banquet."

In Herbert's version, Love does not simply invite a guest who refuses, making excuses, is pronounced unworthy, and replaced by someone else, for the host has given up on him. In Herbert's version, *Love will not be refused.* Like the rejected lover in the Song of Songs, Love is not angered but determined to win him back: "I opened to my beloved, but my beloved had withdrawn himself, and was gone." And so, in Herbert's poem, she lures him, not only to a dinner, but also into a conversation. Marked by a deceptive simplicity, an ease, even grace, at presenting a deep theological and emotional drama, *Love* is often thought of as Herbert's quintessential poem.

*Love (III)*
Love bade me welcome. Yet my soul drew back
                    Guiltie of dust and sinne.
But quick-ey'd Love, observing me grow slack
                    From my first entrance in,
Drew nearer to me, sweetly questioning,
                    If I lack'd any thing.

A guest, I answer'd, worthy to be here:
                    Love said, You shall be he.
I the unkinde, ungratefull? Ah my deare,
                    I cannot look on thee.
Love took my hand, and smiling did reply,
                    Who made the eyes but I?

Truth Lord, but I have marr'd them: let my shame
                    Go where it does deserve.
And know you not, says Love, who bore the blame?
                    My dear, then I will serve.
You must sit down, says Love, and taste my meat:
                    So I did sit and eat.

In Herbert's version, protestations of unworthiness are not dismissed, but they are not punished either. They are heard and they are given a response. When Love asks, maternally, do you lack anything? He replies, "a guest worthy to be here." But Love claims that he *is* such a guest: "You shall be he." The guest responds, predictably, by demurring—no, not me, I am not worthy to look on you, echoing the biblical injunction, "no one can look on the face of God and live." Unflinchingly, Love takes the guest by the hand, smiles, and replies, "who made the eyes but I?" All the while that the guest is trying to back away, Love is holding on to him. She does it by continuing to engage him in conversation. Even so, when the stubborn guest agrees that Love did create him, he still insists that he has marred that created image. Alluding to the original sin, he feels he deserves exile, death, outer darkness. Love does not disagree: the image of God *has* been marred, shame *has* ensued, but Love reminds him that she has "borne the blame." She has paid the price of his sin and granted worthiness to him. This is her gift. But all the while, this conversation is not only a discussion *about* worthiness. In the course of the conversation, a transformation is taking place. The guest *becomes* worthy—first, by acknowledging his lack of worth; then, by listening when he is told that his unworthiness has been accounted for; and finally because he then understands that he belongs at the meal. All of these acknowledgements change him, qualify him, for the communion. The conversation becomes a conversion.

The guest, in this way, is created by dialogue, in conversation. We cannot legitimately ask who is speaking and who is spoken to—as though they are prior and independent of the conversation—for the addresser and addressee, host and guest, only exist as such in conversation. Who is this speaker? One who receives an invitation. And who offers this invitation? Who is the host? God? Christ? Love, but what is Love? That which welcomes, observes, questions, smiles, takes a hand, offers an invitation, in short, loves. The conclusion alludes not only to the Eucharist, but also to the scene in Exodus of the ceremonial meal that the elders have in contrast to the overwhelming experience of God at Sinai, the thunder and lightning, and the terror leading to "I cannot look on thee" (Exod. 33:20). Unlike the violence of those who break the covenant even as it is given to them, these elders are raised to a peaceful communion. The Hebrew describes the elders looking on God, sitting, and eating, with three spare verbs: "they looked on God, they sat and they ate." Herbert's unworthy speaker enters his covenant with "So I did sit and eat."

Herbert's "Love" understands communion as an invitation that is accepted, with the drama of the poem focusing with exquisite intensity on the invitation and the question of its acceptance—not on the menu, certainly not on the bread and wine. Herbert shows no interest here in defining the nature of the meal served—the Eucharistic elements—instead, he attends to the conversation itself. The mystery of communion is that an utterance could ever be heard, that a call could ever be answered, an invitation ever be accepted, a conversation ever take place. In sacramental signification, language is not understood as "standing for things," what is said is less important than the very activity of saying, the dynamic of conversation itself. In conversation, some *thing* is not passed from one to another; rather some one hears and responds. What is heard may be indeterminate, but whatever it is, it is the only utterance we really make while we live: praise, in joy and in pain. In the Hebrew Bible, death is understood as the state when we can longer praise: "For Sheol does not sing thy praise, Death does not celebrate thee" (Isa. 38:18). "The dead, they do not praise Yhwh, nor any who sink to the silent land. But we, we will bless Yhwh from this time forth and for evermore" (Ps. 115:17). To live is to praise.

Much of the current discussion of sacrifice has returned to the question of the *gift*. We are told that the gift must be given with no expectation of return for it to be truly a gift. To give with an expectation of return is not to give a gift but to enter into a kind of contract, or economic exchange. Still others insist on the reciprocity of the gift. In either case, we should be wary of the consequences of framing the discourse of the gift by economy. Instead, we have much to gain by framing the question as Herbert did, not economically, but linguistically. There is a world of difference, for when we shift the trope about love from gift to conversation, we are no longer tempted to imagine an exchange of things nor a measure of quantity; instead, we think of a response that evokes a further response, and this conversation becomes a model both for theology as well as for the love that is its focus. Herbert's achievement is to make this poetry.

In his poetry, not only must we speak to be heard, if we are unable to be heard, we are unable to speak.

> When my devotions could not pierce
>     Thy silent eares;
> Then was my heart broken, as was my verse:
> My breast was full of fears
>         And disorder:
> (Denial, 1–5)

The act of praise, poetry, falls into fragments when unheard. But when our devotions are sincere and we are heard, our petition is granted, our praise finds voice, and the poem succeeds:

> O cheer and tune my heartlesse breast,
>     Deferre no time;

> That so thy favours granting my request,
> They and my mind may chime,
>                 And mend my rime.
> (Denial, 26–30)

For Herbert, sacramental poetics not only offers a vehicle for conversation with his God, but also a mode of expressing gratitude for that conversation. And that conversation, the "mended rime" that is poetry, ultimately constitutes the subject as calling and responding, as hearing and praising, that is, as loving.

## Afterword

In his *The Disenchantment of the World*, Marcel Gauchet distinguishes two ways that meaning can be established: through the figure of the Other or the figure of the Self. In the premodern world, the believer does not actively establish meaning for all that is; it is given to him. Such "givens" include understandings of justice, materiality, love, and language. When he does not receive meaning from the Other, he begins to devise meaning for himself actively; this is what Gauchet calls the figure of the Self. In the modern world, the figure of the Other is gradually replaced by the figure of the Self who defines and controls all he surveys—that is, the modern subject. What had once been Other and inaccessible is now comprehended and grasped.[1]

Nonetheless, resisting the figure of the Self, many early moderns sought to keep alive the figure of the Other. They detected the threat on the horizon of a world emptied of meaning, a godless world. And so, abandoning the idol of Self, they set to work to restore the "icon" that points to the Other—not the visible icons of religion, but cultural icons that point beyond the sayable. They confronted the dilemma of how to think and to portray mystery—without naming, comprehending, or controlling it. They sought to express wonder toward the divine gifts in works of human creativity, and to draw their audiences into participation with this mystery. If the Reformation inaugurated the beginning of modernism—the death of God and the birth of the modern Self—it also transfigured values that in the earlier regime and in another register were conveyed as God-given: justice, love, and a living universe.

Today, we are witnessing a shift in emphasis again, away from the figure of the modern Self and toward the figure of the Other, a shift that, as we have seen, is inflected both philosophically, as given-ness, and theologically, as gift. Before the "object" as understood by modernism, we feel compelled to use, to analyze, and to comprehend. Before the "gift" of postmodernism, we respond with gratitude, responsibility, and wonder. Hence, although I have already joined the widespread contemporary critique of religious idolatry in my critique of possession, here I wanted to elaborate a different religious legacy: not the legacy of possession but of dispossession, not of religious idolatry but of mystery.

I would be surprised if readers did not discern a tone of lament in this study. Is this nostalgia for the "old faith" of a more sacramental Christianity, even for Catholicism? Unlikely from an heir of Judaism. In that tradition, with the conviction that God no longer walks in the garden in the cool of the day comes the conviction that divinity can only be manifest in human acts of goodness. The process of mourning the departure of God from the world issues in an understanding of the revelation as law instead of incarnation. Is it a lament that the departure of transubstantiation at the Reformation signals the departure of the divine, of a world meaning-full replaced by one emptied? Not really: I opened the book by situating it in the context of gods that are *ever*-departing; hence, they are ever-returning only to depart again. Something else, however, is impelling this lament—the departure of a ritual that harbored the potential of reconciliation—and here, as I conclude, I would prefer to express it as a hope instead of as loss. Justice, a life-world, love, and conversation— the departure of these eucharistic impulses would be very much worth lamenting, and these poets offer a reminder of their value as well as the hope that we will continue to desire these and strive for them—however sadly.

When we live in a world of conflicting identities—cultural, national, ethnic, religious, and gendered—each asserting their particularity against another, the result is invariably violent.[2] Conversely, the opposite demand for a universal is attended by another kind of violence, the risks of a political totalitarianism, a global imperialism, a violence that crushes particularity in its relentless drive toward universal control. Another option, a third option, that we could try to imagine is a particular that honors other particulars, one that opens out toward a potential universal without coercion. In the Eucharist, I seek such an example.[3] This is not to pretend that it has not served as the occasion for terrible strife—it has—nor that it has not been used to distinguish between those who are welcome and those who are not—it has done that too. But in its intent to create a community that coheres, not from blood or territorial boundaries, not from history or from political allegiance, but through sharing divinity, it sought to overcome the pain of difference, to achieve reconciliation. The irony that this only led to further strife over the meaning and form of that very ritual is a testimony to the stubbornness of human aggression. Nonetheless, even in the time of greatest conflict over the ritual, early modern thinkers sought to embrace the central impulses of the Eucharist: a life-world instead of a dead universe, justice instead of the triumph of evils, love instead of utility, and conversation instead of conflict. To translate these from a church ritual into more secular, cultural achievements could be, perhaps, to save them for a future time. Then too, perhaps the sacramental poetics conferred to us could be far more than a description of literary arts—a way of regarding the world, other peoples, and one another. I conclude with the hope that the potential of reconciliation harbored by communion could still inspire, in new cultural forms, a world of community.

REFERENCE MATTER

# Notes

PREFACE

1. The separation of Creator and Creation is fundamental to Christianity as well. Indeed, Aquinas argues in the *Summa Theologica*, q. 13 of the *prima pars*, that while our relations with God are real, God's relations with us are unreal. God remains completely outside the created order. The sacrifice of the Mass presumes this absolute and asymmetric disjunction.

2. Jacques Derrida, in his gloss on Mendelssohn in *Glas*, trans. John P. Leavey Jr. and Richard Rand (Lincoln: University of Nebraska Press, 1986), 51a.

3. I allude intentionally not only to the Scriptures but also to the theologian Hans Urs von Balthasar's magisterial trilogy whose first volume is *The Glory of the Lord*, trans. Erasmo Meiva-Merikakis (Edinburgh: T. and T. Clark, 1982, orig. *Herrlickheit: Eine theologisiche Asthetick, I: Schau der Gestalt* [Einsiedeln: Johannes Verlag, 1961]).

CHAPTER I

1. While Milton depicts the departure of the "pagan" deities at the birth of the true God, the Christ-child, his lyric captures a tone of mourning that invites us to see even their departure as a loss for a poet steeped in classical myth from his Renaissance humanist education.

2. "Art and Sacrament," in David Jones, *Epoch and Artist* (London: Faber and Faber, 1959), 155.

3. An important collection of essays entitled *The Poetics of Transubstantiation: From Theology to Metaphor*, eds. Douglas Burnham and Enrico Giaccherini (Aldershot, UK: Ashgate, 2005), came to my attention as this volume was concluded. In it, a group of international scholars investigate the question in fruitful and diverse ways, in essays that range from classical precedents through twentieth-century culture. As Andy Mousley writes, "To understand transubstantiation in a metaphorical

sense is to multiply one's options, in such a way as to release the term from its particular, religious orbit of meaning into such varied analogues, metonyms and metaphors as translation, transition, transsexuality, magic, adaptation, metamorphosis and alchemy. . . . The variety of ways in which the Eucharist can be, and has historically been, understood seems to call for a non-essentialist approach" (55–56).

4. Jones, *Epoch and Artist*, 155.

5. Ibid.

6. Jacques Maritain, "Sign and Symbol," *Journal of the Warburg Institute* 1 (July 1937): 1–11.

7. Augustine, Letter 138, "To Marcellinus cum ad res divinas pertinent," Sacramenta appellantur. *Patrologia Latina*, vol. 33, ed. J. P. Migne (Parisiis: excudebat Migne, 1841), 527.

8. Douglas Burnham, "The Riddle of Transubstantiation," in Burnham and Giaccherini, *The Poetics of Transubstantiation*, 8.

9. Ibid., 5, 6.

10. Samuel Johnson, *The Lives of the English Poets* (London: Oxford University Press, 1968), 180.

11. George Herbert, *The Works of George Herbert*, ed. F. E. Hutchinson (Oxford: Clarenden Press, 1941), 168.

12. Jacques Maritain, *Creative Intuition in Art and Poetry* (New York: Pantheon, 1955), 236.

13. Paul Valéry, *The Art of Poetry*, trans. Denise Folliot (New York: Pantheon, 1958), 256.

14. See also Regina Schwartz, *Transcendence: Philosophy, Literature, and Theology Approach the Beyond* (New York: Routledge, 2005).

15. *Catechism of the Council of Trent,* trans. J. A. McHugh and C. J. Callan (New York: Joseph F. Wagner, 1923), 142.

16. "Since the sanctification of man is in the power of God who sanctifies," writes St. Thomas (ST III:60:5), "it is not in the competency of man to choose the things by which he is to be sanctified."

17. Jean-Louis Chrétien, *Hand to Hand: Listening to the Work of Art*, trans. Stephen E. Lewis (New York: Fordham University Press, 2003), 106.

18. Ibid., 114.

19. While I refer often, and with much gratitude, to the many excellent historical investigations of the Eucharistic controversies, my focus is on the theological and philosophical dimensions of sacramentality.

20. These opposing impulses were made visible both in the Mass and in the Corpus Christi procession of the host which physically joined the guilds to governing bodies of the town. "Natural body and social body indeed reacted to each other with a closeness which approaches identity." Mervyn James, "Ritual, Drama and Social Body in the Late Medieval English Town," *Past & Present* 98, no. 1

(1983): 3–29, esp. 20–23. See also Sarah Beckwith, *Christ's Body: Identity, Culture, and Society in Late Medieval Writings,* (London: Routledge, 1993).

21. Eamon Duffy, *The Stripping of the Altars: Traditional Religion in England c. 1400–c.1580* (New Haven: Yale University Press, 1992), 91–92.

22. *The Works of Richard Hooker,* ed. John Keble (Oxford, UK: Clarendon Press, 1863), 1:xci–xcii.

23. Jean-Luc Marion, *God Without Being,* trans. Thomas A. Carlson (Chicago: University of Chicago Press, 1991), esp. 139–58. Michel de Certeau, *The Mystic Fable: The Sixteenth and Seventeenth Centuries,* trans. Michael B. Smith (Chicago: University of Chicago Press, 1992).

24. De Certeau, *Mystic Fable,* 91–92.

25. And this sacramental presence is not the same as ontological being, although they have been so often equated since Heidegger.

26. This has been elaborated many places, among the most recent, Louis Bouyer's *Eucharist: Theology and Spiritrality of the Eucharistic Prayer* (South Bend, Ind.: University of Notre Dame Press, 1968); orig. *Eucharistie, théologie et spiritualité de la prière eucharistique,* trans. Charles Underhill Quinn (Paris: Desclée, 1966); Graham Ward's *Cities of God* (London: Routledge, 2000); Henri de Lubac's *Corpus Mysticum: l'eucharistie et l'église au Moyen Âge* (Paris: Aubier, 1944); E. Schillebeeckx's *Christ the Sacrament of the Encounter with God,* trans. P. Barrett (New York: Sheed and Ward, 1963); Louis-Marie Chauvet, *Symbol and Sacrament: A Sacramental Reinterpretation of Christian Existence,* trans. P. Madigan and M. Beaumont (Collegeville, Minn.: Liturgical Press, 1995); Marion, *God Without Being.*

27. Martin Heidegger, "Origin of the Work of Art," in *Poetry, Language, Thought,* trans. A. Hofstadter (New York: Harper and Row, 1971), 91.

28. Martin Heidegger, *Gesamtausgabe,* ed. F.-W. von Hermann (Frankfurt-on-Main: Klostermann, 1977), 39:216.

29. Ibid., 39:146.

30. Heidegger, "Origin of the Work of Art," 77.

31. See Charles Taylor, *A Secular Age* (Cambridge: Belknap Press, 2007).

32. Edwin Sandys (Archbishop of York), *Sermons,* Parker Society (Eugene, Ore.: Wipf & Stock, 2007), 88, 89. Sandys also cites Augustine: "Why preparest thou thy teeth? Believe, and thou hast eaten," in John Ev. Tract. I.4 xxv.12

33. Matthew Kellison's attack on Calvinism in *A Survey of the New Religion, Detecting Many Grosse Absurdities which it Implieth* (Douay, 1603), bk. IV, 428–29.

CHAPTER 2

1. Marcel Gauchet, *Disenchantment of the World* (Princeton, N.J.: Princeton University Press, 1999), 36.

2. Ibid., 37.

3. As quoted in Ernst Kantorowicz, *The King's Two Bodies: A Study in Medieval Politcal Theology* (Princeton, N.J.: Princeton University Press, 1957), 194 (my italics). The politicization of the Eucharist has been traced in the classic study by Henri de Lubac, *Corpus Mysticum* (Paris: Aubier, 1944). Both Kantorowicz, in *The King's Two Bodies,* and Michel de Certeau, in *The Mystic Fable,* are indebted to his work.

4. De Certeau, *Mystic Fable,* 86. "In the Third Lateran Council (1179) the church body gathered strength, became clericalized, opaque."

5. An increase in movements labeled " 'heretical' or 'spiritual' then in those of *mystics* or witchcraft, reflects both the tenacity and the instability of the traditional modes of integration that were being thrust aside by the new social order." Ibid., 85, 86.

6. Ibid., 89, 90.

7. Ibid., 86. See Sarah Beckwith, *Christ's Body: Identity, Culture, and Society in Late Medieval Writings* (London: Routledge, 1993), and David Aers, *Sanctifying Signs: Making Christian Tradition in Late Medieval England* (South Bend, Ind: University of Notre Dame Press, 2004).

8. Kantorowicz argues in *The King's Two Bodies,* 7, that this case encoded the political theology that governed Tudor England. In the fourth year of the reign of Elizabeth, the case of the ownership of the Duchy of Lancaster was tried; having been private property of the Lancastrian kings (not as property of the Crown), it was now determined that it also belonged to the Crown. According to Edmund Plowden, "For the King has in him two bodies, *viz.,* a Body natural, and a Body politic. His Body natural (if it be considered in itself ) is a Body mortal, subject to all Infirmities that come by Nature or Accident, to the Imbecility of Infancy or old Age, and to the like Defects that happen to the natural Bodies of other People. But his Body politic is a Body that cannot be seen or handled, consisting of Policy and Government, and constituted for the Direction of the People, and the Management of the public weal, and this Body is utterly void of Infancy, and old Age, and other natural Defects and Imbecilities, which the Body natural is subject to, and for this Cause, what the King does in his Body politic, cannot be invalidated or frustrated by any Disability in his natural Body." See Edmund Plowden, *Commentaries or Reports* (London: S. Brooke, 1816), 212a.

9. Ibid.

10. Calvin's Case (1608) in Sir Edward Coke, *The Reports,* ed. George Wilson (London, 1777), VII:10–10a.

11. Kantorowicz, *King's Two Bodies,* 3.

12. Ibid., 7.

13. Ibid., 19.

14. The art historian Roy Strong has documented the "cult of Elizabeth" in several books, including *Gloriana: The Portraits of Queen Elizabeth* (London: Thames and Hudson, 1997) and *The Cult of Elizabeth: Elizabethan Portraiture and Pageantry* (London: Thames and Hudson, 1977).

15. Kantorowicz, *King's Two Bodies*, 193–94.

16. The lawyer who promulgated it, Plowden, did not find his theological forebears sufficient; his genealogy includes Greek, Roman, British, Saxon, and English monarchs. "In Plowden's hands Ovid's sacrifice of Iphigenia becomes a tragedy of the conflict between the king's two bodies." Marie Axton, *The Queen's Two Bodies* (London: Royal Historical Society, 1977), 26. Scholars have noted that Kantorowicz's own early conservative politics may have attracted him to a doctrine deployed to ground absolute monarchy. David Norbrook could validly assert that "as a model of political coherence, the body has a long tradition of association with hierarchy and opposition to democracy, and it often played that role in the early modern period." David Norbrook, "The Emperor's New Body? Richard II, Ernst Kantorowicz, the Politics of Shakespeare Criticism," *Textual Practice* 10 (1996): 329–57.

17. William Corbett, *A Complete Collection of State Trials* (London: Bredshaw-Longman, 1809–26), 3:1265.

18. *Remonstrance à tous les roys et souverains de l'Europe* (The Hague: L. Breeckevelt, 1649), 12 vols. Cited in Sergio Bertelli, *The King's Body*, trans. R. Burr Litchfield (University Park: Pennsylvania State University Press, 2001), 258.

19. Bertelli, *King's Body*, 262.

20. John Tillotson, *Works*, ed. T. Birch (London: J. F. Dove, 1820), x, 21. See Hooker's *Laws of Ecclesiastical Polity* (Cambridge, Mass.: Belknap Press, 1977–1993), 5:67.12 on the mystery of the communion.

21. S. B. Chrimes, *English Constitutional Ideas in the Fifteenth Century* (Cambridge, UK: Cambridge University Press, 1936), 14n1.

22. Cromwell had decisively refused a crown, insisting that he was the Protector and no King. But this only paved the way for another political use of the theology for its own ends. A republican nationalism instead of a royal one will adopt the figure of the corporate body: "the head of state" will represent its "members (body parts)."

23. Augustine, Sermon 272 as cited in Darwell Stone, *A History of the Doctrine of the Holy Eucharist* (London: Longmans, Green, 1909), 95.

24. *Dialogus cum Tryphone*, 116–17, cited in Darwell Stone, 53.

25. "A Fiery Flying Roll" (1649) in *A Collection of Ranter Writings,* ed. Nigel Smith (London: Junction Books, 1983), 114. Among more recent revolutionary thinkers, Alain Badiou has highlighted the radical potential for egalitarianism in the Pauline formulation, "neither Greek nor Jew, neither slave nor free, neither

male nor female, but we are one in Jesus the Christ," and he has commended its fidelity to a universal "truth-event" that supersedes identitarian politics.

26. In his thoughtful critique of Kantorowicz, Norbrook has offered a dualistic taxonomy: classical republicanism/parliamentarianism vs. the mystical body/absolute monarchy. He even marshals a list of uses of the two-body metaphor by royalists in contrast to the infrequency of such use in the Parliamentary rhetoric. But this classification may be problematic for the hallmark of early modern thought was its reliance upon both the resources of Christian theology and classicism without keeping these traditions distinct (as is so evident in the work of Spenser and Milton, among others). When, for instance, Norbrook notes that the rebel Prynne referred to Parliament as the "head and body of all the realme," this does not lead him to the consideration of how fluid and multivalent the image of the mystical body is, applicable not only to king but to parliament, that Prynne is invoking the theological tradition that stresses the corporate body as the mystical body; instead, he concludes that parliament renounces the image of the sacramental body. More important, in Norbrook's impassioned defense of classical republicanism he fails to take full account of its dangers, for the ways in which it gives rise to a theory of "virtue" that thinly veils a new kind of tyranny. Marx, among other theorists, has unmasked this tyranny in political theory, and Christopher Hill has offered an extensive account of the English revolution that does not simply fall into the traps of classical republicanism. In this light, it is odd that while Norbrook is so eager to expose the conservatism of royal absolutism, he does not expose the inherent conservatism of republicanism, its legitimation of a privileged class under the banner of virtue, and the elaborate mechanism of merit that accompanies it. Norbrook, "The Emperor's New Body?"

27. Christopher Sutton, *Godly Meditations upon the Most Holy Sacrament of the Lord's Supper*, as cited in Stone, *A History of the Doctrine*, 233.

28. Hooker, "Of the Lawes of Ecclesiastical Polity," in *The Folger Library Edition of the Works of Richard Hooker,* 6 vols., ed. W. Speed Hill (Cambridge, Mass.: Belknap Press, 1977–1993) 5:67.2.

29. The three work together in a hypostatic union, as the God and man are joined. Hooker is, indeed, unable to elaborate the nature of the sacraments without clarifying his Christology: the mystery of three in one is that all partake in God, even as all are distinct from one another. In the conjunction of the human and the divine, neither substance loses its properties, and there is neither a transition nor fusion of them. This Christology grounds his sacramentology of participation. The bread does not become the body—they are separate substances, but it does deliver the body and thereby grace to the recipient: "there are three thinges said to make up the substance of a sacrament, namely the grace which is thereby offered, the element which shadoweth or signifieth grace, and the worde which expresseth what is don by the elemente." Ibid., 5:58.2.

30. Ibid., 5:56.5.

31. Edward Elton, *Exposition of the Ten Commandments* (London, 1623), 11–12, cited in Aston, *England's Iconoclasts*, 458.

32. Henry Wilkinson, *Babylon's Ruine* (London, 1644), 31, cited in Aston, *England's Iconoclasts*, 459.

33. George Salteren, cited in Aston, *England's Iconoclasts*, 459n11.

34. Jean-Luc Marion, *Idol and Distance: Five Studies*, ed. John D. Caputo (New York: Fordham University Press, 2001), 7.

35. Ibid., 6.

36. "By establishing such an availability of the divine within the fixed, if not frozen, face of the god, does one not deceitfully but radically eliminate the lofty irruption and the undeniable alterity that properly attest the divine?" Ibid., 7–8.

37. Levinas, "Ethics as First Philosophy," in *The Levinas Reader* (Oxford: Blackwell, 1989), 82, first published in *Justifications de l'ethique* (Bruxelles: Editions de l'Université de Bruxelles, 1984), 41–51.

38. Adrian T. Peperzak, *Beyond: The Philosophy of Emmanuel Levinas* (Evanston, Ill.: Nortwestern University Press, 1997), 34.

39. Ludwig Wittgenstein, *The Big Typescript* (Malden, Mass.: Blackwell, 2005), Manuscripts 213 and 413.

40. In *The Curse of Cain: The Violent Legacy of Monotheism* (Chicago: University of Chicago Press, 1997), I have focused that strange way of worshipping—possessing—and noted the violent cost of that idolatry. When we imagine that we possess God, we can use him as an authorizing instrument for our violence. Such a God can authorize, for us, the slaughter of our enemies. When we imagine that God possesses us, we can explain the terrors of history as his righteous wrath for our infidelity, and the violence of possession proliferates; as God possesses us, so we possess land and men possess women, and all of this ownership leads to anxiety over the borders of possession and eventually violence. If I have been suspicious about the adequacy of narratives about God, it is not only because such narratives tend to be projections of human life, human desire, human possession, and human violence but also because of the idolatry of any such description. To speak of representation as idolatry is not new; it is several thousand years old. But to speak of the idol, not as a visual representation—a statue, a painting—but a verbal one—a narrative—seems to still be somewhat controversial. And yet it is our narrative idolatries that hold us in their grip and it is those that need revision through interpretation.

41. Knox, *The Reasoning Which Was betwix the Abbot of Crosragual and John Knox* (*Works*, VI. 172–73), cited in Jasper Ridley, *John Knox* (Oxford: Clarendon Press, 1968), 413.

42. Cranmer, *The Defence of the True and Catholike Doctrine of the Sacrament of the Body and Blood of Our Savior. . .* (London: Reginald Wolfe, 1550), 116.

43. *The Historie of the Reformation of the Church of Scotland* (London: John Raworth, 1644), 418.

44. Among the important contributions are Eamon Duffy's *Stripping of the Altars*; Margaret Aston's *England's Iconoclasts* (Oxford, UK: Clarendon Press, 1988); Patrick Collinson's *From Iconoclasm to Iconophobia* (Reading, UK: University of Reading Press, 1986); and John Phillips's *The Reformation of the Images* (Berkeley: University of California Press, 1973).

45. Aston, *England's Iconoclasts*, 12.

46. Ibid.

47. G. R. Potter, ed., *Huldrych Zwingli* (London: E. Arnold, 1978), 97–98

48. In September of 1538, the suppression of images that were pilgrimage sites resulted in the stripping of images and feeding them into bonfires.

49. John Ayre, ed., *The Works of John Jewel* (Cambridge, UK: Parker Society, 1847), 2:651–68; Nicholas Sanders, *A Treatise of the Images of Christ and His Saints* . . . , (Louvain, 1567), 109. The queen's image also harks back to the holy majesty of the Byzantine and medieval emperors, sharing a "common debt to sacred imperialism" (Strong, 41). Elizabeth needed religiously and doctrinally diverse people to pledge themselves to her, and the multivocality of her images, marked by the lack of a single predicative meaning, was part of their useful power.

50. Aston, *England's Iconoclasts*, 5.

51. Plate XII in Roy Strong, *Portraits of Queen Elizabeth I* (Oxford, UK: Clarendon Press, 1963).

52. Strong, *Portraits of Queen Elizabeth I*, 32.

53. It is Roy Strong, the art historian and expert on the cult of Elizabeth, who has driven home the religious significance of that cult. Strong notes that "the sacred images of Christ, the Virgin, and saints had been cast out of the churches as so much rubbish, while in their place we see the meteoric rise of the sacred images of the *Diva Elizabetha: Portraits of Queen Elizabeth I*, 36.

54. Hooker, "Of the Lawes of Ecclesiastical Polity," V.57.3.

55. The number of religious festivals was radically reduced in the wake of the Reformation to the Prayer-book calendar—to which was added a new calendar centering on the anniversaries of the monarch. A new festival was instituted in Elizabeth's reign: now the annual concert of bells rang to observe a festal observance not tied to the Christian calendar: "Crownation day" (a corruption of coronation day) referred to, significantly, as the " 'queen's holy day' on 17 November" linked parishes throughout England. David Cressy, *Bonfires and Bells* (Berkeley: University of California Press, 1989), 50–51.

56. Aston, *England's Iconoclasts*, 6.

57. Cited in Strong, *Portraits of Queen Elizabeth I*, 35.

58. Ibid., 35–36.

59. H. McIlwain, ed., *The Political Works of James I* (Cambridge, Mass.: Harvard University Press, 1918), 332. See Jonathan Goldberg, *James I and the Politics of Literature: Jonson, Shakespeare, Donne, and Their Contemporaries* (Baltimore, Md.: Johns Hopkins University Press, 1983) 56.

60. Goldberg, *James I and the Politics of Literature*, 85.

61. "Fame, so suddenly transformed but so transparently the annunciate angel, looks upwards as she calls Heaven to witness the beneficence of a learned British king." David Howarth, *Images of Rule: Art and Politics in the English Renaissance, 1485–1649* (Berkeley: University of California Press, 1977), 120.

62. Goldberg, *James I and the Politics of Literature*, 85–112.

63. Howarth, *Images of Rule*, 143.

64. Ibid., 144.

65. Strong, *Portraits of Queen Elizabeth I*, 39.

66. See J. Bruce and T. T. Perowne, eds., *Correspondence of Matthew Parker* (Cambridge, UK: Parker Society, 1853), 94.

67. Louis Marin, *Portrait of the King*, trans. M. Houle (Minneapolis: University of Minnesota Press, 1988), 169–79. See also Strong, *Portraits of Queen Elizabeth I.*

CHAPTER 3

1. Emmanuel Levinas, "Franz Rosenzweig, une pensée juive moderne," in *Franz Rosenzweig, Les cahiers de la nuit surveillée*, vol. 1 (Quétigny, France: La nuit surveillée et les auteurs, 1982), 74.

2. Emmanuel Levinas, *Beyond the Verse: Talmudic Readings and Lectures*, trans. Gary D. Mole (Bloomington: Indiana University Press, 1994), 107.

3. For a further critique of economic justice, see my "The Cost of Justice and Love in *The Merchant of Venice,*" *Triquarterly* (December, 2005).

4. Levinas offers a radical corrective to the procedural justice embraced by so much political theory: "Justice cannot be reduced to the order it institutes or restores, nor to a system whose rationality commands, without difference, men and gods, revealing itself in human legislation like the structures of space in the theorems of geometricians, a justice that a Montesquieu calls the 'logos of Jupiter,' recuperating religion within this metaphor, but effacing precisely transcendence." Levinas, *Beyond the Verse*, 107.

5. The classic case of retribution, "an eye for an eye," is, as all biblical scholars know, the injunction to refuse economic punishment, as it changes the Babylonian law code that demands payment for injury.

6. D. Bentley Hart, "A Gift Exceeding Every Debt: An Eastern Orthodox Appreciation of Anselm's *Cur Deus Homo,*" *Pro Ecclesia* 7, no. 3 (Summer 1998): 333–49, esp. 334.

7. See also Michael Davies, "The Transubstantial Bard: Shakespeare and Catholicism," in Burnham and Giaccherini, *The Poetics of Transubstantiation*; Clifford Davidson, "The Anti-Visual Prejudice," in *Iconoclasm vs Art and Drama*, eds. Clifford Davidson and Anne E. Nichols (Kalamazoo, Mich.: Medieval Institute Publications, 1988); Michael O'Connell, "God's Body: Incarnation, Physical Embodiment and the Fate of Biblical Theatre in the Sixteenth Century," in *Subjects on the World's Stage*, eds. David Allen and Robert White (London: Associated University Presses, 1995); Joel Altman, " 'Vile Participation': The Amplification of Violence in the Theatre of Henry V," *Shakespeare Quarterly* 42, no. 1 (1991): 1–32. On the importance of an incarnational aesthetic for concepts of the bodily, and materiality in late medieval culture, see Miri Rubin, *Corpus Christi: The Eucharist in Late Medieval Culture* (Cambridge, UK: Cambridge University Press, 1991); Sarah Beckwith, *Christ's Body* (New York: Routledge, 1993); and Carolyne Walker Bynum, *Holy Feast and Holy Fast* (Berkeley: University of California Press, 1987).

8. Stephen Gosson, *Plays Confuted in Five Actions* (1582), facsimile ed. (New York: Johnson Reprint Corp., 1972), sigs C5, G6–G7.

9. Shakespeare, *Hamlet*, 3.2.21.This derives from Donatus on comedy where it is attributed to Cicero ("commoediam esse Cicero ait imitationem vitae, speculum consuetudinis, imaginem veritatis").

10. Jeffrey Knapp, *Shakespeare's Tribe: Church, Nation, and Theater in Renaissance England* (Chicago: University of Chicago Press, 2002), 120. Knapp continues: "Following those Protestants who instead treated the petty materiality of the wafer as proof that the eucharist represented Christ, Henry V suggests that the carnal spectacles of the theater sacramentally highlight, rather than obscure, the operations of the spirit precisely because those spectacles are so conspicuously inadequate to the tales of *Non nobis* and *Te Deum* (4.8.121) they represent" (120). In a similar vein, Stephen Greenblatt speaks of the "emptying out" of ritual as the enabling condition of the "craving" set in motion by theater for effective ritual. Greenblatt, *Shakespearean Negotiations* (Berkeley: University of California Press, 1988), 126–27. Louis Adrian Montrose writes of a transfer of the functions of rites of passage from ritual to the theater in "The Purpose of Playing: Reflections on Shakespearean Anthropology," *Helios* 7, no. 2 (1980):51–74. See also Montrose, *The Purpose of Playing: Shakespeare and the Cultural Politics of Elizabethan Theatre* (Chicago: University of Chicago Press, 1996). Historians concur: "If the opportunity for popular participation in public rituals was . . . largely removed, that especial meaning which sacred ceremonies and popular rites had periodically conferred on the citizens' tangible environment also fell victim to the new 'secular' order." Charles Phythian-Adams, "Ceremony and the Citizen: The Communal Year at Coventry 1450–1550," in *Crisis and Order in English Towns 1500–1700*, eds. P. Clark and P. Slack (London: Routledge and Kegan Paul, 1972), 80. See also C. L. Barbar, *Creating Elizabethan Tragedy* (Chicago: University of Chicago Press, 1988) which, with Montrose, argues that the theater compensates

for affective losses wrought by the elimination of ritual in Protestantism. The account needs nuancing as ritual was not eliminated, but altered and given altered significance.

11. "A Declaration of Egregious Popish Impostures," where Harsnett identifies exorcism with the theater, quoted in Greenblatt, *Shakespearean Negotiations,* 112. See Christopher Hodgkins, "Plays Out of Season: Puritanism, Antitheatricalism, and Parliament's 1642 Closing of the Theaters," in *Centered on the Word: Literature, Scripture, and the Tudor-Stuart Middle Way,* eds. Daniel W. Doerksen and Christopher Hodgkins (Newark: University of Delaware Press, 2004); Margot Heinemann, *Puritanism and Theatre* (Cambridge, UK: Cambridge University Press, 1980); and Jonas Barish, *The Anti-Theatrical Prejudice* (Berkeley: University of California Press, 1981).

12. Greenblatt, *Shakespearean Negotiations,* 125.

13. However, critics can be given to the same equation of ritual and theater but for different reasons: for Julia Houston, Cranmer's innovations in the 1552 *Book of Common Prayer* had the effect of transforming the sacrament precisely into theater: "Transubstantiation and the Sign: Cranmer's Drama of the Lord's Supper," *Journal of Medieval and Renaissance Studies* 24 (1994). On theological "participation" and its relation to theater, see the brilliant essay by Anthony Dawson, "Performance and Participation" in Dawson and Paul Yachnin, *The Culture of Playgoing in Shakespeare's England* (Cambridge, UK: Cambridge University Press, 2001), 11–37. He argues that the theater both encourages and undermines the understanding of bodily participation. See also Rajiva Verma, *Myth, Ritual and Shakespeare* (New Delhi: Spantech Publishers, 1990). Discussions of the importance of the sacrament for drama include David Lee Miller, "Witnessing as Theater in Shakespeare," in *Dreams of the Burning Child* (New York: Cornell University Press, 2003); Herbert Coursen Jr., *Christian Ritual and the World of Shakespeare's Tragedies* (Lewisburg, Pa.: Bucknell University Press, 1976); and A. C. Bradley, *Shakespearean Tragedy* (London: Northrop Frye, 1964).

14. Andrew Gurr, *The Shakespearean Stage 1574–1642* (Cambridge, UK: Cambridge University Press, 1970).

15. Some critics are quite sensitive to the distinction: "Playgoing is a little like churchgoing. It is a public act for private ends. It is a private act performed publicly. It is intimate and individual. It is impersonal and communal. It brings us nearer to the apprehension of our own godhood while at the same time it reinforces awareness of the transitory properties of our flesh. Yet likeness is not identity. Playgoing is a surrender to illusion while churchgoing is a ritual embodiment of a higher truth. Through churchgoing we hope to step from one truth to *the* truth. Playgoing holds out the possibility that we can slip through fancy to a lookout upon truth." Bernard Beckerman, "Shakespearean Playgoing Then and Now," in *Shakespeare's More Than Words Can Witness: Essays on Visual and Nonverbal*

*Enactment in the Plays*, ed. Sidney Homan (Lewisburg, Pa.: Bucknell University Press, 1980), 142.

16. As cited in Montrose, "The Purpose of Playing," 58, from a 1597 London Petition.

17. Rubin, *Corpus Christi*.

18. The discourse on Shakespeare and religion is extensive; among other works, it includes Roland Mushat Frye, *Shakespeare and Christian Doctrine* (Princeton, N.J.: Princeton University Press, 1963); Coursen, *Christian Ritual and the World of Shakespeare's Tragedies*; Roy Battenhouse, ed., *Shakespeare's Christian Dimension: An Anthology of Commentary* (Bloomington: Indiana University Press, 1994); Francis Dolan, *Whores of Babylon: Catholicism, Gender, and Seventeenth-century Print Culture* (Ithaca, N.Y.: Cornell University Press, 1999); Judy Kronenfeld, *King Lear and the Naked Truth: Rethinking the Language of Religion and Resistance* (Durham, N.C.: Duke University Press, 1998); Debora K. Shuger, "Subversive Fathers and Suffering Subjects: Shakespeare and Christianity," in *Religion, Literature and Politics in Post-Reformation England, 1540–1688*, eds. Donna Hamilton and Richard Strier (Cambridge, UK: Cambridge University Press, 1996), 46–69; Lowell Gallagher, *Medusa's Gaze: Casuistry and Conscience in the Renaissance* (Stanford, Calif.: Stanford University Press, 1991); Dennis Taylor and David Beauregard, eds., *Shakespeare and the Culture of Christianity in Early Modern England* (New York: Fordham University Press, 2003); Maurice Hunt, *Shakespeare's Religious Allusiveness: Its Play and Tolerance* (Aldershot, UK: Ashgate, 2004); and see below, note 29.

19. Martin Luther, "A Prelude on the Babylonian Captivity of the Church" [1520], in *Works of Martin Luther*, vol. 2 (Grand Rapids, Mich.: Baker Book House, 1982), 201.

20. John Calvin, *Institution of the Christian Religion*, 1536 edition (Atlanta: John Knox Press, 1969), 160.

21. *The Work of Thomas Cranmer* (Appleford, UK: Courtenay Press, 1964), II:55, 56.

22. Ibid., 215.

23. *Liturgiae Britannicae, or, the Several Editions of the Book of Common Prayer of the Church of England* (London: William Pickering, 1842), 215.

24. John Jewel, *The Apology of the Church of England*, ed. William R. Whittingham (New York: H.M. Onderdock, 1846), 55.

25. Richard Hooker, *Ecclesiastical Polity* (London: Everyman, 1907), V.lvii.6.322–23.

26. Ibid., lxvii.12.330–31.

27. Ibid., 35. Susan Zimmerman's *The Early Modern Corpse and Shakespeare's Theatre* (Edinburgh: Edinburgh University Press, 2005) includes an excellent discussion of the Reformers' aversion to the materiality of medieval religious thought. See especially chapter 2, "Body Imaging and Religious Reform: The Corpse as Idol," 24–89.

28. Inst. IV.17.3, my italics. Calvin joined in with vehemence against the Catholic Mass, attacking the "mass-Doctors" who purport to be the agents of grace instead of Christ: "While they have fashioned themselves a god after the decision of their own lust, they have forsaken the living God. Indeed, they have worshipped the gifts instead of the giver. In this there is a double transgression: for both the honor taken from God has been transferred to the creature [cf. Rom. 1:25], and he himself also has been dishonored in the defilement and the profanation of his gift, when his holy sacrament is made a hateful idol" *Institution*, 148.

29. With the stakes high that England's "national poet" does or does not represent England's national religion, the discussion of his greater or lesser sympathy to Catholicism is of considerable interest. See Peter Milward, *Shakespeare's Religious Background* (Chicago: Sidgwick & Jackson, 1973); Richard Wilson, *Secret Shakespeare: Studies in Theatre, Religion, and Resistance* (Manchester, UK: Manchester University Press, 2004); Arthur Marotti, *Religious Ideology and Cultural Fantasy: Catholic and Anti-Catholic Discourse in Early Modern England* (South Bend, Ind.: University of Notre Dame, 2005) and *Catholicism and Anti-Catholicism in Early Modern English Texts* (New York: Macmillan, 1999). Historical re-examinations of the nature and extent of the Reformation have altered the assumption that the religious landscape quickly and decisively converted to Protestant ritual and doctrine. See Eamon Duffy, *Stripping of the Altars*; Jon Bossy, *The English Catholic Community 1570–1850* (New York: Oxford University Press, 1976); and Christopher Haigh, *English Reformations: Religion, Politics, and Society under the Tudors* (Oxford, UK: Oxford University Press, 1993). Arthur Marotti has concluded that the categories of Catholic and Protestant are too rough-hewn to describe the beliefs and practices of those in Shakespeare's audience who constituted a "great muddled middle in English Christianity," "Shakespeare and Catholicism," in *Theatre and Religion: Lancastrian Shakespeare*, eds. Richard Dutton, Alison Findlay, and Richard Wilson (Manchester, UK: Manchester University Press, 2003), 218–41, 219. See also Debora Kuller Shuger, *Habits of Thought in the English Renaissance: Religion, Politics and the Dominant Culture* (Berkeley: University of California Press, 1990) and *The Renaissance Bible: Scholarship, Sacrifice, and Subjectivity* (Berkeley: University of California Press, 1994). For studies of Shakespeare's Protestantism, see the important studies by Huston Diehl, *Staging Reform, Reforming the Stage: Protestantism and Popular Theater in Early Modern England* (Ithaca, N.Y.: Cornell University Press, 1997); and Donna Hamilton, *Shakespeare and the Politics of Protestant England* (Lexington: University Press of Kentucky, 1992).

30. For considerations of religion and *Othello*, see Eric Griffin, "Un-sainting James: or Othello and the 'Spanish Spirits' of Shakespeare's Globe," *Representations* 62 (Spring 1998): 58–99; Huston Diehl, *Staging Reform*, 125–55; Robert Watson, "Othello as Protestant Propaganda" in *Religion and Culture in Renaissance England*, eds. Claire McEchern and Debora Shuger (Cambridge, UK: Cambridge

University Press, 1997), 234–57; Richard Mallette, "Blasphemous Preacher: Iago and the Reformation," 382–414, and Paula McQuade, "Love and Lies: Marital Truth-Telling, Catholic Casuistry, and *Othello*," in *Shakespeare and the Culture of Christianity in Early Modern England*, eds. Dennis Taylor and David Beauregard (New York: Fordham University Press, 2003), 415–38; excerpts from David L Jeffrey and Patrick Grant, Joan Ozark Holmer, and Roy Battenhouse in Battenhouse, *Shakespeare's Christian Dimension*, 415–29.

31. Shakespearean allusions to assassins taking the sacrament prior to their crime include Henry VI 4.2.28; Richard III I.4.191; King John 5.2.6, and Richard II 5.2.97–99.

32. This inadequacy was felt by the radical Reformers themselves, figures like Menno who needed to solve the problem through a God-man whose heavenly rather than earthly flesh offered man the chance to be perfected through communion with that flesh.

33. Gabriel Biel, *Expositio sacri canonis missae* (c. 1488), Brescia edition, 1576, Lectio LVII. lit.D, as quoted in Francis Clark, *Eucharistic Sacrifice and the Reformation* (Baltimore: Newman Press 1960), 180.

34. Ibid., as quoted in Clark, *Eucharistic Sacrifice*, 88.

35. Herbert Coursen Jr.'s "Introduction" to his *Christian Ritual and the World of Shakespeare's Tragedies* includes a fine discussion of the importance of communion to the Elizabethan: "it is in the receiving of the sacraments and not in the consecration of the elements that the fusion of Christ and communicant, blood and wine occurs. . . . It is more important, says Hooker, to 'meditate with silence what we have by the sacrament, and less to dispute the matter how' " (5–6). He concludes that "the 1559 Prayer Book's confirmation of the individual's role in Communion was bound to affect, if not determine, the drama that emerged in the late sixteenth and early seventeenth centuries" (8).

CHAPTER 4

1. Of course, *Paradise Lost* also portrays the honors of human history in its final two books.

2. "De Doctrina Christiana," in *Complete Prose Works of John Milton*, trans. John Carey (New Haven, Conn.: Yale University Press, 1973), VI:554. He is alluding to the Council of Trent's wording, that Jesus is "really and substantially contained under the appearance of those physical things." The authorship of this work has recently been questioned by some Milton scholars, with others vigorously defending it as Milton's.

3. See Susannah B. Mintz, *Threshold Poetics: Milton and Intersubjectivity* (Newark: University of Delaware Press, 2003); Beverley Sherry, "Not by Bread Alone: The Communication of Adam and Raphael," *Milton Quarterly* 13 (1979): 111–14.

4. See John C. Ulreich Jr., "Milton on the Eucharist: Some Second Thoughts about Sacramentalism," in *Milton and the Middle Ages*, ed. John Mulryan (Lewisburg, Pa.: Bucknell University Press, 1982), 32–56; Marshall Grossman, "Milton's 'Transubstantiate': Interpreting the Sacrament in Paradise Lost," *Milton Quarterly* 16, no. 2 (1982): 42–47, where Grossman seeks to refigure what Milton means by "transubstantiation"; and Claude N. Stulting Jr., " 'New Heav'ns, New Earth': Apocalypse and the Loss of Sacramentality in the Postlapsarian Books of Paradise Lost," in *Milton and the Ends of Time*, ed. Juliet Cummins (Cambridge, UK: Cambridge University Press, 2003), 184–201.

5. This interpretation departs markedly from the explanation offered by John N. King. He rightly notes how central the issue of communion was for Milton, paying heed, importantly, to Milton's revision in the 1674 edition of *Paradise Lost* where he substitutes the following passage for V. 637–39 in the first edition.

> They eat, they drink, and *in communion* sweet
> *Quaff immortality and joy, secure*
> *Of surfeit where full measure only bounds*
> *Excess,* before the all bounteous King, who showered
> With copious hand, rejoicing in their joy.
> (V. 637–41)

"Italics highlight the new wording. . . . The revision valorizes Holy Communion as a worldly analogue to angelic dining, in particular Raphael's transubstantiation of his Edenic meal." King, "Miltonic Transubstantiation," *Milton Studies* 36 (1998): 41–58, esp. 45. But then King's analysis embraces one of the two options for understanding Milton's allusions to liturgy that have been laid out by Miltonists. One option is that these are straightforward liturgical allusions which, however, fail to refer to any particular liturgical practice. Another, that he endorses, is that Milton is engaged in church satire. The evidence offered for satire seems specious: that Milton puts a Latinate term (*transubstantiate*) in the midst of otherwise simple language, that Milton's verse relies on repetition (the word *table*)—both techniques used far too commonly by Milton with high seriousness to signal satire with any certainty. We would not want to reduce *Samson Agonistes* to a satire on classical tragedy, although Milton creatively reworks the tradition, or see *Paradise Lost* as a satire on Greek and Latin epics or *Paradise Regained* as a satire of the gospels, although his allusions are never orthodox in any of those cases. And even if Milton seems playful to have his minister serving naked (in light of Puritan critiques of vestments), that does not preclude a creative understanding of the rite that includes pure innocence just as alluding to private parts as "mysteries" need not reduce the mystery of the sacrament, but can instead attach the mystery of the Eucharist to sexuality, as Donne does. This is not to read without a sense of humor, but to read with delight in his alternative world, rather than simply seeing him as more or less angry with the social practices around him.

6. Stephen Fallon, *Milton Among the Philosophers: Poetry and Materialism in Seventeenth-Century England* (Ithaca, N.Y.: Cornell University Press, 1991), 80; Phillip J. Donnelly, "'Matter' Versus Body: The Character of Milton's Monism," *Milton Quarterly* 33, no. 3 (1999): 79–85; Michael Lieb, "Reading God: Milton and the Anthropopathetic Tradition," *Milton Studies* 25 (1989): 213–43; John Rumrich, "Milton's Theanthropos: The Body of Christ in Paradise Regained," *Milton Studies* 42 (2003): 50–67; and Raymond B. Waddington, "'All in All': Shakespeare, Milton, Donne and the Soul-in-Body Topos," *English Literary Renaissance* 20, no. 1 (1990): 40–68.

7. John Eck, *De Sacrificio Missae Contra Lutheranos* (Ingolstadt, 1526), 69.

8. John Hales, in *Four Tracts . . .* (London, 1677), 62.

9. John King has contributed a different approach to this question, regarding Milton's allusion to transubstantiation as wholly ironic, in "Miltonic Transubstantiation," 41–58 (see note 4 above). See also John Ulreich Jr.'s discussion of Haemony as a eucharistic symbol in "A Bright Golden Flow'r: Haemony as a Symbol of Transformation," *Studies in English Literature, 1500–1900* 17, no. 1, *The English Renaissance* (Winter 1977), 119–28.

10. See Michael Schoenfeldt, "'That Spectacle of Too Much Weight': The Poetics of Sacrifice in Donne, Herbert, and Milton," *Journal of Medieval and Early Modern Studies* 31, no. 3 (2001): 561–84.

11. Thomas Cranmer, *Writings and Disputations of Thomas Cranmer*, ed. J. E. Cox (Cambridge: Parker Society, 1844), 229.

12. Calvin, *Institution* IV.48.160.

13. As Tyacke points out, "During the 1630's, the . . . parish churches were transformed more radically than at any time since the Elizabethan settlement of religion. This chiefly involved the conversion of communion tables into altars, permanently railed in at the east ends of chancels." Nicholas Tyacke, *Anti-Calvinists: The Rise of English Arminianism c. 1590–1640* (Oxford, UK: Clarendon Press, 1987), 199.

14. For instance, at St. Gregory's Church, which adjoined St. Paul's Cathedral in London, the communion table had been moved to the east end of the chancel and rails had been added to cordon it off. Five parishioners appealed that it had been moved unlawfully, citing the Elizabethan injunction of 1559 wherein it was ordered that "the holy table in every church" should be "set in the place where the altar stood . . . saving when the communion of the sacrament is to be distributed; at which time the same shall be so placed in good sort within the chancel, as whereby the minister may be more conveniently heard of the communicants in his prayer and ministration, and the communicants also more conveniently, and in more number communicate with the said minister. And after the communion done, from time to time the same holy table to be placed where it stood before." E. Cardwell, *Documentary Annals of the Reformed Church of England* (Oxford, 1844), I. 234,

quoted in Tyacke, 200–201. On November 3, 1633, the Privy Council ruled against the five parishioners. King Charles wanted the table to be where the altar once was, in other words, to be an altar—and by 1635 Archbishop Laud had ordered all communion tables to be moved to the east end of the chancel and railed in, separated and sanctified by separation. He reasoned that as daughter churches, parishes should imitate their mother churches, the cathedrals, and he defended his policy at the famous trial of the radicals, Bastwick, Burton, and Prynne.

Mr. Burton says the placing of the holy table altarwise "is done to advance and usher in Popery."

To this I answer, that tis no Popery to set a rail to keep profanation from that Holy Table; nor is it any innovation to place it . . . as the Altar stood . . . in the King's royal chapels and divers cathedrals. . . .

And though it stood in most parish churches the other way, yet whether there be not more reason the parish churches should be made conformable to the Cathedral and Mother Churches, than the Cathedrals to them, I leave to any reasonable man to judge. (William Laud, *Liturgy, Episcopacy and Church Ritual* [Oxford: John Henry Parker, 1840], 383.)

And yet, despite Laud's best efforts, by January 1636, historians count that only 140 out of 469 parishes had moved their communion tables "altarwise." At St. Lewes, one of the churchwardens moved the communion table from the altar position back to the middle of the chancel in the middle of the night. At St. Peter's, Nottingham, the parish fought with a delaying action, and when many parishioners were "presented" for not communicating, they argued in their defense that the church was unusually crowded and that decent administration in the legal place was difficult. When further orders were given to the churchwardens to provide a rail, this was done, but then the table was found standing outside it! Upon the breakdown of Laud's ecclesiastical machinery, the vicar of Stanton-on-the-Wolds violently moved the table from its place behind the rails. In practice, apparently, this peripatetic table did not journey up and back, but was left in the middle of the chancel. The ecclesiastical canons of 1604 did not bother to specify where the table should be when communion was not taking place. Tyacke, 199–209.

15. "Of Reformation," in *Complete Prose Works of John Milton,* ed. Maurice Kelley (New Haven, Conn.: Yale University Press, 1973), I.547–48.

16. Milton, "De Doctrina Christiana," in *Complete Prose*, VI.

17. See John Rogers's important study of vitalism, *The Matter of Revolution: Science, Poetry and Politics in the Age of Milton* (Ithaca, N.Y.: Cornell University Press, 1996); for Milton and monism, see Dennis Danielson, *Milton's Good God: A Study in Literary Theodicy* (Cambridge, UK: Cambridge University Press, 1982); on Milton and alchemy, see Michael Lieb, *The Dialectics of Creation: Patterns of Birth and Regeneration in Paradise Lost* (Amherst: University of Massachusetts Press, 1970).

18. Jason Rosenblatt has persuasively shown how extensive Milton's debt to Torah was in his brilliant *Torah and Law in Paradise Lost* (Princeton, N.J.: Princeton University Press, 1994); William B. Hunter Jr., "The Obedience of Christ in Paradise Regained," in *Calm of Mind: Tercentenary Essays on Paradise Regained and Samson Agonistes in Honor of John S. Diekhoff*, eds. Joseph A. Wittreich Jr., James G. Taaffe, and Jane Cerny (Cleveland and London: The Press of Case Western Reserve University Press, 1971), 67–75.

19. John Milton, *Areopagitica,* in *Complete Poems and Major Prose of John Milton*, ed. Merritt Hughes (New York: Odyssey Press, 1957), 742.

20. Michael Lieb, *Milton and the Culture of Violence* (Ithaca, N.Y.: Cornell University Press, 1994).

21. Jean-Louis Chrétien, *The Unforgettable and the Unhoped For*, trans. Jeffrey Bloechl (New York: Fordham: 2002), 125.

22. Ibid., 124. An impossibly distant past opens onto the present along with an interminable future, all made present in the promise, in which "we receive more than we receive, by opening all of the future to receive it" (ibid., 125).

23. See the invaluable study by Michael Lieb, *Theological Milton: Deity, Discourse and Heresy in the Miltonic Canon* (Pittsburgh: Duquesne University Press, 2006).

24. John Karl Franson, "Bread and Banquet as Food for Thought: Experiential Learning in *Paradise Regained*" in *Milton Reconsidered: Essays in Honor of Arthur E. Barker* (Salzburg: University of Salzburg, 1976), 154–92; Denise Gigante, "Milton's Aesthetics of Eating," *Diacritics: A Review of Contemporary Criticism* 30, no. 2 (2000): 88–112; Ann Torday Gulden, "Milton's Eve and Wisdom: The 'Dinner-Party' Scene in *Paradise Lost*," in *Self-Fashioning and Metamorphosis in Early Modern English Literature*, eds. Olav Lausund and Stein Haugom Olsen (Oslo, Norway: Novus, 2003), 209–19; Michael Schoenfeldt, "Fables of the Belly in Early Modern England" in *The Body in Parts: Fantasies of Corporeality in Early Modern Europe*, eds. David Hillman and Carla Mazzio (New York: Routledge, 1997), 243–62; Schoenfeldt, *Bodies and Selves in Early Modern England: Physiology and Inwardness in Spenser, Shakespeare, Herbert, and Milton* (Cambridge, UK: Cambridge University Press, 1999).

25. Regina Schwartz, "Milton on the Bible" in *A Companion to Milton*, ed. Thomas Corns (Oxford: Blackwell, 2001), 37–54.

26. Jean-Luc Marion and Jacques Derrida debate gift theory in *God, the Gift, and Postmodernism*, ed. John Caputo (Bloomington: Indiana University Press, 1999). For Marion, when the phenomenon of the absolute gift is "understood unconditionally, without any a priori and according to its pure givenness alone, any theological identification of the gift or its giver would become impossible. . . . Characterized by its remaining unforeseeable, nonpresentable and nonrepeatable for the intentional subject of consciousness, such a givenness would indicate the

radical possibility 'of the impossible itself.' " Thomas Carlson, *Indiscretion: Finitude and the Naming of God* (Chicago, University of Chicago Press, 1999), 192. See also Marion, "Metaphysics and Phenomenology: A Relief for Theology," *Critical Inquiry* 4 (1994): 572–91.

27. For further discussion of interpreting the Bible according to principles of scarcity and plenty, see Schwartz, *The Curse of Cain*, esp. chapter 1.

28. James E. Johnston, "Milton on the Doctrine of the Atonement," *Renascence: Essays on Values in Literature* 38, no. 1 (1985): 40–53; C. A. Patrides, "Milton and the Protestant Theory of the Atonement," *PMLA: Publications of the Modern Language Association of America* [hereafter *PMLA*] 74, no. 1 (1959): 7–13; and Alinda Summers, "The Banqueting Scene in *Paradise Regained*: Milton's Temptation to the Anti-Puritan Appetite," in *Praise Disjoined: Changing Patterns of Salvation in 17th-Century English Literature*, ed. William P. Shaw (New York: Peter Lang, 1991), 273–302.

29. Irenaeus, *Against Heresies*, in *Sancti Irenaei . . . Adversus Haereses*, vol. 2 ed. W. W. Harvey (Cambridge, 1857), 2:368.

30. Jaroslav Pelikan, *The Christian Tradition: The Emergence of the Catholic Tradition (100–600)* (Chicago: University of Chicago Press, 1975), 150.

31. Martin Luther, *Commentary on Galatians* (Grand Rapids, Mich.: Revell, 1998), cf. Pelikan, 162.

32. Susan Schreiner, *Where Shall Wisdom Be Found?: Calvin's Exegesis of Job from Medieval and Modern Perspectives* (Chicago: University of Chicago Press, 1994), 104.

33. All of these functions of salvation, so alien to *Paradise Regained*, are detailed in *De Doctrina Christiana*, leaving us to ask how he could have written that section and *Paradise Regained*. The authorship of this theological treatise is a vexed problem and scholars at least agree that it is a deeply heterogeneous text, not the record of a single or even a handful of amanuenses. Without commenting on the whole of the theological treatise's authorship, I discern that the presuppositions of what constitute the regaining of paradise in *De Doctrina Christiana* are precisely the ones the author of *Paradise Regained* does not embrace.

34. Irenaeus, *Adversus Haereses*, 2:100 (my italics), as quoted in Pelikan, *The Christian Tradition*, 150.

35. Irenaeus, *Adversus Haereses*, 5:388–89.

36. Irenaeus, *Proof of the Apostolic Preaching* (Demonstratio apostolicae praedicationis), in *Ancient Christian Writers* (Westminster, Md.: The Newman Press, 1952), 68.

37. Pelikan, *The Christian Tradition: The Emergence of the Catholic Tradition*, 141.

38. Irene Samuel, "Milton on Learning and Wisdom," *PMLA* 64, no. 4 (1949): 708–23. See also my discussion of knowledge in *Paradise Lost*, chapter 3 of

*Remembering and Repeating: On Milton's Theology and Poetics* (Chicago: University of Chicago Press, 1990).

39. Hence, making the stubborn scholarly focus on the problem of "identity" in *Paradise Regained*, only another category of being, is so misguided.

40. See Marc Geisler, "'Join Voices all Ye Living Souls': Renunciation and Gathering in Milton's Invocations," *Hellas: A Journal of Poetry and the Humanities* 6, no. 2 (1995): 48–68.

41. Northrop Frye, "The Typology of *Paradise Regained*," *Modern Philology* 53, no. 4 (1956): 235.

42. Barbara Lewalski has organized the second part of *Milton's Brief Epic: The Genre, Meaning, and Art of Paradise Regained* (Providence, R.I.: Brown University Press, 1966) on Christ's identity and his work, around the positive roles for Savior of prophet, king, and priest, gleaned from Milton's discussion of redemption in *De Doctrina Christiana.*

43. Milton's apophaticism, his desire to allow mystery to remain mystery, emerges in his discourse on the Incarnation: "Since then this mystery is so great, we are admonished by that very consideration not to assert any thing respecting it, rashly or presumptuously . . . not to add anything . . . of our own . . . what is mysterious would be suffered to remain inviolate." *The Works of John Milton* (New York: Columbia University Press, 1931–1940), XV:273. Milton concludes, on the mystery of the God/man question: "it behooves us to cease from devising subtle explanations, and to be contented with remaining wisely ignorant." If he echoes Raphael's advice to Adam in *Paradise Lost* to "be lowly wise," he also echoes Nicholas of Cusa's "on learned ignorance."

44. *Mystical Theology* 1025A, in *Pseudo-Dionysius: The Complete Works*, trans. Colm Luibhéid (New York: Paulist Press, 1987), 138. For Milton and the question of the mystical, see Michael Lieb, *The Sinews of Ulysses* (Pittsburgh: Duquesne University Press, 1989); Stephen R. Honeygosky, *Milton's House of God: The Invisible and Visible Church* (Columbia: University of Missouri Press, 1993); Joseph A. Wittreich Jr., *Visionary Poetics: Milton's Tradition and His Legacy* (San Marino, Calif.: Huntington Library, 1979); William Kerrigan, *Prophetic Milton* (Charlottesville: University of Virginia Press, 1974); and Ken Simpson, "The Rituals of Presence in *Paradise Regained*," in *Wrestling with God: Literature and Theology in the English Renaissance*, ed. Mary Ellen Henley et al. *Early Modern Literary Studies* (May 2001): 14.1–33.

45. *Mystical Theology* 1033C, 139.

46. Ibid., 1048A, 1048B, 141.

47. Ken Simpson, "Lingering Voices, Telling Silences," *Milton Studies* 35 (1997): 179–95, has also read *Paradise Regained* with apophatic lenses: "Christ is charged to represent the unrepresentable while transcending representation himself since his identity as 'God-man' is a mystery of faith" (180). Simpson's insight-

ful essay on silence in *Paradise Regained* traces it back to Pseudo-Dionysius and the apophatic tradition. Focusing rigorously and convincingly on literal silence, he does not link "unsaying" to the renunciations of Jesus. Everything Satan says is unsaid by Christ; renunciation characterizes the entire poem. But Simpson wants to distinguish between the silencing of Satan and the silence of Jesus: "The silencing of Satan and the silence of Jesus on the pinnacle are two completely different events: the first reveals the emptiness of words not linked to the Word; the second reveals the saving power of the Word as well as the inability of words to present God's presence" (180). I see them as completely implicated in one another. Jesus must unsay Satan's words to arrive at his own silence. On language and *Paradise Regained*, see Steven Goldsmith, "The Muting of Satan: Language and Redemption in Paradise Regained," *SEL: Studies in English Literature, 1500–1900* [hereafter *SEL*] 27, no. 1 (1987): 125–40; Stanley Fish, "Inaction and Silence: The Reader in Paradise Regained," in *Calm of Mind: Tercentenary Essays on Paradise Regained and Samson Agonistes*, ed. Joseph A. Wittreich Jr. (Cleveland, Ohio: Case University Press, 1971), 25–47; Leonard Mustazza, "Language as Weapon in Milton's Paradise Regained," *Milton Studies* 18 (1983): 195–216; Douglas Wurtele, " 'Persuasive Rhetoric': The Techniques of Milton's Archetypal Sophist," *ECS* 3 (1977): 18–33; and Henry J. Laskowsky, "A Pinnacle of the Sublime: Christ's Victory of Style in *Paradise Regained*," *Milton Quarterly* 15 (March 1981): 10–13.

48. That is the argument of my book *Remembering and Repeating: On Milton's Theology and Poetics* (Chicago: University of Chicago Press, 1993), 19.

49. Denys Turner, *Eros and Allegory: Medieval Exegesis of the Song of Songs* (Kalamazoo, Mich.: Cistercian Publications, 1995), 54.

50. Ibid., 56.

51. Louis Martz understood *Paradise Regained* as a poem of renunciation in *Milton: Poet of Exile* (New Haven, Conn.: Yale University Press, 1980), 247–71.

52. David Loewenstein, "The Kingdom Within: Radical Religious Culture and the Politics of Paradise Regained," *Literature and History* 3, no. 2 (1994): 63–89. Irene Samuel has charged her reading of *Paradise Regained* with an optimism that sounds more like the youthful Milton who would spread his mighty wings than the weary, soul-battered poet of the Restoration: "everything said [by Jesus] has established that man as man is wholly adequate to be, say, think, do all that man must to recover Eden, his full human heritage." With complete confidence in the efficacy of reasoned argument—"saying is itself a doing" (Samuel, 131)—she concludes that Milton "creates a highly Socratic Saviour to enact through dialogue the adequacy of 'mere man' to the regaining of the fully human Paradise" (134). Samuel has perhaps produced the most powerful secular reading of *Paradise Regained*: it is a moral poem, its protagonist is a man, like all men, not higher than all men, and its lessons are offered as "reasoned arguments," not as mysteries. "Milton's [protagonist] is willing to go on talking, even to the Devil,

confident that out of right talk can come a vision of 'something better' which man will then 'strive to bring into existence.'" What this persuasive secular argument misses is that there is no reasoned argument on how to regain paradise: there is no argument to be made at all. It is only possible because of a mystery, and that mystery is completely unsayable. Thus, Milton's protagonist can indeed talk and talk and go on talking, but he reduces the words of his opponent—indeed, the reasoned arguments of his opponent—to nothingness.

53. Irenaeus, 4.14.1.

54. When we move beyond the controversies over the person of Christ and refocus our attention on the question of paradise regained, we do more than attend to Milton's chief concern in his epic and thereby adhere more faithfully to his poetry. We allow one of the most contentious debates in the history of Western religious thought—one that split the Western church from the East, that allowed many a pious person to be accused of heresy, and that required many a so-called heretic to endure grotesque physical violence and appalling murder—to rest in peace.

CHAPTER 5

1. Sermon preached May 8, 1625, in *John Donne: The Major Works*, ed. John Carey (Oxford, UK: Oxford University Press, 2000), 360.

2. Sermon preached at Whitehall, March 8, 1622, ibid., 305–6.

3. As Albert C. Labriola has noted, "[T]he argument that spiritual love may manifest itself corporeally is developed, by implication, against a frame of reference involving the love of the godhead for humankind" (79). Labriola's fine essay "This Dialogue of One: Rational Argument and Affective Discourse in Donne's 'Aire and Angels,'" *John Donne Journal* 9, no. 1 (1990): 77–83, is one of the readings that deals most explicitly with the theological context of the poem. His focus is on ways the scholastic understanding of analogy informs Donne's lyric. See Felicia Wright McDuffie, *To Our Bodies Turn We Then: Body as Word and Sacrament in the Works of John Donne* (New York: Continuum, 2005), a sustained treatment of Donne on the body as a sign and sacrament, 69–77. "Donne's most distinctive focus is the embodiment of the Word in body itself, not only in the incarnation of Christ, but in the bodies of all of humanity" (69).

4. Raymond-Jean Frontain and Frances M. Malpezzi, eds., *John Donne's Religious Imagination: Essays in, in Honor of John T. Shawcross* (Conway, Ark: UCA Press, 1995), 2–3.

5. On Donne and religion, see *John Donne and the Protestant Reformation: New Perspectives*, ed. Mary Arshagouni Papazian (Detroit, Mich.: Wayne State University Press, 2003), 293–313; R. V. Young, *Doctrine and Devotion in Seventeenth-century Poetry: Studies in Donne, Herbert, Crashaw, and Vaughan* (Cambridge and

Rochester, N.Y.: D. S. Brewer, 2000); Frontain and Malpezzi, *John Donne's Religious Imagination;* and Paul Cefalu, *Moral Identity in Early Modern English Literature* (Cambridge, UK: Cambridge University Press, 2005). And among many essays that take up the question of Donne's affiliation with a religious confession, see Murray Roston, "Donne and the Meditative Tradition," *Religion and Literature* 37 (2005): 45–68; John Stachniewski, "John Donne: The Despair of the 'Holy Sonnets,'" *ELH* 48, no. 4 (1981): 677–705; Richard Strier, "John Donne Awry and Squint: The 'Holy Sonnets,' 1608–1610," *Modern Philology* 86, no. 4 (1989): 357–84; and Anthony Low, "Absence in Donne's Holy Sonnets: Between Catholic and Calvinist," *John Donne Journal: Studies in the Age of Donne* 23, no. 10 (2004): 95–115.

6. Sermon on Christmas Day 1626, in Carey, *John Donne: The Major Works*, 375.

7. Ibid.

8. *The Sermons of John Donne*, eds. George Potter and Evelyn Simpson (Berkeley: University of California Press, 1953–1962), V:135.

9. Critical literature on Donne and the sacrament includes Robert Whalen, *The Poetry of Immanence: Sacrament in Donne and Herbert* (Toronto: University of Toronto Press, 2002); Theresa M. DiPasquale, *Literature and Sacrament: The Sacred and the Secular in John Donne* (Pittsburgh, Pa.: Duquesne University Press, 1999); Eleanor McNees, *Eucharistic Poetry: The Search for Presence in the Writings of John Donne, Gerard Manley Hopkins, Dylan Thomas, and Geoffrey Hill* (Lewisburg, Pa.: Bucknell University Press, 1992); and Andy Mousley, "Transubstantiating Love: John Donne and Cultural Criticism," in Burnham and Giaccherini, *The Poetics of Transubstantiation*, 55–62. For the argument that Donne sees sacraments in conjugal terms, see Theresa DiPasquale, "Ambivalent Mourning: Sacramentality, Idolatry, and Gender in 'Since she whome I lovd hath payd her last debt,'" *John Donne Journal: Studies in the Age of Donne* 10, nos. 1–2 (1991): 45–56; Anne Barbeau Gardiner, "Donne and the Real Presence of the Absent Lover," *John Donne Journal: Studies in the Age of Donne* 9, no. 2 (1990): 113–24; Helen B. Brooks, "'Soules Language': Reading Donne's 'the Extasie,'" *John Donne Journal: Studies in the Age of Donne* 7, no. 1 (1988): 47–63; and Elizabeth Hodgson, *Gender and the Sacred Self in John Donne* (Newark: University of Delaware Press, 1999) (my italics).

10. Carey, *John Donne: The Major Works*, 14.

11. See especially Carey's excellent introduction to the collected works. There he writes, "The belief that 'all the soul does, it does in, and with, and by the body' (324), which the sermons persistently endorse, is recognizable as the conclusion to 'The Ecstasy.'" Ibid., xxxi.

12. Donald Guss, *John Donne, Petrarchist: Italianate Conceits and Love Theory in The Songs and Sonets* (Detroit, Mich.: Wayne State University Press, 1966);

Theresa M. DiPasquale, "Donne's Catholic Petrarchans: The Babylonian Captivity of Desire," in *Renaissance Discourses of Desire*, eds. Claude J. Summers and Ted-Larry Pebworth (Columbia: University of Missouri Press, 1993), 77–92; and Heather Dubrow, *Echoes of Desire: English Petrarchism and Its Counterdiscourses* (Ithaca, N.Y.: Cornell University Press, 1995).

13. Guss, *John Donne, Petrarchist*, 129.

14. Mario Equicola, *Libro di natura d'amore* Venice, 1536 fol., 199v, cited in Guss, *John Donne, Petrarchist*, 143.

15. See Bernard McGinn's magisterial multivolume work on Christian mysticism: *The Foundations of Mysticism* (London: SCM Press, 1992); *The Growth of Mysticism* (New York: Crossroad, 1994); *The Flowering of Mysticism* (New York: Crossroad, 1998). Denys Turner asks with appropriate wonder, "why did Bernard, and before him Gregory, and Origen, hold that, of all the great canticles of the hebrew and christian scriptures—songs of victory, of exhortation, of aggression, of rejoicing and of gratitude—this song of uninhibited eroticism in which there is not a single mention of Israel's God, was nonetheless the highest of all songs, *the* Song of Songs?" Turner, *Eros and Allegory*, 26, 41–42.

16. Other critics have noted that Donne "presents himself as at once resident and alien in the realms of Petrarchism" (Dubrow, *Echoes of Desire*, 207). And Petrarch presents *himself* that way, renouncing his love for Laura as profane and substituting the Virgin at the end of the *Canzoniere*, only to revive a heavenly Laura in the *Trionfi*.

17. On love and Donne, see Catherine Belsey, "John Donne's Worlds of Desire," in *John Donne*, ed. Andrew Mousley (New York: St. Martin's Press, 1999), 63–80; Ronald Corthell, *Ideology and Desire in Renaissance Poetry: The Subject of Donne* (Detroit, Mich.: Wayne State University Press, 1997); William Shullenberger, "Love as a Spectator Sport in John Donne's Poetry," in Summers and Pebworth, *Renaissance Discourses of Desire*, 46–62; Kitty Datta, "Love and Asceticism in Donne's Poetry: The Divine Analogy," *Critical Quarterly* 19, no. 2 (1977): 5–25; Peter De Sa Wiggins, "'Aire and Angels': Incarnations of Love," *English Literary Renaissance* 12, no. 1 (1982): 87–101; Benjamin Saunders, "Circumcising Donne: The 1633 Poems and Readerly Desire," *Journal of Medieval and Early Modern Studies* 30, no. 2 (2000): 375–99; David Buck Beliles, *Theoretically-Informed Criticism of Donne's Love Poetry: Towards a Pluralist Hermeneutics of Faith* (New York: Peter Lang, 1999); Catherine Gimelli Martin, "The Erotology of Donne's 'Extasie' and the Secret History of Voluptuous Rationalism," *SEL* 44, no. 1 (2004): 121–47; Achsah Guibbory, "Fear of 'Loving More': Death and the Loss of Sacramental Love," in *John Donne's "Desire of More": The Subject of Anne More Donne in His Poetry*, ed. M. Thomas Hester (Newark: University of Delaware Press, 1996), 204–27; Joan Faust, "Donne on Love: Sometimes the End Just Doesn't Justify the Means," in *Fault Lines and Controversies in the Study of Seventeenth-Century English Literature*, eds. Claude J. Summers and Ted-Larry Pebworth

(Columbia: University of Missouri Press, 2002), 170–86; Anne D. Ferry, *All in War with Time: Love Poetry of Shakespeare, Donne, Jonson, and Marvell* (Cambridge, Mass.: Harvard University Press, 1975); Kenneth Gross, "John Donne's Lyric Skepticism: In Strange Way," *Modern Philology* 101, no. 3 (2004): 371–99; M. Thomas Hester, "'Miserrimum Dictu': Donne's Epitaph for His Wife," *Journal of English and Germanic Philology* 94, no. 4 (1995): 513–29; Anthony Low, *The Reinvention of Love: Poetry, Politics and Culture from Sidney to Milton* (New York: Cambridge University Press, 1993); Lindsay A. Mann, "Sacred and Profane Love in Donne," *Dalhousie Review* 65, no. 4 (1985): 534–50; Dennis J. McKevlin, *A Lecture in Love's Philosophy: Donne's Vision of the World of Human Love in Songs and Sonets* (Lanham, Md.: University Press of America, 1984); Helen Wilcox, "Miracles of Love and Wit: John Donne's 'The Relic,'" *GRAAT: Publication des Groupes de Recherches Anglo-Américaines de l'Université François Rabelais de Tours* [hereafter *GRAAT*] 25 (2002): 119–37; R. V. Young, "Love, Poetry, and John Donne in the Love Poetry of John Donne," *Renascence: Essays on Values in Literature* 52, no. 4 (2000): 251–73; Mary E. Zimmer, "'In Whom Love Wrought New Alchimie': The Inversion of Christian Spiritual Resurrection in John Donne's 'A Nocturnall upon S. Lucies Day,'" *Christianity and Literature* 51, no. 4 (2002): 553–67; and Gordon Braden, *Petrarchan Love and the Continental Renaissance* (New Haven, Conn.: Yale University Press, 1999).

18. Carey, *John Donne: The Major Works*, 400.

19. The Christian paradox of necessity and freedom is helpfully understood by the erotic tradition, in which "eros imposes obligations more binding—and so in a sense more 'necessary'—than any which the force of moral laws could impose; and yet, within *eros*, the language of 'imposition' and 'obligation' is wholly inappropriate . . . lover and beloved exchange with one another the gift of their own freedom, so each lives within the one freedom of both." Turner, *Eros and Allegory*, 58–59.

20. *The Sermons of John Donne*, VI. 163.

21. Noting that Donne's love poetry is preoccupied with fidelity, John Carey interprets this as a symptom of his infidelity to the Catholic Church. He imagines that Donne "transferred this disloyalty to women and directs the execrations against them which he could be seen as meriting" (Carey, *John Donne: The Major Works*, 38). On the other hand, Carey also gives a more positive spin to "infidelity." In "Change" and "Woman's Constancy," the speaker changes to become like her, embracing change. "Though Donne eventually came to accept Anglicanism, he could never believe that he had found in the Church of England the one true church outside of which salvation was impossible. To have thought that would have meant consigning his own family to damnation" (29).

22. John Donne, *Selected Poetry*, ed. John Carey (Oxford: Oxford University Press, 1998), "Holy Sonnet XVII."

23. Not all critics see "The Indifferent" as a libertine poem. Arthur Marotti writes that "the speaker's earlier smug libertinism is threatened by the experience

of actually falling in love with a particular woman." Arthur F. Marotti, *John Donne, Coterie Poet* (Madison: University of Wisconsin Press, 1986), 78.

24. In Philip Schaff, *The Creeds of Christendom* (New York: Harper, 1877), 42.

25. Sermon preached before King Charles I on April 15, 1628, in Carey, *John Donne: The Major Works*, 388.

26. Critics agree that he is celebrating the Countess of Bedford, who moved to Twickenham Gardens in 1607.

27. John Milton, *Complete Prose Works* (New Haven, Conn.: Yale University Press, 1959), 2: 228.

28. On Milton and charity, see Regina Schwartz, "Milton on the Bible," in *A Companion to Milton*, ed. Thomas Corns (Oxford, UK: Blackwell, 2001), 37–54.

29. Meat, instead of the elements or bread and wine, is precisely the way that Herbert refers to the body of Christ in his eucharistic lyric, "Love," in *The Temple*. See chapter 6 on conversation and the Eucharist in Herbert.

30. See Adam Potkay, "Spenser, Donne, and the Theology of Joy," *SEL* 46, no. 1 (2006): 43–66.

31. The "nothing" that is negative love recurs in the "Nocturnal upon St. Lucy's Day" where it is associated with dissolution, death, and grief, and in "Air and Angels" where it is associated with the soul. Kate Gartner Frost, "Preparing towards Her" in Hester, *John Donne's "Desire of More,"* 161. "The Nocturnal [upon St. Lucy's Day] thus presents a kind of liturgical / alchemical anti-epithalamion: a religious divorce and remarriage of the kind entailed in the movement from profane to sacred love. . . . All three contexts [for the poem]—the alchemical, liturgical and arithmetical—manifest Donne's anguish at his lone state, bereft of that other half of himself, Anne More. But he has seen his bereavement as an opportunity, quite in traditional terms, to turn his life to penitence, purification, and the works of his clerical profession . . . Donne is reduced to a near-to-nothing material to be worked upon by God's process" (165).

32. Jean-Luc Marion, *In Excess: Studies in Saturated Phenomena* (Bronx, N.Y.: Fordham University Press, 2002).

33. Sermon preached on Easter Monday, 1622, in Carey, *John Donne: The Major Works*, 311.

34. Ibid., 311.

35. Sermon preached before King Charles I in April 1629, in ibid., 392.

36. Ibid., 311. On Donne and the mystical tradition, see Harry J. Brown, "'Soul's Language Understood': John Donne and the Spanish Mystics." *Q/W/E/R/T/Y: Arts, Littératures & Civilisations du Monde Anglophone* 11 (2001): 27–35; Elizabeth Teresa Howe, "Donne and the Spanish Mystics on Ecstasy," *Notre Dame English Journal: A Journal of Religion in Literature* 13, no. 2 (1981): 29–44; Merritt Y. Hughes, "Some of Donne's 'Ecstasies,'" *PMLA* 75, no. 5

(1960): 509–18; John J. Pollock, "A Mystical Impulse in Donne's Devotional Poetry," *Studia Mystica* 2, no. 2 (1979): 17–24; and John T. Shawcross, "The Meditative Path and Personal Poetry," *John Donne Journal: Studies in the Age of Donne* 19 (2000): 87–99.

37. Origen, *Commentary on the Song of Songs*, prologue, English translation by Roland Greer, and Origen, *An Exhortation to Martyrdom, Prayer and Selected Works* (Mahwah, N.J.: Paulist Press, 1979), 217.

38. *Bernard of Clairvaux: Selected Works*, eds. Jean Leclercq and Ewert Cousins, trans. G. R. Evans (Mahwah, N.J.: Paulist Press, 1987), 211.

39. See Bernard McGinn, "The Language of Inner Experience in Christian Mysticism," *Spiritus* 1 (2001), 156–71.

40. Origen, *Commentarium in Canticum Canticorum*, ed. W. A. Baehrens, 194, 6–13 trans.; and Origen, *The Song of Songs, Commentary and Homilies*, ed. R. P. Lawson (Westminster, Md.: Newman Press, 1957), 198.

41. McGinn, "The Language of Inner Experience," 162.

42. *Bernard of Clairvaux: Selected Works*, 5.

43. See Achsah Guibbory, " 'The Relique,' the Song of Songs, and Donne's Songs and Sonets," *John Donne Journal: Studies in the Age of Donne* 15 (1996): 23–44.

44. *Bernard of Clairvaux: Selected Works*, 212.

45. Ibid., 213.

46. Ibid., 214, 215.

47. The distinguished Bernard scholar Jean Leclercq has even concluded that Bernard "sees man's redemption more in terms of the incarnation than of Christ's death and resurrection." *Bernard of Clairvaux: Selected Works*, 46.

48. Ibid., 50

49. Sermon preached before the King at Whitehall, February 24, 1625, in Potter and Simpson, eds., *Sermons*, VII:87–88.

50. *Sermons*, VIII:94–95

51. Sermon preached in 1618 at Essex house, in Potter and Simpson, eds., *Sermons*, V:169.

52. On the sanctification of every man, Donne writes, "As though the glory of heaven were too much for God alone, God hath called up man thither, in the ascension of his Son, to partake thereof; and as though one God were not enough for the administration of this world, God hath multiplied gods here upon earth, and imparted, communicated, not only his power to every magistrate, but the divine nature to *every sanctified man*." Sermon preached on May 8, 1625, in Carey, *John Donne: The Major Works*, 361. His body will be ingrafted onto the body of God and thereby be made eternal "As when my true repentence hath re-ingraffed me in my God, and reincorporated me in my Saviour, no man may reproach me, and say, Thou wast a sinner: So, since all these dead bodies shall be restored by the power, and are kept alive in the purpose of Almighty God, we cannot say, *They*

*are*, scarce that they were dead" (365). See also Sermon preached on January 16, 1626, 382–83.

53. *Bernard of Clairvaux: Selected Works*, 50.

54. McGinn, "The Language of Inner Experience," 157. Jean Daniélou, *Platonisme et théologie mystique: essai sur la doctrine spirituelle de Saint Grégoire de Nysse* (Paris: Aubier, 1944), is foundational.

55. Sermon no. 3, preached at Saint Dunstons, April 11, 1624 (the first sermon at that church, as vicar). Potter and Simpson, eds., *Sermons*, VI:81–82 (my italics).

56. Sermon no. 3, preached on November 19, 1627, in ibid., VIII:99 (my italics).

57. Ibid., VIII:94.

58. On the body in Donne, see McDuffie, *To Our Bodies Turn We Then*; Thomas Hester, " 'Impute this Idle Talke': The 'Leaven' Body of Donne's 'Holy Sonnet III,' " in *Praise Disjoined: Changing Patterns of Salvation in 17th-Century English Literature*, ed. William P. Shaw (New York: Peter Lang, 1991), 175–90; Christopher Ricks, "Donne After Love," in *Literature and the Body: Essays on Populations and Persons*, ed. Elaine Scarry (Baltimore, Md.: Johns Hopkins University Press, 1988), 33–69; Elaine Scarry, "Donne: 'But Yet the Body Is His Booke,' " *Literature and the Body,* op.cit., 70–105; Michael Schoenfeldt, "Thinking Through the Body: Corporeality and Interiority in Donne," *GRAAT* 25 (2002): 25–35; and Nancy Selleck, "Donne's Body," *SEL* 41, no. 1 (2001): 149–74.

59. See Labriola, note 3 above.

60. Quoted in Jaroslav Pelikan, *The Christian Tradition*, 3:138.

61. *Liturgy of Basil,* quoted in Pelikan *The Christian Tradition*, 2:138.

62. Potter and Simpson, eds., *Sermons*, VII:103 (my italics).

63. Ibid.

64. Sermon no. 3, preached on November 19, 1627, in Potter and Simpson, eds., *Sermons*, VIII:98.

65. Robert E. Wagoner, *The Meanings of Love: An Introduction to the Philosophy of Love* (Westport, Conn.: Praeger, 1997), 65.

66. Denis de Rougemont, *Love in the Western World*, trans. Montgomery Belgion (Princeton, N.J.: Princeton University Press, 1983), 42–46.

CHAPTER 6

Early versions of this chapter were presented at the conference on Mystics at the University of Chicago and the conference on Questioning God at Villanova University. I want to thank Jacques Derrida, David Tracy, Susan Schreiner, and Jean-Luc Marion for their helpful responses.

1. My debt is to the biblical understanding of praise as celebration, praise that is not part of an economic exchange or engages in the determinations that mark such exchanges. Here, I depart from Jacques Derrida's distinction between

"praise" and "prayer" in which he assigns this noninstrumental role to prayer, and not to praise, in "Comment ne pas parler: Dénégations" in *Psyché: Inventions de l'autre* (Paris: Galilée, 1987), 535–95. Trans. as "How to Avoid Speaking: Denials" by Ken Frieden, in *Languages of the Unsayable: The Play of Negativity in Literature and Literary Theory*, eds. Sanford Budick and Wolfgang Iser (New York: Columbia University Press, 1989), 3–50. For Derrida, "the encomium qualifies God and *determines* prayer, determines the other, Him to whom it addresses itself, refers . . ." (42). Derrida understands prayer as *to*, and praise as *of*, whereas in the Bible praise is offered without a request and prayer is a supplication *for some thing*. My exchange with Derrida on this issue can be found in *Questioning God*, ed. John Caputo, et al. (Bloomington: Indiana University Press, 2001), 230–34.

2. Hans Urs von Balthasar, *Theo-drama: Theological Dramatic Theory*, trans. Graham Harrison (San Francisco: Ignatius Press, 1988), 1:15.

3. Jean-Luc Marion reiterates this recurring theological theme in *God Without Being*, trans. Thomas A. Carlson (Chicago: University of Chicago Press, 1991).

4. In *Laudem Caesarii*, quoted in Louis Bouyer, *The Christian Mystery: From Pagan Myth to Christian Mysticism*, trans. Illtyd Trethowan (Edinburgh: T. and T. Clark, 1990), 168.

5. Louis Martz, *The Poetry of Meditation: A Study in English Religious Literature of the Seventeenth Century*, rev. ed. (New Haven, Conn.: Yale University Press, 1962), 280; and Barbara Kiefer Lewalski, *Protestant Poetics and the Seventeenth-Century Religious Lyric* (Princeton, N.J.: Princeton University Press, 1979), 300. Chana Bloch, *Spelling the Word: George Herbert and the Bible* (Berkeley: University of California Press, 1985); and Heather A. R. Asals, *Equivocal Prediction: George Herbert's Way to God* (Toronto: University of Toronto Press, 1981) have also written of Herbert's poetry as psalmody, demonstrating the analogies between his verse and the biblical psalms. See also the classic studies by Stanly Fish, *The Living Temple: George Herbert and Catechizing* (Berkeley: University of California Press, 1978); Daniel Doerksen, *Conforming to the Word: Herbert, Donne, and the English Church before Land* (Lewisburg Pa.: Bucknell University Press, 1997); and Richard Strier, *Love Known: Theology and Experience in George Herbert's Poetry* (Chicago: University of Chicago Press, 1983).

6. Among Herbert's precedents, it is Sir Philip Sidney's *Psalms* (1–43) that are indeed the closest approximation in poetry to Herbert's *The Temple*. Sidney translated the first forty-three and his sister, the Countess of Pembroke, the rest, and they were printed in 1823; nonetheless, they were widely circulated in manuscript earlier, in Herbert's time. Sidney's translations—which moved John Donne to write a poem in praise of them—were based on the Coverdale and Geneva Bibles and are marked by such simplicity of phrasing and metrical variety (especially different stanza forms) that one critic was prompted to describe them as beginning a new school of English versification.

7. Both Barbara Lewalski in *Protestant Poetics* and Mary Ann Radzinowicz in *Toward Samson Agonistes: The Growth of Milton's Mind* (Princeton, N.J.: Princeton University Press, 1978) have demonstrated the biblical inheritance in the verse of the period. Arthur L. Clements's *Poetry of Contemplation: John Donne, George Herbert, Henry Vaughan, and the Modern Period* (Albany: State University of New York Press, 1990) is a deeply thoughtful study of the widespread and important influence of mystical theology on religious poetry. See also Margaret J. Oakes, "'To Be Thy Praise,'" *Texas Studies in Literature and Language* 47, no. 2 (2005): 120–38; Martin Elsky, "Polyphonic Psalm Settings and the Voice of George Herbert's *The Temple*," *Modern Language Quarterly: A Journal of Literary History* 42, no. 3 (1981): 227–46; and Bloch, *Spelling the Word*.

8. See Martin Elsky, "The Sacramental Frame of George Herbert's 'the Church' and the Shape of Spiritual Autobiography," *Journal of English and Germanic Philology* 83, no. 3 (1984): 313–29; Ryan Netzley, "'Take and Taste': Sacramental Physiology, Eucharistic Experience, and George Herbert's *The Temple*," in *Varieties of Devotion in the Middle Ages and Renaissance*, ed. Susan C. Karant-Nunn (Turnhout, Belgium: Brepols, 2003), 179–206; Robert Whalen, *The Poetry of Immanence: Sacrament in Donne and Herbert* (Toronto: University of Toronto Press, 2002); and Edith Whitehurst Williams, "From Sacrifice to Communion: The Eucharist in Two Periods of English Verse," *Journal of Evolutionary Psychology* 18, nos. 1–2 (1997): 21–33.

9. On sacraments and Herbert, see especially William Bonnell, "Anamnesis: The Power of Memory in Herbert's Sacramental Vision," *George Herbert Journal* 15, no. 1 (1991): 33–48 and "The Eucharistic Substance of George Herbert's 'Prayer' (I)," *George Herbert Journal* 9, no. 2 (1986): 35–47; Elsky, "The Sacramental Frame"; Jeanne Clayton Hunter, "'With Winges of Faith': Herbert's Communion Poems," *Journal of Religion* 62, no. 1 (1982): 57–71; Jeannie Sargent Judge, "Accepting the Flesh: George Herbert and the Sacrament of Holy Communion," in *Images of Matter: Essays on British Literature of the Middle Ages and Renaissance*, ed. Yvonne Bruce (Newark: University of Delaware Press, 2005), 136–52; Jeannie Sargent Judge, *Two Natures Met: George Herbert and the Incarnation* (New York: Peter Lang, 2004); William Kerrigan, "Ritual Man: On the Outside of Herbert's Poetry," *Psychiatry: Interpersonal and Biological Processes* 48, no. 1 (1985): 68–82; Christopher Hodgkins, *Authority, Church, and Society in George Herbert: Return to the Middle Way* (Columbia: University of Missouri Press, 1993); Netzley, "Take and Taste"; William Shullenberger, "The Word of Reform and the Poetics of the Eucharist," *George Herbert Journal* 13, nos. 1–2 (1989): 19–36; Whalen, *The Poetry of Immanence*; R. V. Young, "Herbert and the Real Presence," *Renascence: Essays on Values in Literature* 45, no. 3 (1993): 179–96 and *Doctrine and Devotion in Seventeenth-century Poetry: Studies in Donne, Herbert, Crashaw, and Vaughan* (Cambridge and Rochester, N.Y.: D. S. Brewer, 2000).

10. MLA 1986, New York. Some of these debates continue in the *George Herbert Journal* 11, no. 1 (1987). See also Daniel W. Doerksen, *Conforming to the Word*.

11. Christopher Hodgkins argues that Herbert's poetry should not be used to systematize theology or to make claims about religious doctrine and identity in his *Authority, Church, and Society in George Herbert*. See also Elizabeth Clarke, *Theory and Theology in George Herbert's Poetry: 'Divinitie, and Poesie, Met.'* (Oxford, UK: Clarendon Press, 1997); Jeannie Sargent Judge, "Beyond the Branches: The Nature of George Herbert's Protestantism," *Cithara: Essays in the Judaeo-Christian Tradition* 29, no. 2 (1990): 3–19; Bruce A. Johnson, "Theological Inconsistency and its Uses in George Herbert's Poetry," *George Herbert Journal* 15, no. 2 (1992): 1–18; and Louis L. Martz, "Donne, Herbert, and the Worm of Controversy," in *Wrestling with God: Literature and Theology in the English Renaissance: Essays to Honor Paul Grant Stanwood*, ed. Mary Ellen Henley et al. (Vancouver: M. E. Henley, 2001), 11–25.

12. *Institutes*, Book 4.

13. Letter to Peter Martyr (August 8, 1555), in *Elijah Waterman, Memoirs of the Life and Writings of John Calvin* (Hartford: Hale & Hosmer, 1813), 378.

14. See William Nestrick, "George Herbert: The Giver and the Gift," *Ploughshares* 2, no. 4 (1975): 187–205.

15. Oakes, "To Be Thy Praise"; Christene Yule, "The Art of Praise: The Poetry of George Herbert," in *From Dante to Solzhenitsyn: Essays on Christianity and Literature*, ed. Robert M. Yule (Wellington, New Zealand: Tertiary Christian Studies Program, Victoria University of Wellington, 1978), 73–95; and Thomas B. Stroup, " 'A Reasonable, Holy, and Living Sacrifice': Herbert's 'the Altar,' " *Essays in Literature* 2 (1975): 149–63.

16. Jean-Luc Marion, *Idol and Distance: Five Studies*, trans. Thomas A. Carlson (New York: Fordham University Press, 2001), 9.

17 Marion, *Idol and Distance*, 5.

18. For discussions of Herbert and language, see Heather Asals, "The Voice of George Herbert's 'the Church,' " *English Literary History* [hereafter *ELH*] 36, no. 3 (1969): 511–28; P. G. Stanwood, "Time and Liturgy in Herbert's Poetry," *George Herbert Journal* 5, nos. 1–2 (1981): 19–30; Elizabeth Clarke, "Silent, Performative Words: The Language of God in Valdesso and George Herbert," *Literature & Theology: An International Journal of Theory, Criticism and Culture* 5, no. 4 (1991): 355–74; Mark A. Eaton, " 'Brittle, Crazy Glass': George Herbert's Devotional Poetics," *Christianity and Literature* 43, no. 1 (1993): 5–20; Thomas F. Merrill, "George Herbert's 'Significant Stuttering,' " *George Herbert Journal* 11, no. 2 (1988): 1–18; John Savoie, "The Word Within: Predicating the Presence of God in George Herbert's *The Temple*," *George Herbert Journal* 23, nos. 1–2 (1999): 55–79; Robert B. Shaw, "George Herbert: The Word of God and the Words of Man," in *Ineffability: Naming the Unnamable from Dante to Beckett*, eds. Peter S. Hawkins, Anne Howland Schotter, and Allen Mandelbaum (New York: AMS Press, 1984),

81–93; and P. S. Weibly, "George Herbert's 'Heaven': The Eloquence of Silence," *George Herbert Journal* 4, no. 2 (1981): 1–9.

19. Elizabeth Clarke has an important discussion of Juan de Valdes, the Catholic reformer, whose *The Hundred and Ten Considerations* was published by Nicholas Ferrar with Herbert's explicit enthusiasm. See her *Theory and Theology in George Herbert's Poetry*, 179–267.

20. Pseudo-Dionysius, *The Divine Names*, in *The Complete Works*, trans. Colm Luibhéid (New York: Paulist Press, 1987), 701C.

21. Bloch, *Spelling the Word*, 60.

22. Pseudo-Dionysius, *Divine Names*, ch. I, 592A, 52

23. Anselm, *Proslogion,* chapter 15 in *Monologion and Proslogion*, trans. Thomas Williams (Indianapolis: Hackett Publishing, 1996), 108.

24. Herbert, *Works*, ed. F. E. Hutchinson (Oxford: Clarendon Press, 1941), 304, 305. Elizabeth Clarke writes, "Like that of Savonarola, and Francois de Sales, Valdes's spirituality aspires towards the closest possible unity between God and the believer, which is possibly the reason why the author of 'Clasping of Hands' and 'The Search' was attracted to all three writers" (*Theory and Theology in Herbert's Poetry*, 189). She does not argue for a direct influence, but for their compatibility.

25. This submission of the speaker's will is apparent in many Herbert lyrics, among them, "The Reprisal" and "The Altar."

26. Henri de Lubac, *The Mystery of the Supernatural,* trans. Rosemary Sheed (New York: Herder and Herder, 1967), 272. Orig. *Le Mystère du surnaturel* (Paris, 1965).

27. William Nestrick, "George Herbert," noted the configuration of the personal pronoun.

28. See Jean-Luc Marion, *Étant Donné: essai d'une Phénoménologie de le donation* (Paris: Presses Universitaires de France, 1997).

29. Sigmund Mowinckel, *The Psalms in Israel's Worship*, trans. D. R. Ap-Thomas, 2 vols. (New York: Abingdon Press, 1962), 2:3–43.

30. Gerhard von Rad, *Old Testament Theology*, vol. 1, trans. D. M. G. Stalker (New York: Harper and Row, 1962), orig. *Theologie des Alten Testaments* (Munich: Kaiser Verlag, 1957).

31. Pseudo-Dionysius, *Divine Names*, 1:588A, 49.

32. Pseudo-Dionysius, *Divine Names*, 701C–704A.

33. As the third poem on "Love" in *The Temple*, it is often designated as Love III. In reading *Love* I as a poem about the Eucharist, I am in line with the consensus among Herbert critics. Heather A. R. Asals, *Equivocal Predication*; Joseph H. Summers, *George Herbert: His Religion and Act* (London: Chatto and Windus, 1954), 88–89; Roger B. Rollin, "Self-Created Artifact: The Speaker and Reader in 'The Temple,'" in *"Too Rich to Clothe the Sunne": Essays on George Herbert*, eds. Claude J. Summers and Ted-Larry Pebworth (Pittsburgh: University of Pitts-

burgh Press, 1980), 156–57; Bloch, *Spelling the Word*, 100–104; and Lewalski, *Protestant Poetics*, 288. Richard Strier maintains that it is not about the Eucharist on the grounds that the poem speaks of sitting rather than kneeling to accept the meal (in MLA debate about *Love*, 1997), but that argument contradicted his otherwise consonant reading of Herbert in *Love Known: Theology and Experience in George Herbert's Poetry* (Chicago: University of Chicago Press, 1983), which stresses Herbert's theological debt to the Lutheran justification by faith.

34. Bloch, *Spelling the Word*, 100.

35. *Book of Common Prayer*, 1604.

36. "Holy Scriptures I."

AFTERWORD

1. Marcel Gauchet, *The Disenchantment of the World: A Political History of Religion* (Princeton, Pa.: Princeton University Press, 1999).

2. I have explored some of the logic and rhetoric of such identity violence in *The Curse of Cain: The Violent Legacy of Monotheism* (Chicago: University of Chicago Press, 1997). An effort to find in religious discourse a model for reconciliation produced this subsequent book. I caution readers from assuming that this is Christian triumphalism, however, and they can turn to my exposition of the identity of justice and the Law in "Revelation and Revolution," in *Theology and the Political*, ed. Creston Davis (Duke University Press, 2004), 102–26, for the example of Judaism.

3. The philosopher Alain Badiou has sought such a "particular universal" and for him, its exemplary figure is St. Paul with his "neither Jew, nor Greek." See his *St. Paul: The Foundation of Universalism*, trans. Ray Brassier (Stanford, Calif.: Stanford University Press, 2003). My reservations with understanding Paul in this way stem from his complex relation to Judaism, but this does not dim my enormous respect for Badiou's project. See Schwartz, "Revelation and Revolution."

# Index

*Cultural Memory* | *in the Present*

Herlinde Pauer-Studer, ed., *Constructions of Practical Reason: Interviews on Moral and Political Philosophy*

Jean-Luc Marion, *Being Given That: Toward a Phenomenology of Givenness*

Theodor W. Adorno and Max Horkheimer, *Dialectic of Enlightenment*

Ian Balfour, *The Rhetoric of Romantic Prophecy*

Martin Stokhof, *World and Life as One: Ethics and Ontology in Wittgenstein's Early Thought*

Gianni Vattimo, *Nietzsche: An Introduction*

Jacques Derrida, *Negotiations: Interventions and Interviews, 1971–1998*, ed. Elizabeth Rottenberg

Brett Levinson, *The Ends of Literature: The Latin American "Boom" in the Neoliberal Marketplace*

Timothy J. Reiss, *Against Autonomy: Cultural Instruments, Mutualities, and the Fictive Imagination*

Hent de Vries and Samuel Weber, eds., *Religion and Media*

Niklas Luhmann, *Theories of Distinction: Re-Describing the Descriptions of Modernity*, ed. and introd. William Rasch

Johannes Fabian, *Anthropology with an Attitude: Critical Essays*

Michel Henry, *I Am the Truth: Toward a Philosophy of Christianity*

Gil Anidjar, *"Our Place in Al-Andalus": Kabbalah, Philosophy, Literature in Arab-Jewish Letters*

Hélène Cixous and Jacques Derrida, *Veils*

F. R. Ankersmit, *Historical Representation*

F. R. Ankersmit, *Political Representation*

Elissa Marder, *Dead Time: Temporal Disorders in the Wake of Modernity (Baudelaire and Flaubert)*

Reinhart Koselleck, *The Practice of Conceptual History: Timing History, Spacing Concepts*

Niklas Luhmann, *The Reality of the Mass Media*

Hubert Damisch, *A Theory of /Cloud/: Toward a History of Painting*

Jean-Luc Nancy, *The Speculative Remark: (One of Hegel's bon mots)*

Jean-François Lyotard, *Soundproof Room: Malraux's Anti-Aesthetics*

Jan Patočka, *Plato and Europe*

Hubert Damisch, *Skyline: The Narcissistic City*